Languages of Politics in Nineteenth-Century Britain

Also by David Craig

ROBERT SOUTHEY AND ROMANTIC APOSTASY: Political Argument in Britain 1780–1840

Also by James Thompson

BRITISH POLITICAL CULTURE AND THE IDEA OF 'PUBLIC OPINION'

Languages of Politics in Nineteenth-Century Britain

Edited by

David Craig
Lecturer in Modern British History, University of Durham, UK

and

James Thompson
Senior Lecturer in Modern British History, University of Bristol, UK

palgrave
macmillan

First published 2013 by
PALGRAVE MACMILLAN

Palgrave Macmillan in the UK is an imprint of Macmillan Publishers Limited, registered in England, company number 785998, of Houndmills, Basingstoke, Hampshire RG21 6XS.

Palgrave Macmillan in the US is a division of St Martin's Press LLC, 175 Fifth Avenue, New York, NY 10010.

Palgrave Macmillan is the global academic imprint of the above companies and has companies and representatives throughout the world.

Palgrave® and Macmillan® are registered trademarks in the United States, the United Kingdom, Europe and other countries

ISBN: 978–0–230–30402–4

This book is printed on paper suitable for recycling and made from fully managed and sustained forest sources. Logging, pulping and manufacturing processes are expected to conform to the environmental regulations of the country of origin.

A catalogue record for this book is available from the British Library.

A catalog record for this book is available from the Library of Congress.

Contents

Acknowledgements

We would like to thank Jon Lawrence, Cherry Leonardi, Andrzej Olechnowicz, Miles Taylor, Philip Williamson and the anonymous referee for advice and comment during the gestation of this book. We owe a special debt to Jonathan Parry, partly for hosting a workshop for the contributors at Pembroke College, Cambridge, in August 2011 – which enabled many of us to sharpen our ideas – but especially for generously providing comments on many drafts, and giving the editors a much needed sense of urgency.

Notes on Contributors

David Craig is Lecturer in History at the University of Durham. He is the author of *Robert Southey and Romantic Apostasy: Political Argument in Britain 1780–1840* (2007) and is currently working on the emergence of the language of 'liberalism' in Britain from the late eighteenth century.

Ben Griffin is Fellow and Lecturer in History at Girton College, University of Cambridge. He is the author of *The Politics of Gender in Victorian Britain: Masculinity, Political Culture and the Struggle for Women's Rights* (2012) and co-editor, with Lucy Delap and Abi Wills, of *The Politics of Domestic Authority in Britain since 1800* (2009). He is currently writing a history of family law in Britain since the middle of the eighteenth century.

Anthony Howe is Professor of Modern History at the University of East Anglia. His publications include *Free Trade and Liberal England, 1846– 1946* (1998); *The Letters of Richard Cobden (1804–65): Volume 1 1815–1847* (2007); *Volume 2 1848–1853* (2010) and, with Simon Morgan, *Volume 3 1854–1859* (2012).

Matthew Kelly is Senior Lecturer in History at the University of Southampton. He is the author of *The Fenian Ideal and Irish Nationalism, 1882–1916* (2006) and *Finding Poland: From Tavistock to Hruzdowa and Back Again* (2010), and he has written a number of articles on mid-Victorian Irish nationalism. He is currently writing a history of modern Dartmoor.

Jonathan Parry is Professor of Modern British History at the University of Cambridge. His four books on nineteenth-century British politics include *The Politics of Patriotism: English Liberalism, National Identity and Europe, 1830–1886* (2006). He is currently working on aspects of the Victorian engagement with the Middle East.

Robert Saunders is Lecturer in Modern British History at Queen Mary, University of London. He is the author of *Democracy and the Vote in British Politics, 1848–1867: The Making of the Second Reform Act* (2011) and co-editor, with Ben Jackson, of *Making Thatcher's Britain* (2012). He is currently writing about the 1975 referendum on British membership of the European Community.

Simon Skinner is Fellow and Tutor in History at Balliol College, Oxford, and CUF Lecturer in History at the University of Oxford. His book *Tractarians and the 'Condition of England':The Social and Political Thought of the Oxford Movement* was published in 2004.

James Thompson is Senior Lecturer in Modern British History at the University of Bristol. He is the author of *British Political Culture and the Idea of 'Public Opinion'* (2013). He is working on the visual culture of British politics from the 1860s to the 1930s and has developed an interest in the history of numeracy.

Jon Wilson is Senior Lecturer in History at King's College London. He is the author of *The Domination of Strangers: Modern Governance in Eastern India, 1785–1830* (2008). He is currently writing a history of the practice of colonial governance in India, to be published by Simon and Schuster in 2015.

Introduction

David Craig and James Thompson

Some would say that the study of nineteenth-century politics is just now in a curiously unsatisfactory condition. Other areas seem more dynamic. Many scholars have moved towards research in twentieth-century history while others now focus principally upon Victorian culture. Undergraduate courses feature less nineteenth-century British politics than was once the case. It would be wrong, though, to attribute the problematic state of the field simply to neglect. After all, a fair amount of work continues to be produced on nineteenth-century political history. Those coming to the period for the first time are unlikely to be struck by the absence of writing on late Victorian liberalism or on the career of Disraeli. Indeed, the last 30 years have seen the publication of numerous important works that taken together have fundamentally altered our picture of the political history of nineteenth-century Britain. And yet few would deny that the field faces difficult times.

The study of nineteenth-century British politics suffers in part from its very success and longevity. Decades of scholarship have bequeathed a daunting legacy of detailed studies of individual politicians, movements and episodes. Our current understanding of central issues in nineteenth-century politics reflects debates that have persisted for generations. The wealth of valuable publications since the 1980s has advanced our knowledge considerably, but this very proliferation has also served to fragment the field and to render it less approachable. Those who (still) teach nineteenth-century political history know how challenging this can be: the period can appear to students either misleadingly proximate – the view familiar from the heritage industries that the Victorians were just like us; or bafflingly distant – stuffy old men in strange hats banging on about religion.

1

The confused state of the field is not only a product of its antiquity; the difficulties faced by newcomers are not wholly reducible to the extent and density of the historiography. The 'cultural turn' has fostered some highly creative writing, especially but not exclusively, about popular politics, which has rightly been well received. In some respects, however, the underlying architecture of our understanding of nineteenth-century politics has remained fairly constant over time. This is not primarily a matter of particular politicians or elections continuing to seem important. It is rather that the categories and chronologies within which textbooks are written, and nineteenth-century political history is taught, have not caught up with the implications of the research of the last 30 years. The complexity of the field has not encouraged integrative efforts, and the relative paucity of such initiatives has effectively enabled older syntheses to retain a currency that can no longer be justified.

The aim of this book is to offer a map – far from the only possible one – of politics in Britain's long nineteenth century that embodies and extends the work of the last 30 years. It aims in particular to examine the attitudes and assumptions that underpinned political behaviour and experience. We do not so much mean the coherent bodies of thought to which intellectual historians are drawn, as the loose clusters of beliefs and arguments – sometimes seemingly common sense – that made up the world-viewed of political persons, that shaped what they did, and enabled them to evaluate the words and deeds of others.[1] A language of politics was not only a view of the world, but also a tool for getting things done: justifying lines of action and criticising forms of behaviour. Such a language might in fact be the highest ideals of the sincerest politician, but it need not – a language could still act as a regulator of political conduct even to someone who didn't believe a word of it: no one existed in a vacuum, and even the shifting and shuffling politician knew that wider norms and values limited what he or she might do. In ranging across the whole of the century, our objective is to assess the longevity, durability and malleability of these languages. Some were tenacious because of their close links to numerous related – and highly esteemed – values, while others evolved considerably, often because of shifts in associated discourses.

The purpose of this introduction is to provide a fuller sense of what we mean by languages and to explain in what ways this approach can enrich our understanding of nineteenth-century Britain. In the first section, therefore, we consider some of the methodologies associated with the study of political languages. There has, of course, been huge interest in language since at least the 1980s, and it is fair to say that few fields of history have been left unaffected by this 'linguistic turn'.[2] Our purpose is not to survey all the forms which this has taken – that would be beyond the scope of this volume – but rather to indicate the evolution of and justification for studying 'languages' and to note the origins of this approach in the study of the history of political thought.

The second section then assesses the impact of this work on political historians working on the nineteenth century, suggesting that its effects have been more muted than is commonly claimed. We particularly wish to stress the fractured nature of the field of political history – the legacy of earlier disputes between different styles and approaches continues to be felt. The effect has been, on the one hand, to enable fairly traditional styles of political history to continue unhampered while, on the other, new approaches have sometimes lost their anchoring in a set of compelling historical problems and processes. The final section turns to the content of this book, introducing the main themes of our chapters, and situating them within their broader contexts.

The language of 'languages'

Historians of nineteenth-century Britain will be most familiar with 'languages' because of the work of Gareth Stedman Jones in the early 1980s. Emerging out of debates among social historians, *Languages of Class* argued that political consciousness could not be read off from supposedly objective social conditions and group interests. Hence, famously, the Chartists could not be understood purely by reference to their real social conditions, because their 'interests' were defined through the political languages they were immersed in. It therefore followed that one should study how such languages produced 'interest, identification, grievance and aspiration', and, further, to map out how they related to each other and succeeded one another.[3] Although the object of intemperate debate in Britain, *Languages of Class* was part of a wider questioning of the methods of social history at this time. William Sewell, for instance, had in 1980 explored *The Language of Labor from the Old Regime to 1848* by turning to the work of Clifford Geertz to help reconstruct the 'ideological discourse' of the working class of Marseilles. If all experience was 'construed experience' it ought to be possible to examine not just written texts for meanings but also 'activities, events, and institutions...of *all* kinds of working-class experience'.[4] Similarly, Lynn Hunt's *Politics, Culture and Class in the French Revolution* proposed not a narrative of the 1790s, but an exposure of the 'values, expectations, and implicit rules that expressed and shaped collective intentions and actions'.[5] *Languages of Class* was clearly part of a much wider movement within social history which took it a step closer to the concerns of political historians.

The specific interest in 'languages', however, has an older ancestry. In the 1960s the methodological writings of the intellectual historian J.G.A. Pocock offered all the central elements for thinking about the study of a political language. Drawing on Collingwood and Oakeshott, Pocock was trying specifically to historicise the study of political thought, but his arguments had implications for historians more generally. From the outset he was critical of those who argued that political thinking could be explained by reference to social structure or political situation and pointed out that even the authors of such studies were puzzled by the vagueness of the connections they uncovered. The point, he argued, was not to assume that thought 'reflected' society, but to recognise 'how far language is from a simple mirror of unmediated experience of aspiration'.[6] To this end he argued that the historian of thought should look at the activity 'of thinking, of conceptualising, of abstracting ideas from particular situations and traditions' – in this way society produced the 'concepts with which to discuss its political affairs' and it linked them together to form 'groups or languages'.[7] While the preferred term was 'languages', he could happily accept synonyms: idioms, rhetorics, even vocabularies.[8] There might be several of them – sometimes they might emerge from highly specialised and technical fields, such as theology, and at other times from more practical branches of activity, such as law. Their relations to each other might be quite complex and they could operate at different levels of abstraction: 'The languages of politics, then, must be thought of as plural, flexible and non-final; each must permit of both responses and other speech acts which will modify it from within, and of various forms of interaction with other language-structures which will modify it from without.'[9] Nevertheless, Pocock also firmly believed that the task of the intellectual historian first and foremost was to investigate the fortunes of these languages rather than the individuals whose repeated speech acts sustained them.

This approach to languages was enormously influential across the field of the history of political thought, as evidenced by the 1987 collection of essays, *The Languages of Political Theory in Early-Modern Europe*, which included further methodological reflections by Pocock. What was unclear, however, was at what level of abstraction these 'languages' should be conceptualised. The editor's introduction made a case for there being four central languages in the early modern period: natural law, classical republicanism, political economy and the science of politics.[10]

Aside from the internal and relational complexities of each, it is not apparent why languages should be pitched at this level of abstraction rather than another. This is perhaps one reason why some historians have preferred instead to trace the history of concepts. This popular approach has taken a number of forms, including the often-criticised 'unit ideas' of A.O. Lovejoy, and the increasingly influential school of *Begriffsgeschichte*, particularly associated with Reinhart Koselleck.[11] Quentin Skinner has been critical of some strands of this approach, arguing that there is a tendency to see concepts as having some separate existence from their actual usage, though in recent writings he has been more circumspect, arguing that such histories may be legitimate as long as they attend to the contexts of concepts and the way they were used in arguments.[12] Others, such as Michael Freeden, have developed their own approach to studying concepts, and have mounted sophisticated methodological arguments about the way they could be collected into ideologies, his preferred term for what others call languages.[13]

It is important to be aware of some of the criticisms that have been made of a 'languages' approach, even of the fairly weak kind advocated here. An important complaint – often levelled at Pocock – is that languages become reified.[14] Skinner has argued that if we focus only on the appearance of a vocabulary associated with a language, we may become insensitive to the novel ways in which it was being used. It was not enough 'merely to indicate the traditions of discourse to which a given writer may be appealing, but also to ask what he may be *doing* when he appeals to the language of those particular traditions'.[15] So, to take a well-known example, Skinner's argument about Lord Bolingbroke's opposition to the Walpolean regime was not simply that he used a 'country' language to articulate his grievances, but that he chose such a language not so much because he truly believed in it – he probably did not – but because it was most likely to resonate with the audience to which he appealed.[16] To put it another way, we need to know 'who says what to whom, for what purposes, in what situations, through what channels and in what codes'.[17] This is as true for ordinary speakers as for sophisticated thinkers: whether in elite or popular circles – or anything in between – political actors might deploy political languages for any number of purposes in any range of situations. This is a theme increasingly stressed by historians inspired by performative approaches to language. Willibald Steinmetz, for instance, has contrasted a diachronic approach – 'investigating the changing meanings of single or clustered keywords or concepts over a long time-span' – with 'a synchronic, or micro-synchronic, approach to communicative practices in specific historical settings'.[18] It is only the beginning to trace out languages, for from there we must 'start to find out more about what particular political actors said and did in response to the specific questions they faced'.[19]

The state of political history

What impact have these methodological trends had on the practice of political history in the nineteenth century? On first reflection, one might assume that it has been extensive, that linguistic approaches to politics have become the norm, and even that it might now be time to turn attention elsewhere. This would be a mistake. In fact, the impact of languages on political history has been distinctly patchy, as evidenced by the fractured nature of the field.[20] In some areas research continues within well-worn grooves – biographies of leaders, studies of policies and so on – with only cursory nods to recent developments, while in other parts the interest in languages has been widespread, but has sometimes been imposed on top of a conventional, but outmoded, historiography.[21]

Before turning to 'mainstream' political history, we need to consider whether languages have had as much effect on historians of modern political thought as on their early-modernist colleagues. Surprisingly, this is not the case. Some have argued that the sort of languages analysed by Pocock are unhelpful guides to the period because of the way that political theory became a more deductive enterprise less indebted to traditional concepts.[22] On the other hand, there has been a much greater awareness of the need to approach texts and authors historically and to situate writings in richly delineated contexts. Still, the uncertain disciplinary identity of political thought has tended to mean that at the modern end these historical studies increasingly slide into philosophy, or, at best, histories of philosophy. As Stefan Collini has recently remarked, despite the historical turn in the study of political thought, it remains the case that much of it is actually rather poor as history.[23] There are important exceptions: some historians have effectively tried to 'democratise' the history of political thought by expanding vastly the scope of the source material analysed, and moving beyond a relatively established range of thinkers. In the work of Gregory Claeys, Eugenio Biagini and Dror Wahrman, the attention to the complexity of debate has thickened considerably our understanding of arguments about socialism, liberalism and class.[24] There is a great need for further such studies, but a caution must be registered. How far do they explore languages *of* politics as opposed to languages *in* politics? Pocock's whole approach was predicated on a distinction between the historian of thought and the historian of action. While the latter looked at how ideas, beliefs and arguments enabled us to understand political behaviour, the former – the intellectual historian – was interested in the process of abstraction and reflection: 'studying the regular employment of relatively stable concepts'.[25] This has tended to mean that histories of languages seem to float above the fray, and, in practice, have not tended to help with the task of 'putting ideas back into politics'.

Turning now to political history, it may be useful to consider historiographical trends over a longer term. While the Namierite assault on Whig history had the advantage of dissipating naive and anachronistic progressivism from political histories, it seemed to replace them with a sort of atomism: histories constructed around the collisions and coagulations of politicians motivated purely by narrow self-interest. There was little scope for party allegiance, let alone adherence to political principles. The gain in archival nuance seemed to be balanced by loss in explanatory power.[26] The work of Maurice Cowling in the 1960s and 1970s modified this approach and stressed more the complex and fluctuating pressures that party exerted on political leaders and policy makers.[27] Many students of the 'high politics' approach have subsequently developed these insights further – in particular Michael Bentley and Jonathan Parry have demonstrated the ways in which political ideas could actually be incorporated into the flow of parliamentary and governmental life.[28] Like Namier they were sceptical about an easy correspondence between political belief and political action, but unlike him, they refused simply to dismiss the problem. One of their chief insights was the centrality of religion to political argument and calculation – whether in formulating economic policy, or in considering how to 'civilise' the expanding demos.[29] While they may not have written about 'languages', these historians were nevertheless interested in the way that the attitudes and assumptions of politicians affected their leadership. Unfortunately the nuances of these approaches have sometimes been lost on other historians, who have preferred instead to see in 'high politics' simply the persistence of Namierism.

Admittedly the potential of this approach has been hindered by arguments about the supposedly closed world of 'high politics' and its imperviousness to popular pressure. Those social historians of the 1970s and 1980s interested in the development of popular politics found this particularly galling, and it confirmed their suspicions that traditional political history was congenitally elitist and methodologically impoverished – the achievements of great men and the fortunes of parties.

These historians were receptive to new approaches which questioned economic reductionism – it was here that the 'languages' of Stedman Jones made their strongest impact. Indeed, it was quickly argued that such approaches needed to be taken much further. Patrick Joyce drew on a wide range of non-traditional sources to expose the rhythms of popular political culture, while James Vernon argued that the formal emergence of democratic institutions closed down other forms of popular expression which might be found, for example, in oral and visual sources.[30] Meanwhile Joan Scott was among the most influential of gender historians who emphasised the constructed and indeterminate nature of the public/private distinction and showed that seemingly neutral political concepts – such as citizenship – encoded gendered assumptions at their very core.[31] However, while these pioneering works have added considerable texture to the understanding of political culture, their concern has generally continued to be with popular politics. The divisions between studies of 'high' and 'low' politics have remained stubbornly entrenched, despite pleas from Lawrence Goldman, Jon Lawrence and others, that these very connections are themselves ripe for sustained enquiry.[32] This has meant that political histories have tended to evolve along different routes, exacerbating sub-disciplinary identities, fracturing the field and impeding the ability of each side to learn from the other and to dissolve their differences.

This problem is particularly evident in one area: the endurance of party as an organising concept. While Namier's scepticism towards party was taken too far, there was some truth in his broader points. Party has remained a central category of enquiry and as a result shapes our narratives of the century – the periodisation of continuity and change, the classification of political struggles. If anything, the growing interest in political languages has helped strengthen the weight attached to party. So, for instance, Stedman Jones wanted to explain why working-class activism was co-opted by liberalism at mid-century, and this led him back to early nineteenth-century radicalism. By the 1840s its critique of the state seemed increasingly implausible, and so the 'language of radicalism' lost credibility, to be replaced by liberalism. Eugenio Biagini and Alastair Reid modified this argument to draw attention to the points of similarity between radicalism and liberalism, and so explain their congruence after Chartism.[33] This approach has been extremely influential and may be seen as part of a wider revival of interest in 'liberal languages' after the relatively dismissive view of the 1960s and 1970s.[34] While conservatism has been much less a beneficiary of these revisionist trends, it is nevertheless the case that study of the languages of party has shaped the work of these historians. There is, however, a real danger that these approaches will give greater coherence in space, and endurance over time, than is warranted – radicalism, liberalism and conservatism must not become the new master-narratives of political history. This is true of any period. Stedman Jones recognised this when he described party as a 'vacant centre'. It is a 'space traversed or tenanted by groups possessing different and sometimes incompatible political languages of widely varying provenance, a changing balance of forces and their discursive self-definitions, defined primarily from without'.[35] It is even more true of the nineteenth century: there remained a well-articulated suspicion of party until at least the middle of the century, and, some have suggested, beyond.[36] While it was recognised that some form of party affiliation was essential to the working of the constitution, at the individual level this attachment could be fairly loose – a matter of family traditions, personal preferences and expedient slogans. At any given point, these attachments could be subject to a wide variety of pressures, which means that, over time, the history of any party – and, accordingly, the relations that made up the party system as a whole – is likely to be a contingent and winding affair. If not, how could we explain the fortunes of the numerous political leaders – Melbourne, Peel, Derby, Aberdeen, Palmerston, Disraeli and Gladstone – who appeared to have 'jumped ship' from one party to another? We need instead to examine how assertions of party coherence were made plausible and how, at various points, they were marked off from other party groupings.

So, to summarise, our argument is that nineteenth-century political history remains a fractured field. Some parts of it pursue and defend a fairly traditional definition of their subject matter, and continue to produce biographies of politicians, studies of policies and narratives of parties where the proliferation of detail can act as a substitute for explanation. The main danger here is that ossification sets in and that the interest of researchers turns elsewhere. Meanwhile, other parts of the field have adopted more theoretically innovative methodologies, but have sometimes also remained stuck with topics and problems of concern to an earlier generation. It would be too pat to say that each side needs to hear what the other is saying. This is true, but much more importantly both sides in fact need to listen to what their subjects were saying.

In this book we stress the contribution that languages can make to this task. Building on the arguments above, we suggest four ways in which this approach may be fruitful. First, examining languages moves us away from the schools of thought typically studied by historians of philosophy. Such approaches tend to concentrate on the intellectual coherence of a body of thought – say, utilitarianism – but can have the unfortunate effect of encouraging reification. It is important to ask how such theories were understood and experienced historically, for they may turn out to have been disjointed and discontinuous – and this could have consequences for the way they were used. We therefore consider the looseness of bundles of beliefs, attitudes and assumptions, even as they may have been shared fairly widely and experienced as fairly unified. Second, these languages may enable us to identify broad traditions that informed political understanding and which lay behind political action. There is no reason to assume party division was crucial here – indeed the very idea of politics requires a measure of consensus and the social elites who dominated nineteenth-century politics shared quite a lot. We must not think of party as a 'total' world view and there may be continuities which its presence belies. Third, and related, we also need to identify how various languages could be put to use by different groups, both within and across parties. This might sometimes open up new lines of thinking and create further possibilities for collaboration. At the same time, however, it could also have the opposite effect of closing down other avenues of inquiry and partnership. Every time an argument was made, and especially if it was repeatedly made, the possibility existed that social understanding might be changed and political practice altered. Fourth, considering a language can provide a way of connecting different parts of the political sphere. If it is rooted deeply in culture or widely in society, a politician might in effect have to adhere to its norms. Sometimes this could be an opportunity – exploiting such a language might be a useful way to legitimate a controversial line of action. Equally, it could also be a hindrance, either preventing a politician from doing something, or at least requiring him or her to try to re-describe it in more acceptable terms. As a result we need to be aware of the social locations of these languages: while an undifferentiated 'public' might be one source, in this period we can also see anxieties about the clash between the expectations of traditional aristocratic culture and the culture of the middle classes. Such an approach may help us clarify – and even rethink – the connections between 'the high' and 'the low'.

Obviously we are not arguing that this approach represents the totality of political history, but we do claim that it is an integral part of it. We cannot understand politics without attending to the attitudes and arguments of its practitioners – whether they believed them or not, or even whether they were strongly conscious of them. How we incorporate such knowledge into our histories will depend on what we wish to explain. In this volume we have deliberately focused on tracking various languages over the long term. This enables us to consider continuities across the nineteenth century and to suggest particular periods when their scope and appeal was put under pressure. In this sense the volume is broadly diachronic. That does not mean, however, that synchronic approaches are not equally important: political historians will also need to attend closely to the ways that languages were used in political debates and struggles and with what consequences. Furthermore, we must also be aware of the multiple locations of such debates and struggles – political change does not occur solely in a parliamentary environment and languages may have a very different salience in alternative contexts, whether regional or institutional. Finally, and contrary to a commonly held view, a languages approach need not deny the significance of social, economic and structural factors, though it does have theoretical implications for how we conceive them.[37]

An overview

The chapters in *Languages of Politics* explore many leading aspects of political understanding in the nineteenth century. They may be read on their own or as part of a connected sequence which stresses the links and tensions between and within languages. As we explained above, our chief concern is to unearth the assumptions and attitudes which underlay political behaviour. These languages guided and shaped action, but they were sufficiently flexible that agile agents and groups could, at times, put them to innovative use. In analysing the two sides of this constraining/enabling relationship, some of the chapters pay close attention to the language of political leaders, while others adopt a broader frame and try to chart the languages to which such leaders found themselves subject. Inevitably, it has not been possible to be exhaustive and there are some areas which have not been pursued in depth. It may be time, for example, to return to the language of class, and while the state and the law are recurring themes, it has not been possible to consider them separately here.[38] Furthermore, we have deliberately restricted ourselves to a fairly formal – and largely textual – approach to languages, not because the study of visual and oral signs is unimportant, but simply to impose some order on our necessarily large subjects.[39]

We begin with chapters on 'Good Government' and on 'Statesmanship', which explore the various ways in which the business and practice of politics was understood. Curiously, these are neglected themes within the recent historiography. While historians of political thought have traditionally been more preoccupied with the theoretical aspects of the state, historians of politics have tended to focus on the practical aspects of government. The division is starkly illustrated by the terms of debate about the 'revolution in government' that preoccupied scholars in the mid-twentieth century. On the one hand were those who argued for the crucial role of utilitarian administrators in channelling the activity of the state, while on the other were those who stressed pragmatic factors and a febrile public opinion.[40] What was missing was much sense of the way that government, administration and leadership were actually understood and evaluated. While recent studies inspired by Foucauldianism have been suggestive, there is still a need for further attention to the evolving *tecnhe* of rule if the experience of 'modernisation' is to be fully captured.[41] This was, after all, a period when monarchical power declined, politics slowly became professionalised, the administration and its responsibilities expanded and the whole edifice was increasingly, so it was claimed, subject to the power of public opinion. James Thompson argues that the language of 'good government' initially drew on eighteenth-century thinking about virtuous leadership and the common good, to which was later added concerns drawn from utilitarianism about maximising happiness. By mid-century invocations of business efficiency were common, but there was also a stronger emphasis on the moral health of nation and citizenry. At the end of our period, however, while these themes did not disappear, they resonated less in an electoral politics concerned with social questions of wealth and welfare. In addition, the figures who seemed to represent good government – or indeed bad government – were themselves the subjects of intense discussion. The traditional political leaders largely survived a century of potential challenges to their authority, and they did so, as David Craig argues, by plausibly embodying a series of qualities that could transcend their class and even party backgrounds. They had to have principles, and an acute sense of judgement to know when and how to act on them. The assurance of this was character – developed moral qualities – but also a good temper. Finally they had to be able to persuade, and while the obsession with oratory evolved, it did not diminish over this period.

Next, we turn to three languages which were, in various ways, central to claims of political virtue and competence. In other words, any aspirant to a position of political authority had to be able to be trusted with the nation's interest, with its religion, and with its economy. At the same time, each area was also obviously highly debateable and potentially divisive and could be made the subject of party disagreement at various points. We begin with Jonathan Parry's chapter on 'Patriotism'. This topic was in fact the subject of one of the earliest explicit treatments of a political language. Hugh Cunningham noted how eighteenth-century patriotism had been central to radical attacks on the elite and argued that by the end of the following century this had evolved into a nationalist discourse which was effectively monopolised by the forces of conservatism: 'militarism, royalism and racialism'.[42] Since then, political historians have become increasingly bold in challenging this argument, showing that patriotism was central to liberal and left argument as well.[43] Building on his recent monograph, Parry argues that patriotism was affected by the growing acceptability of party after 1832. This made it much harder for any group to claim the patriotic high-ground without being ridiculed by opposing groups. That said, the ideal of patriotism – of acting above party interest – remained present and at periods of anxiety about sectionalism, it tended to reappear with vigour. In addition, and in contrast to earlier orthodoxy, it was not primarily invoked in opposi-tion to foreign 'others', in large part because Britain's enemies tended to fluctuate over time. Instead it was linked to the constitutional ideals that remained familiar from the preceding century. The exception to this was Ireland, but even the ability of this 'other' to galvanise domestic sentiment was complicated by the way Irish MPs deployed this language to show the hollowness of constitutionalism beyond Britain's borders. Ultimately, 'patriotism' remained a constitutional ideal to which most politicians cleaved, but which could not be used to extract substantial political capital from opponents.

Turning now to 'Religion', we see similar attempts – with similarly ambiguous results – to exploit confessional differences. The importance of religion to politics – both high and low – has become increasingly apparent since the 1980s, and historians have focused fruitfully on concern about the shape and nature of Anglicanism and its relation-ship to Nonconformity.[44] As Simon Skinner shows, religion was never far from the surface of political debate, and, as a parliamentary ques-tion, it remained contentious for much of the period. The religious reforms that seemed to mark the end of the *ancien régime* in 1828–9 in fact opened up a swathe of further grievances which progressives would agitate over the next half century, among them church rates, burials, education, the Irish Church and, for some, disestablishment. Much of the labour of revisionists has been devoted to exploring the imagi-native way in which Liberals responded to these issues, but it should be remembered that Conservatives could find mileage in exploiting religious positions, especially at times when Liberal policies opened it to charges of consorting with enemies of the Church, as in the 1860s and 1880s. Skinner indicates that by the end of the century, with the virtual exhaustion of dissenting grievances, the denominational heat of politics died away, although ethical and emotional overtones continued to resonate into the twentieth century.

Questions of economic language are obviously central to politics, and yet until recently were not really a subject of enquiry. Outside of formal accounts of classical economics, there was a tendency to assume that a fairly schematic idea of laissez-faire pushed its way into economic policy between the 1820s and 1840s, and was in turn, slowly pushed out from the 1880s by the 'rise of collectivism'. Since the 1980s this account has been deconstructed. Among intellectual historians, political economy has been properly contextualised and placed within the broader frame of the 'noble' science of politics, while political historians – such as Boyd Hilton and E.H.H. Green – have examined the particular forms that economic opinion took, and the ways it actually affected party policies.[45] Historians have begun to trace the way that conceptions of economics – often liberal rather than socialist – put down deep roots into popular political culture.[46] Anthony Howe's chapter on 'Popular Political Economy' shows that part of the early success of free trade was its ability to appeal to pre-existing languages and to new audiences – in doing so it became, he argues, the 'core component' of popular liberalism. It remained central to the end of our period and fought off sustained assaults from fair trade, tariff reform and socialism because of its links to powerful themes such as harmony, co-operation and justice. While it was ironic that what had originally seemed a supremely bourgeois language had become central to working-class Edwardians, it was nevertheless the case. This was, then, a language of politics that could be considerably more contentious than, say, 'Patriotism', but which also had the range and power to invalidate the claims of alternatives.

The next set of chapters considers the various forms of social division that might threaten prevailing institutions and norms. Both 'Democracy' and 'Women's Suffrage' challenged existing views of inclusion within the constitution. As historians of radicalism have argued, constitutionalism became a 'master narrative' through which political identities and struggles could be articulated.[47] Its inherent flexibility – due to its disputed historical forms – was an asset: fierce opposition to the status quo could be clothed in seemingly loyal garb. It could be a language of inclusion even as it railed against existing exclusion from the polity. Robert Saunders examines this issue from the point of view of the language of democracy. Surprisingly, such an important subject has attracted little sustained attention despite its obvious shifts in meaning. After all, for at least the first half of the century 'democracy' belonged either to the past or to other countries. Even after the Second Reform Act, politicians remained fearful of what it portended. Nevertheless from the 1880s there was a growing sense across parties that rather than opposing this language, it was better to stake a claim to it: all manner of political controversies were suffused with this terminology. Hence, Saunders argues, there was no single moment when Britain 'became' a democracy – instead, there was a 'prolonged negotiation' between this language and traditional ways of understanding politics. Ben Griffin turns his attention to the way that arguments about women's suffrage were affected – and in turn impacted upon – changing conceptions of liberal and conservative representative government. In particular, he stresses that the way politicians conceptualised the basis for the vote (classes, communities, taxpayers?) affected how easy it was to move towards accepting the vote for women. So, if politicians believed in representation by classes, it was necessary to persuade them that women were a class. This was a difficult case to make, even into the 1870s. Thereafter, matters started to change: Liberals, piece by piece, moved towards an effectively democratic basis for the franchise, while Conservatives spoke of representation of communities and property as the proper basis of 'fitness'. Both developments provided opportunities for supporters of female suffrage and cut the ground away from opponents who were now reduced to arguing that active citizenship depended solely on sexual difference.

Finally, the last two chapters extend the national frame of reference. By considering some of the more troubled parts of the British empire, it becomes possible to see the ways that political languages could either be put to very different uses outside Britain, or may indeed have had limited applicability beyond its shores. While recent work has stressed the increasing importance of 'Britishness' within parts of the settlement empire, our chapters on 'Ireland' and India indicate some of the limits to the inclusiveness of liberal constitutionalism.[48] Matthew Kelly shows the anxieties that nationalists in Ireland had in articulating a unified case for separation from Britain. The lack of recognition from European nationalists was galling, especially in the way that they failed to see that British liberalism was a 'carapace' for imperial self-interest. If, in the hands of moderates, Home Rule was about creating the conditions for concord and progress, for Parnell it could also be used to evoke a purer form of nationalism. The language of 'confrontation, defiance, distrust, and opposition' could be apparent even as he called for a 'union of hearts'. If, in his final crusades, Gladstone did not concede self-determination, he nevertheless went far in accepting that Britain had misgoverned Ireland and recognising that nationality had its place. No such recognition was accorded India. Jon Wilson, in 'The Silence of Empire: Imperialism and India', argues that ultimately the political languages of empire were incapable of capturing what was actually happening in India. There remained throughout the century a vibrant conservative tradition which defended conquest and eulogised martial vigour and virtue, but the contrasting liberal language struggled to offer a cogent narrative. It could easily articulate the view that empire corroded constitutional liberty in the metropole, but the transformative potential of liberal imperialism was surprisingly short-lived, and by the second half of the century had been replaced with 'unease and silence'. These were languages that said more about politics in Britain than practice in India.

Ultimately *Languages of Politics* seeks to develop three broad – and perhaps obvious – claims. First, politics matters. If we define politics not just as 'conflict over the mastery and uses of governmental power' but also as 'struggle over the resources and arrangements that set the basic terms of our practical and passionate relations' we have a description that can bring together all parts of the field, from those primarily concerned with the daily struggles of ordinary people right through to those fascinated by the opaque operations of formal institutions.[49] It is important that political historians think hard about the nature of their discipline, and not let it be subsumed by variants of cultural history or political science. One aspect of this will need to be reconstructions of the political imaginary – shared understandings of the contexts and settings of political struggles, as well those struggles themselves. Second, therefore, language matters. It is not enough to examine epistemes or discourses alone – certainly, these form a crucial background to behaviour, but we need to drill down to look at how individuals thought and behaved if we are to credit them with agency. This is not, as some historians fear, an attempt to reduce political to intellectual history, but rather to recognise that everyone has ideas – views, attitudes, assumptions, prejudices, whatever – which affect what they do, whether they conform to norms, resist them or seem largely indifferent either way. There is no shortcut to such understanding: while much will be lost to the historian, much also can be gained by observing the traces that remain. This leads on to the third point – that the period matters. The nineteenth century is now too far away to be part of our present, but still too close to be appealingly alien. Yet its centrality as a period of transition is self-evident. Unfortunately the familiar terms used by social and political scientists to understand this process (capitalism, modernisation, class, party, bureaucracy, rationalisation etc.) are themselves largely products of a rickety social theory which cannot sustain the empirical riches which have been heaped on top of it. However, rather than simply stretch a 'long' eighteenth century ever further into the nineteenth century, we need to bring it back from 'suspended animation'.[50] Exploring its languages enables us to see how practices and institutions were embodied, how power and struggle were understood and how change was resisted and accommodated. While mapping the multiple languages of politics is only a part of what is needed, it is, nonetheless, a necessary start.

Notes

1. See C. Taylor, *Modern Social Imaginaries* (Durham NC, 2004), chs. 2–3.
2. For surveys see L. Hunt, ed., *The New Cultural History* (Berkeley, 1989); T.J. McDonald, ed., *The Historic Turn in the Human Sciences* (Ann Arbor, 1996); L. Hunt and V. E. Bonnell, eds, *Beyond the Cultural Turn: New Directions in the Study of Society and Culture* (Berkeley, 1999).
3. G. Stedman Jones, *Languages of Class: Studies in English Working Class History* (Cambridge, 1983), p. 22. For an overview see the 'Introduction' to D. Feldman and J. Lawrence, eds, *Structures and Transformations in Modern British History* (Cambridge, 2011), pp. 1–23.
4. W. Sewell, *Work and Revolution in France: The Language of Labor from the Old Regime to 1848* (Cambridge, 1980), pp. 9, 10, 11.
5. L. Hunt, *Politics, Culture, and Class in the French Revolution* (Berkeley, 1984), p. 10.
6. J.G.A. Pocock, *Political Thought and History: Essays on Theory and Method* (Cambridge, 2009), p. 17.
7. Ibid., pp. 13, 14.
8. Ibid., pp. 71, 77.
9. Ibid., p. 74.
10. A. Pagden, 'Introduction' in idem, ed., *The Languages of Political Theory in Early-Modern Europe* (Cambridge, 1987), pp. 1–17.
11. See M. Richter, *The History of Political and Social Concepts: A Critical Introduction* (Oxford, 1995).
12. Q. Skinner, *Visions of Politics I: Regarding Method* (Cambridge, 2002), pp. 175–87.
13. M. Freeden, *Ideologies and Political Theory: A Conceptual Approach* (Oxford, 1996).
14. See especially M. Bevir, *The Logic of the History of Ideas* (Cambridge, 1999), chs. 2, 5.

15. Q. Skinner, 'Some Problems in the Analysis of Political Thought and Action' in J. Tully, ed., *Meaning and Context: Quentin Skinner and His Critics* (Cambridge, 1988), p. 107.

16. Q. Skinner, *Visions of Politics II: Renaissance Virtues* (Cambridge, 2002), pp. 344–67. See also *Visions I*, pp. 145–57.

17. P. Burke cited in M. Sonenscher, 'The Sans-Culottes of the Year II: Rethinking the Language of Labour in Revolutionary France', *Social History* 9 (1984), 302.

18. W. Steinmetz, 'Introduction' in idem, ed., *Political Languages in the Age of Extremes* (Oxford, 2011), pp. 49–50.

19. M. Sonenscher, 'Enlightenment and Revolution', *Journal of Modern History* 70 (1998), 308.

20. There has, however, been growing interest in political *speech*. See J. Meisel, *Public Speech and the Culture of Public Life in the Age of Gladstone* (New York, 2001) and P. Readman, 'Speeches' in M. Dobson and B. Ziemann, eds, *Reading Primary Sources: The Interpretation of Texts from Nineteenth and Twentieth Century History* (London, 2008), pp. 209–25. For the potential of quantifying political speeches see L. Blaxhill, 'Quantifying the Language of British Politics', *Historical Research* 86 (2013), 1–34.

21. A point made by J. Lawrence and M. Taylor, 'The Poverty of Protest: Gareth Stedman Jones and the Politics of Language – A Reply', *Social History* 18 (1993), 1–15.

22. M. Francis and J. Morrow, *A History of English Political Thought in the Nineteenth Century* (London, 1994), pp. 3–4.

23. S. Collini, 'Postscript: Disciplines, Canons, and Publics: The History of "The History of Political Thought" in Comparative Perspective' in D. Castiglione and I. Hampsher-Monk, eds, *The History of Political Thought in National Context* (Cambridge, 2001), p. 302.

24. See, for instance, G. Claeys, *Citizens and Saints: The Politics and Anti-Politics in Early British Socialism* (Cambridge, 1989); E.F. Biagini, *Liberty, Retrenchment and Reform: Popular Liberalism in the Age of Gladstone, 1860–1880* (Cambridge, 1992); D. Wahrman, *Imagining the Middle Class: The Political Representation of Class in Britain, c. 1780–1840* (Cambridge, 1995). The editors' recent work may also be seen in this tradition: D.M. Craig, *Robert Southey and Romantic Apostasy: Political Argument in Britain, 1780–1840* (Woodbridge, 2007); J. Thompson, *British Political Culture and the Idea of 'Public Opinion'* (Cambridge, 2013).

25. Pocock, *Political Thought*, pp. 13–14.

26. Though see L. Colley, *Namier* (London, 1989), pp. 46–71.

27. D.M. Craig, '"High Politics" and the "New Political History"', *Historical Journal* 53 (2010), 453–75.

28. See, for example, M. Bentley, 'Party, Doctrine, and Thought' in M. Bentley and J. Stevenson, eds, *High and Low Politics in Modern Britain* (Oxford, 1983), pp. 123–53; J. Parry, *Democracy and Religion: Gladstone and the Liberal Party 1867–1875* (Cambridge, 1986).

29. For example, B. Hilton, 'Peel: A Reappraisal', *Historical Journal* 22 (1979), 585–614; J. Parry, *The Politics of Patriotism: English Liberalism, National Identity and Europe, 1830–1886* (Cambridge, 2006), ch. 1.

30. P. Joyce, *Visions of the People: Industrial England and the Question of Class, 1848–1914* (Cambridge, 1991); J. Vernon, *Politics and the People: A Study in English Political Culture, c. 1815–1867* (Cambridge, 1993).

31. J. W. Scott, *Gender and the Politics of History* (New York, 1988); C. Hall et al., *Defining the Victorian Nation: Class, Race, Gender and the Second Reform Act of 1867* (Cambridge, 2000).

32. L. Goldman, *Science, Reform, and Politics in Victorian Britain: The Social Science Association 1857–1886* (Cambridge, 2002), pp. 7–11; J. Lawrence, 'Political History' in S. Berger et al., *Writing History: Theory and Practice* (London, 2003), pp. 183–202.

33. E. F. Biagini and A. J. Reid, eds, *Currents of Radicalism: Popular Radicalism, Organised Labour and Party Politics in Britain, 1850–1914* (Cambridge, 1991). Useful surveys of revisionism are R. McWilliam, *Popular Politics in Nineteenth-Century England* (London, 1998) and M. Roberts, *Popular Movements in Urban England, 1832–1914* (Basingstoke, 2009).

34. For example, M. Freeden, *Liberal Languages: Ideological Imaginations and Twentieth-Century Progressive Thought* (Princeton, 2005).

35. Stedman Jones, *Languages of Class*, p. 22.

36. J. Lawrence, *Speaking for the People: Party, Language and Popular Politics, 1867–1914* (Cambridge, 1998).

37. See Taylor, *Modern Social Imaginaries*, pp. 31–3 and, more extensively, R. Unger, *Social Theory: Its Situation and Its Task* (Cambridge, 1987). Indeed Unger's broader work suggests that an interest in languages of politics can be reconciled with Susan Pedersen's concerns about lack of attention to structural questions. See 'What is Political History Now?' in D. Cannadine, ed., *What is History Now?* (Basingstoke, 2002), pp. 36–56.

38. See the essays by Philip Harling, Peter Baldwin, and Margot Finn in P. Mandler, ed., *Liberty and Authority in Victorian Britain* (Oxford, 2006).

39. For the question of visual culture, see J. Thompson, '"Pictorial lies"?: Posters and Politics in Britain, 1880–1914', *Past and Present* 197 (2007), 177–210.

40. See the debate generated by O. MacDonagh, 'The Nineteenth Century Revolution in Government: A Reappraisal', *Historical Journal* 1 (1958), 52–67.

41. See, for example, S. Gunn and J. Vernon, eds, *The Peculiarities of Liberal Modernity in Imperial Britain* (Berkeley, 2011).

42. H. Cunningham, 'The Language of Patriotism, 1750–1914', *History Workshop Journal* 12 (1981), 24.

43. P. Ward, *Red Flag and Union Jack: Englishness, Patriotism and the British Left, 1881–1924* (London, 1998); P. Readman, *Land and Nation in England: Patriotism, National Identity, and the Politics of Land, 1880–1914* (Woodbridge, 2008).

44. See J. Parry, *The Rise and Fall of Liberal Government in Victorian Britain* (New Haven, 1993).

45. S. Collini, D. Winch and J. Burrow, *That Noble Science of Politics* (Cambridge, 1983); B. Hilton, *The Age of Atonement: The Influence of Evangelicalism on Social and Economic Thought, 1795–1865* (Oxford, 1988); E.H.H. Green, *The Crisis of Conservatism: The Politics, Economics and Ideology of the British Conservative Party, 1880–1914* (London, 1995).

46. See A. Howe, *Free Trade and Liberal England, 1846–1946* (Oxford, 1997); F. Trentmann, *Free Trade Nation: Commerce, Consumption, and Civil Society in Modern Britain* (Oxford, 2008).
47. Vernon, *Politics and the People*; idem, ed., *Re-Reading the Constitution* (Cambridge, 1996).
48. See J. Darwin, *The Empire Project: The Rise and Fall of the British World-System, 1830–1970* (Cambridge, 2009), ch. 4; U. Mehta, *Liberalism and Empire: A Study in Nineteenth-Century British Liberal Thought* (Chicago, 1999); J. Pitts, *A Turn to Empire: The Rise of Imperial Liberalism in Britain and France* (Princeton, 2005).
49. Unger, *Social Theory*, p. 145.
50. M. Taylor, 'Bring Back the 19th Century', *London Review of Books*, 22 June 2000.

1
Good Government

James Thompson

This chapter examines debates about the purpose of politics. It does so by reconstructing the language of 'good government' that provided an important and enduring means whereby Britons discussed politics and politicians through the long nineteenth century. The theme tackled is a large one, and could encompass a vast, indeed endless, range of arguments about what constitutes desirable political action. The approach taken here is to concentrate upon the notion of 'good government' as a useful way into nineteenth-century discussions of the ends of politics that yields insights into the periodisation and character of British political debate over the long run.

While the question of what constituted good government is in one sense an obvious, even inescapable one, for a book about nineteenth-century languages of politics, it has arguably not received the coverage that one might expect. As the introduction to this book argues, much writing about nineteenth-century politics has been organised through the history of parties and their ideologies. This chapter, along with the others in the book, seeks to offer a different perspective, firmly anchored in the political discourse of the period, by recovering a number of political languages that often cut across party allegiances. Much recent and often very good writing about Victorian politics has been concerned with questions of citizenship and belonging often approached through debates about the constitution in general and the franchise in particular.[1] There has lately been less attention given to the matter of the ends of politics, to debates about what it is for, and what counted as doing it well. There is certainly a long established and important historiography focusing upon ideas about the state in which the late nineteenth century features as a turning point towards a more interventionist conception of the role of the state.[2] This has though often focused primarily upon the contemporary discussions of the size of the state, and upon the merits of social legislation, rather than upon evaluations of what counted as good government, and more general discussions of what government and politics was for.

This chapter, like the rest of the book, is concerned with periodisation, and more particularly with the legacy of eighteenth-century modes of thinking about politics for the nineteenth century, and with changes in political culture in the later nineteenth century. The nineteenth-century language of good government was, like the idiom of patriotism explored by Jonathan Parry, one indebted to eighteenth-century precedents. Indeed, the roots of nineteenth-century invocations of good government are much older. One set of sources was classical, nicely encapsulated in Ambrogio Lorenzetti's fourteenth-century frescoes in the Palazzo Publico in Sienna. In Lorenzetti's paintings, good government is identified with the pursuit of the common good. Good government is virtuous government that delivers peace, prosperity and justice. Scholars differ somewhat over which virtues are presented as most crucial to the achievement of good government, but prudence and fortitude are generally thought to be among them. The bequests of good government are seen as extensive, embracing glory and greatness. In one well-known interpretation, the maintenance of good government and through it the common good is portrayed as depending upon the active self-government of the people of Sienna themselves.[3]

Fourteenth-century Sienna may seem very distant from the world of nineteenth-century Britain. This might, however, be misleading. In his 1893 penny pamphlet for the Liberal Unionist Association, Hugh Seymour Tremenheere sought to explain *How Good Government Grew Up and How To Preserve It*. For Tremenheere, the existence of good government brought prosperity and was founded upon just laws. Its erection depended upon the courage and wisdom of past generations and its preservation required the active and educating citizenship of public men. Tremenheere strenuously upheld the value of 'mixed' government. In support of his views, he quoted at length from Plato and especially from Goethling's 1824 edition of Aristotle's *Politics* upon the object of government, urging that 'just pride' should be inspired by the realisation that England was unique in safeguarding the principles of government dear to 'three of the greatest minds that ever adorned humanity – Solon, Plato, and Aristotle'.[4] Much of Tremenheere's pamphlet was devoted to such disparate contemporary issues as the eight-hour day, which he opposed, or the advantages of Belgian midwifery schools, which he praised. In the ideal and language of good government upon which it drew, however, it owed much to the classical inheritance. In his panoramic account of the birth of the modern world, C.A. Bayly argues that a conception of 'good government' that he links to 'civic republicanism' was widespread in eighteenth-century Europe and America. Indeed, for Bayly, this way of thinking about good government – with its emphasis upon political engagement and the claims of community – was also evident in the 'patriotic communitarianism' that was a feature of Indian, Islamic, African and East Asian societies. In Bayly's grand vision, liberalism emerges as in part an extension of these established traditions that was able to 'reinvigorate and sharpen the older discourse on good government', but that was at its most disruptive when it focused in on the importance of individual rights.[5] This chapter's scope will be singularly parochial in comparison to Bayly's portrait of global trends, but his work reminds us of both the broad European inheritance upon which British debates about 'good government' drew and the parallels between that inheritance and political languages beyond Europe. It was perhaps amongst British imperial administrators and politicians that a more traditional idiom of good government would prove most persistent.

The other much older set of sources for nineteenth-century appeals to good government was religious in origin. Eighteenth- and nineteenth-century sermons could make good government their theme, sometimes taking Isaiah as their text, with its emphasis on 'reigning in righteousness' or Timothy with its appreciation of the peaceable life.[6] In this tradition, good government was godly government. Here, too, there was an emphasis upon the moral qualities required of the governor and indeed the governed. Within the classical inheritance, good government was sharply contrasted with corrupt government, or government that was factional in its favours. Similarly, the ideals of good government rooted in Christianity apparent in eighteenth-century moral philosophy distinguish it strongly from corrupt or tyrannical rule.

Many of these associations had a very long shelf life in the Anglophone political world. Movements to cleanse big city politics in the United States of jobbery and graft often adopted the language of good government, apparent in the pamphlets of the National Municipal League with their emphasis on improving urban political morality in the name of Christianity.[7] The language and ideals of good government also provided a means of discussing issues of what might now be called corporate governance, and the proper running of civic associations. At the heart of the idiom of 'good government' was a cluster of values – about virtuous conduct, about devotion to the common good, about disinterested service – that had long histories. Whereas it might seem at first sight that 'good government' was a purely consequentialist idiom, solely concerned with assessing the effects of government, whether through administration or legislation, it was in fact intimately connected to the qualities possessed and the attitudes espoused by those in government.

The rest of this chapter is in three parts. These serve to trace ways in which the language of good government was contested and developed over the century. It is, to some extent, a story of the declining purchase of the inherited conceptions of good government outlined above. The first section explores the early part of the nineteenth century, including the different, but also overlapping, ways in which radicals and Whigs construed good government. It re-examines in particular the language of utilitarianism with its highly consequentialist approach. The historiographical tide has, for some time now, been running towards a downplaying of the influence of utilitarianism in nineteenth-century politics.[8] There is much that is right in this reassessment. There is, however, a danger that it rests upon too narrow a focus upon full-blown adherence to the felicific calculus. Utilitarians could recast the language of good government in their own image, and in these less philosophically sophisticated ways, contribute to a conception of 'good government' that came to identify its appearance closely with the supposedly hard-headed virtues of the English.

The second section focuses upon mid-Victorian discussions of 'good government'. It examines the relationship between the language of good government and the notion of politics as a kind of business. More generally, it develops the earlier account of Whig and liberal invocation of good government, tracing its evolution in the 1850s and 1860s. It focuses on contemporary debates about government performance, and about the kind of government that was most appropriate to the age. The broader intellectual context is one in which the need for politics to adapt to changing mores, and the importance of national character in determining the possibilities of political action, were much stressed. Debate about good government often addressed the form of government, and in these years institutional analysis was often informed by a pretty positive view of British arrangements in comparison to those abroad, which was bolstered by an equally benign view of the social and psychological bases for politics.

The third part concentrates upon the last third of the nineteenth century, and the early years of the twentieth. As we have noted, the idea of just rule, and of governing for the common good, were integral to traditional conceptions of good government. In the last part of the nineteenth century, the claims of justice came for some to require a notably more active role for central government. The strengthening of party loyalties and organisations offered a challenge to inherited models of good government that could emphasise consensus, and an administrative rather than legislative vision of political action. It was perhaps those less comfortable with party government, such as Liberal Unionists, for whom older understandings of good government proved most resonant. Similarly, the ideal of disinterested, almost un-politicised, service that some versions of good government conveyed may have been more congenial to the official mind of Whitehall than the Westminster politician for whom detachment from the vibrant, but pressing, world of popular politics was increasingly unavailable. Hence, too, the enduring appeal of the language of good government for some imperial administrators.

The emergence of social politics in the last years of the nineteenth century recast debates about good government, but also reduced the relevance of an older language. Champions of the new liberalism, notably J.A. Hobson, summarised the liberalism that needed to be left behind in ways that were strikingly similar to older understandings of the nature of good government.[9] An emphasis upon fostering the good life for all, and ensuring its material basis, could be conveyed in the terminology of good government, but the more expansive, and social, agenda involved strained the conventional boundaries of this language.[10] It would, though, be wrong to present the final years of the nineteenth century and the first of the twentieth as simply witnessing the disappearance of good government as a language of politics. Promotion of the common good and the improvement of material conditions as part of that were expressed within the language of good government earlier in the nineteenth century. Opposition to tariff reform sometimes stressed its corrupting and factional tendencies in contrast to a notion of free trade as preserving an even-handed state in a fashion that echoed previous appeals to the virtues of good government. Nor indeed, in the era of the South African war, did interest in administrative competence disappear.[11] It was, though, nonetheless the case that the discursive terrain of politics was shifting, and that emerging concerns with democratic citizenship, new conceptions of welfare, and a programmatic politics of legislation were usually articulated in terms somewhat distant from the inherited language of good government.

Whiggism, utilitarianism and the art of governing

The most familiar understanding of nineteenth-century politics is one in which laissez-faire looms large. This view has been very seriously modified in the last 40 years.[12] Historians increasingly emphasise the exceptions contemporaries made to minimalist conceptions of the role of government, and the extent to which older accounts of the ubiquity of laissez-faire failed to look beyond economics in charting contemporary views of the role of government. One important source of this shift has been the restoration of Whig liberalism to a central position in our understanding of the governing ethos of Victorian Britain. The work of Jonathan Parry especially has been crucial in this process.[13] In recovering the Whig perspective, historians have disclosed a strong attachment to good government, in which good government depended upon good leadership, also known as the leadership of good Whigs. In an important essay Parry has shown how central the promotion of Christian and moral values was to Lord John Russell, and brought out how deeply his conception of good government resonated amongst Liberals, so helping to explain his appeal.[14] The habit of local self-government was seen as crucial in inculcating political virtue. As Peter Mandler forcefully argued, the politics of the Whig aristocracy did not tend to the view that good government was synonymous with less government. The Whig tradition upheld a vision of politics as a creative act that identified, as in the Holland circle, good government with un-corrupt service, but which also insisted that politics was capable of making a difference, and that Parliament should be central and active, not passive and peripheral. Indeed, Mandler quotes Lord John Russell identifying good government with 'the greatest improvement in the comforts and well being of the people'.[15]

The Whig dialect of good government was one in which the quality of leadership was crucial. It was also one in which politics was very much an art, requiring a complex array of qualities, of judgment and prudence, but also of courage and risk-taking. A somewhat different version emerges in the writings of James Mill. In his famous essay on government, Mill repeatedly deployed the language of good government. He took 'the question' of government to be one of the 'adaptation of means to an end'. In this starkly instrumental, and self-consciously disenchanted, approach to politics, Mill swiftly argued for the greatest happiness of the greatest number attained by ensuring to 'every man the greatest possible quantity of the produce of his labour' as the aim of government. He did hint that this view had a longer history, traceable to Locke's focus on 'the public good', but its validity was presented as a logical deduction from the basic and constant facts of human nature. He dismissed talk of the balance between democracy, aristocracy and monarchy as impossible, casting representative government as 'the grand discovery of modern times'. A broad franchise allied to efficient delegation of responsibility to the government would ensure effective rule.[16]

Mill's conception of good government, like that of the Whigs, was anchored in an account of the human qualities necessary to its provision, but that account was different. Mill was rather less impressed by the characteristics of aristocrats than were the Whigs. Strikingly, he noted that prudence – traditionally seen as an important virtue underpinning good government – was more common amongst those without fortune, who were not subject to its corrupting effects. Furthermore, it was those outside of the charmed aristocratic embrace who had the greater interest in justice and the pursuit of the common good with which good government was identified. Mill argued that 'intellectual powers are the offspring of labour' and offered a lengthy and well-known elegy to the middle ranks. Historians have differed over the exact sociological referent for Mill's category, but it does seem clear that the group was found between 'rich manufacturers' and 'poor workmen', embodied science and art, and set the tone for 'the great majority of the people'. So, whilst Mill's was a strictly utilitarian and consequentialist account of what constituted good government – maximising the greatest happiness of the greatest number – the possibility for its achievement rested upon the emergence of that middle rank that was 'numerous' in Great Britain, which was 'the chief source of all that has exalted and refined human nature' and which would, if the franchise was extended, supply 'the opinion that would ultimately decide'.[17]

As political and intellectual historians have effectively demonstrated in recent years, programmatic doctrinal utilitarianism was a distinctly acquired and minority taste in early and mid-nineteenth century Britain. While James's son John Stuart Mill came, certainly in the 1850s and 1860s, to exert a far greater influence than his exacting father, he did so through a recasting of utilitarianism that very significantly distanced his thinking from that of earlier philosophical radicals. Indeed, the changing emphases in scholarship on John Stuart Mill – towards, for instance, stressing his agonistic conception of citizenship, and the 'positive' elements of his view of liberty – exemplify the broader shift away from a picture of nineteenth-century political thought with utilitarianism near its centre.[18]

This lower estimate of the impact of utilitarianism is essentially correct, but we do need to attend to the ways in which philosophic radicals did help shape the everyday language of good government as a means of discussing and evaluating politics. In his influential *Lectures on the Relation of Law to Public Opinion*, A.V. Dicey argued that 'Benthamism or Individualism' was the ruling creed of early nineteenth-century Britain. Dicey nostalgically portrayed 'the Benthamism of common sense' as apparent throughout British life from the 1820s to the 1860s. It was compatible with 'the best ideas of the English middle classes'. Dicey grossly over-estimated the purchase of utilitarian ideas, but the manner in which he identified them with English virtues is suggestive of the means by which a more homespun concern for utility could inflect considerations of good government.[19]

This was apparent, for example, in some discussions of colonial government. The philosophic radical Charles Buller's important pamphlet of 1840, *Responsible Government for Colonies*, was styled as 'a contribution to the cause of good government in all the colonies'. Buller argued for the devolution of government towards the colonies, but was concerned to present this as a temperate proposal. His proposals involved an element of representation. He was though careful to argue that responsible government did not require fully fledged representation, rather that establishing a representative dimension was one of the 'guarantees of good government in our colonies'. It was central to Buller's argument that while he fully acknowledged the efficacy of enlightened opinion, he felt that British opinion could not be seriously brought to bear upon events in such distant places. Originally published as a series of articles in the *Colonial Gazette*, Buller's intervention exemplifies the philosophic radical employment of the goal of good government.[20] In the aftermath of the collapse of the philosophic radical grouping in Parliament, Buller moved towards the Whigs – a transition perhaps already presaged in aspects of his political language.

The crusade against 'old corruption' was clearly one of the dominant motifs of British politics in the early nineteenth century.[21] For radicals especially, the untrammelled power of the Crown and the executive needed disciplining through the extension of the franchise, the intensification of parliamentary scrutiny, the increased frequency of elections, and so on.[22] For these critics, the structures of *ancien régime* Britain were thoroughly incapable of delivering good government. They were also, it could be argued, wrong in themselves, in that they denied individuals a political voice that was theirs by right. It is though the failure to secure good government that is of concern here.

The failure was multifaceted. The charge of old corruption cast government as an exercise in rewarding fellow aristocrats and clients rather than an attempt to pursue the common good.[23] The allegation was one of clannishness, but also of incompetence. It was argued that such deficiencies were inevitable, given the closed and interconnected character of British institutions. In order to secure good government, greater transparency was required, but also greater popular involvement in the polity, so harnessing larger energies and hence raising performance.

Many historians now argue that this critique came to seem less persuasive over time, in part because of the ways in which the governing classes became more conscientious in their approach to governing, and the manner in which the state increasingly sought to operate more neutrally between groups.[24] There, are, though, some difficulties here, given the enduring reality of aristocratic power, and indeed, in comparative terms, Britain's increasingly undemocratic arrangements when contrasted with the rest of Europe. In some respects, the language of 'old corruption' still seemed pretty serviceable at the end of the nineteenth century to radicals dispirited by the dominance of the Cecil clan and the reactionary character of British politics at home and abroad.[25] The importance for us, however, is the way in which the language of good government was, in some ways, bolstered by the radical critique, and the manner in which mid-Victorian visions of good government did come to stress a business-like competence. It is to these that we now turn.

Administration, competence and participation

Few people can have written more essays with government in the title than Walter Bagehot. It was perhaps Bagehot more than any other mid-Victorian writer who wryly enunciated the doctrine that 'politics are a kind of business'. This was, for Bagehot, one of the many important things that the English understood but other nations did not. It was a sobering but also reassuring thought, Bagehot argued, that politics 'bear the characteristics, and obey the laws' inherent to the world of business. In an essay on 'Dull Government', Bagehot argued that dullness was in fact evidence of excellence in parliamentary government, since 'all the best business is a little dull'. Indeed, in Bagehot's sardonic take on good government, it was candidly acknowledged that 'no lofty and patriotic execution' of its tasks was appropriate to times of peace. Governance should reflect the developing character of the nation: 'we are now arrived at the business statesman – or rather, the business speaker'.[26]

Bagehot wrote very extensively about politics and politicians, and his fertile production of phrases and judgments reflects the demands of journalism. It is, though, evident that a vision of good government emerges from his writings. This image was not one of simple-minded minimalist administration. On more than one occasion, Bagehot stressed the dangers of an excessive enthusiasm for reducing the size and reach of the central state, and for adhering instinctively to local solutions. In an essay on 'Shabby Government', he sketched the dangers of overly reducing government expenditure, noting how official parsimony might be 'injurious to the public interests as it is unfair to the individual sufferers'.[27] The proper conduct of administration was undoubtedly a pre-requisite for government to be good in Bagehot's eyes. He insisted in 1874, no doubt with the first Gladstone government in mind, that 'legislation never ought long to be, and never permanently can be, the main business of Parliament'.[28] In a revealing essay from the mid-1860s on 'Politics as a Profession', Bagehot equated 'statesmanship' with 'political business', and agreed with Gladstone that statesmanship was a distinct profession that needed to be learnt when young through a 'practical apprenticeship', and that only in the House of Commons could this training be had.[29] The last point reminds us that Bagehot's conception of politics was a broad one, in which speaking in Parliament was of considerable educative value in itself. This reflected the links between society and politics through the force of national character and public opinion that he articulated in both *The English Constitution* and *Physics and Politics*.[30]

The ideal of good government, it has been suggested, was strongly linked to the notions of justice and the common good. There is a very great deal that could be said about each of these, but a brief consideration will have to suffice. In the mid-Victorian language of good government, the demands of justice are perhaps primarily those of impartiality, of some notion of even-handedness between different groups of people, evident in the construction and presentation of taxation policy under Gladstone.[31] Rhetorically, the stress is upon fair transactions between free individuals, though, as Paul Johnson has recently reemphasised, the realities of the market as enforced by the law could be brutal and discriminatory.[32] This is, roughly speaking, justice as guaranteeing formal legal equality, the security of property, and the rights of contracting individuals: it is more of a commutative than a distributional conception. Relatedly, the underlying notion of the common good is perhaps best understood in terms of what was regarded as its antithesis. It was the pursuit of selfish gain for an individual or a group and the privatising of public resources that were most sharply contrasted with the common good. There is, though, also a lingering sense of a good that was meaningfully shared, and hence perhaps not a question of material resources, but was rather a good for the community as a whole, from which all benefited, if not necessarily equally.[33] Established notions of good government, as Bagehot was well aware, linked it closely to local government. Joshua Toulmin Smith made the case at great length in his account of *Local Government and Centralisation* in 1851, in which the virtues of the former were held to be inexhaustible, those of the latter, meagre to non-existent. Local government was, for Toulmin Smith, a rigorous school in the active citizenship required to combat the forces of selfish materialism and to preserve liberty. He regarded bureaucracy as another form of despotism, but one more dangerous for its ability to masquerade as a free constitution.[34] The centrality of liberty to his political language is well established, but it needs noting that he saw vigorous localism as essential to both good and free government. Toulmin Smith held that the conservation of person and property was not incompatible, in the absence of true local government, with the reduction of the people to 'a nation of slaves'. He took the essential purpose of the polity to be that of enabling 'the fullest scope … to the healthy development of the faculties of every one of those members'. He argued, reflecting here at least widely held views in nineteenth-century Britain, that 'the highest self-interest and the public good can never be antagonistic, but always go together'. He approvingly quoted F.W. Newman's maxim that 'to centralize is the art and trick of despots, to decentralize is the necessary wisdom of those who love good government'.[35]

In the language of good government inherited from the eighteenth century, localism was seen as the strongest guarantee of a well-informed and genuinely responsible approach to political problems.[36] The middle of the nineteenth century saw intense debate over how best to deliver the administrative competence central to 'good government' in the face of significant challenges, notably in the 1850s. This was the era of the Administrative Reform Association and the heyday of politics-as-business rhetoric.[37] An emphasis upon the effective dispatch of administration was not novel, and Bagehot's portrait of Peel made much of his gifts as 'a man of business'.[38] The waging of war, as it would at the end of the century, proved fertile ground for a renewed emphasis upon business-like virtues through the language of good government.[39] For the protagonists of the Administrative Reform Association, renewed independent parliamentary scrutiny was necessary to restore the quality of government. As, however, the limited success of the Association suggests, business-like methods and business-friendly policies did not exhaust the mid-Victorian meanings of good government. Palmerston influentially insisted that more traditional virtues, associated with a landed aristocratic governing class, remained crucial, not least as good government necessitated an encompassing sense of the common good scarcely fostered by the moneyed interest.[40]

Much debate in the mid-Victorian period was directed towards the franchise in particular, and, more broadly, to the relationship between politics and the attributes of the citizenry. These discussions involved much more than the question of how best to secure good government. Indeed, champions of enfranchisement could argue that justice required its granting rather than basing their case upon the consequences of an enlarged electorate. Many, however, did claim that the spread of good character amongst the population meant that a larger electorate would lead to better government.[41] More generally, it was increasingly common to relate the quality of government more strongly to the capacities of the people. John Stuart Mill's claim that good government rested principally upon the 'qualities of the human beings composing the society over which the government is exercised' had broad resonance, and gained further adherents over time.[42]

Mid-century assessments of the human beings composing society in Britain were generally upbeat, particularly in comparison to human beings elsewhere. This encouraged support for extensions of the franchise on the basis that a more inclusive politics would, at least in Britain, improve decision making. The idea that good government was rooted in the characteristics of the broader population was certainly not new. *Bradshaw's Journal* approvingly quoted Robert Hall in 1842 arguing that 'the true prop of good government is opinion; the perception, on the part of the subjects, of benefits resulting from it; a settled conviction, in other words, of its being a public good'.[43] This knowledge was a product of a free constitution to be contrasted with the fear upon which tyranny depended. Established Whig doctrines had attributed a role to an active citizenship, mediated through Parliament, in ensuring high-quality governance.

Within the language of good government, the link between a politically alert citizenry and an able political class persisted. However, in the mid-century, the importance attributed to 'public opinion' in shaping politics was growing. In debates about the form of government, it became increasingly common to stress the significance of national character, and to argue that the functionality of the polity could only be judged in relation to the historical trajectory of a given society.[44] Eighteenth-century political thought was castigated for its alleged abstraction and adherence to fixed conceptions of human nature.[45] More dynamic, inclusive and progressive notions of history were popularised.[46] The implications for politics of such understandings could be evaluated in a variety of ways. It might, however, be suggested that these more demotic conceptions of politics had the potential to make good government as the sensible conduct of business appear narrow in its ambitions and social basis. This reflection leads naturally to a consideration of the final third of the nineteenth century.

Citizenship, good government and the social

In his *Political Studies* of 1879, George Brodrick distinguished between the school of thought that focused purely on the ends of government, defined in terms of public safety and material prosperity; and that which regarded 'the process of government, as a means of moral training' which 'denies the title of "good Government" to polities in which the noblest faculties of the citizens are left unemployed'.[47] As we have seen, the inherited terminology of good government did not necessarily preclude concern for 'moral training', but the idiom was certainly well suited to articulating a focus on effective processes and readily observable outcomes. By the early twentieth century, more progressive liberals could chafe at the apparently Whiggish constraints of the language of good government. In his 1911 study of *Liberalism*, L.T. Hobhouse conceded that 'good government is much', but proceeded to insist that 'the good will is more' and that 'even the imperfect, halting, confused utterance of the common will may have in it the potency of higher things than a perfection of machinery will ever attain'.[48]

Hobhouse's recognition of both the imperfection and the essential value of the 'utterance of the common will' remains striking, but more significant for our purposes is his equating of good government with effective institutions. The legacy for Liberals of the dark years of the 1890s was evident in his earlier acknowledgment in *Liberalism* that 'even in this country it is a tenable view that the extension of the suffrage in 1884 tended for some years to arrest the development of liberty'.[49] Hobhouse was not simply denying the worth of good government, nor was he ignorant of the capacity of reactionary politics to mobilise popular support. It was, however, only 'a social democracy', as he put it in *Social Evolution and Political Theory*, published in the same year as *Liberalism*, which could by 'the organized expression of the collective will ... remodel society in accordance with humanitarian sentiment'.[50] In doing so, it realised the harmonious inter-dependence between persons embodied in social evolution.

Hobhouse's metaphysics were complex, and the intricate structure of his political theory was scarcely representative of everyday political discourse. He was, however, more typical of changes in political discourse in his sense of the limitations of a tight focus on good government in defining the ends of politics. His fellow new liberal J.A. Hobson forcefully argued in 1909 that liberalism must advance beyond a faith in 'mere economy, in good administration at home, peace abroad, in minor legislation' if it was to remain relevant.[51] By the early twentieth century, dismissal of Whig ideas was a common refrain across the political spectrum. The conservative and historian Keith Feiling's *Toryism: A Political Dialogue* portrayed Whig ideas as a shallow individualism whose incorporation into elements of the Conservative Party distracted from an older, more glorious tradition of organic, righteous Tory belief.[52] Widespread attacks on 'individualism' in these years also identified Benthamism with an overly narrow account of the scope of government, as the radical conservative F.E. Smith did in distinguishing unionist social reform from the failings of laissez-faire on the one hand, and socialism on the other.[53] Feiling was content to take fitness to deliver 'good government' as a test for determining the electorate at both local and national level.[54] Nonetheless, in Edwardian Britain, debates over the purpose of politics routinely evoked more expansive, and interventionist, goals than those associated with the established discourse of good government.

These developments in the language of politics in Britain are illuminated by Dicey's much-cited *Lectures on the Relation between Law and Public Opinion*. Dicey was unimpressed by what he saw as a growth in collectivist sentiment in late nineteenth-century Britain. This neglected, he insisted, the fundamental truth that 'for the ultimate cure of social diseases we must trust to general good-will', and especially, to 'individual energy and self-help'. Indeed, Dicey insisted on the inescapable relevance for statesmen of original sin as a fact of human nature. He was unsympathetic to many of the intellectual trends of the late nineteenth and early twentieth century, cleaving to the superior wisdom of earlier times. He tended, accordingly, to identify good government with 'what any Benthamite liberal' would understand by it. This was a consequentialist, self-consciously realistic but inclusive conception of good government, evident in his citation of Sydney Smith on the myriad benefits of parliamentary reform to 'the hewer of wood and the drawer of water'.[55]

The last third of the nineteenth century by no means witnessed the demise of the language of good government. There were, though, aspects of the period that made the idiom more problematic. The emergence of a more legislative, programmatic approach to governance implied greater dynamism than the deliverance of good government. As Anthony Howe argues in his chapter, free trade proved a powerful popular language for understanding economic life. It was, though, challenged more strongly from the 1880s, and while free traders' response to this challenge was notable, the debate made it harder to present good government as simply the competent application of settled principles.[56] Similarly, discussion of socialism from the 1880s highlighted basic questions about the role of the state and the nature of society.[57] The shared liberal values underlying much of British political culture encouraged a robust public debate in which significant differences of policy and principles were fully ventilated. The very ferocity of disagreement over Ireland was in part a result of a shared adherence to constitutionalism expressed in sharply clashing understandings of what was the properly constitutional course of action. Dispute over the purpose of the state and the meaning of the constitution was not resolvable through the inherited language of good government.

The spread of party organisation from the 1870s served to energise political controversy and perhaps to foster greater concern with defining and distinguishing political creeds.[58] Debate about the identity of liberalism, or socialism, became more prevalent. This did not, of course, extinguish the language of good government. Indeed, the consolidation of party government inspired considerable misgivings. As Dicey put it, 'no one can help feeling that there is a sense in which government by Party is an evil, even though it be necessary evil'. He remarked that 'there is something irrational in the supposition that for the promotion of good government it is essentially necessary that there should be a constant conflict between the men in office & the men out of office'. Dicey noted that in England it was often assumed that 'defined parties', which some continental countries unfortunately lacked, were required to make parliamentary government work.[59] It was, though, clear that for Dicey, as for Henry Maine, the intensification and nationalisation of party conflict was troubling.[60]

For Dicey's fellow Liberal Unionist, Hugh Seymour Tremenheere, wirepulling was primarily a radical sin, and the quality of parliamentarians in the 1890s remained high. Preserving mixed, rather than unlimited government, was, he felt, crucial to preserving the established benefits of good government.[61] Related to the debate over party government was concern about the advent of 'one-man rule'.[62] Some argued that increasingly centralised parties along with the expansion of extra-parliamentary speaking enabled political leaders to exercise very considerable power, as, for his opponents, Gladstone showed. The increased authority of the Commons and the growth of the electorate from the mid-1880s exacerbated fears for some about a loss of balance within the constitution. Traditionally good government was often seen as the product of strong parliamentary scrutiny from independent MPs allied to institutional checks upon executive power. Here, Tremenheere espoused a constitutionalist account of good government of a kind that Hobson or Hobhouse might have seen as overly preoccupied with machinery.

However, in articulating his vision of how good government arose and could be sustained, Tremenheere combined this older picture with newer elements. He praised the work of public men whose speeches had helped to educate the people, contributing to 'the formation of the good sense and matured opinion which is the real ruling power of the country'. He argued 'by these means that the voters in our Parliamentary contests may be now brought to distinguish well-considered measures having for their object the true interests of the whole, from the narrow, selfish, visionary notions of "faddists"'. This happy state of affairs owed much to the legacy of good government, which had 'greatly raised the national character'.[63] His emphasis upon the power of opinion, and the need for government to deliver for the nation as a whole, were key tropes in late nineteenth-century political debate.

The provision of just rule, and a care for the common good, were established elements of the language of good government, whose centrality to political debate was if anything greater at the close of the century. Tremenheere presented good government as the foundation of general prosperity. By securing property and liberty through the impartial administration of the law, the basis was laid for the accumulation of capital and the flourishing of industry.[64] Tremenheere offered a version of the origins of prosperity and the operation of capitalism that was much contested in late Victorian Britain. He was, though, representative in his view that successful government led to material gains, and that bad government did the opposite. While such concerns were scarcely novel, economic performance and the distribution of resources became increasingly salient politically in the last part of the century.[65] This had important consequences for discussions of good government, and for the language of politics more generally.

Renewed attention to poverty from the 1880s, and the emergence of unemployment as a clearly defined political problem from the 1890s, significantly recast the political agenda.[66] Other issues, of course, remained prominent, and many of these, such as Home Rule or House of Lords' reform, were of long-standing. There was, however, a distinct shift in the political terrain whereby 'social' issues, particularly housing and the fate of the unemployed, assumed a more central position. These matters were discussed in variety of idioms, and echoes were evident of earlier periods, notably the condition of England debates of the 1840s. Nonetheless, real changes occurred in political discourse. The popularisation and conceptualisation of 'unemployment' as a distinct economic phenomenon provides one example. As Michael Freeden has noted, 'welfare' gained currency as a political goal that combined an aggregate and a distributive dimension on the basis that a given gain had greater impact at the bottom than the top.[67] Discussion of material realities was not necessarily secularised; clergy were often instrumental in anti-poverty campaigns, and religious language was frequently deployed. The growing prominence of the incarnation in much contemporary Christianity inspired hope of building the kingdom of heaven upon earth, by insisting on the common spark of the divine amongst men regardless of circumstance.[68]

Alongside such distributional debates, the late nineteenth century saw sharper discussions of economic performance. Comparisons with other countries were rife and could be unflattering. The riposte to tariff reformers mounted by free traders was certainly impressive, and fiscal issues continued to be freighted with moral and symbolic significance.[69] The language of good government with its connotations of impartiality and fair dealing could be mobilised against tariff reform, presented as a corrupting force that would cause sectional interests to besiege the state seeking favours. Discussion of relative performance was, however, multifaceted, incorporating worries about education, entrepreneurship, industrial training and animal spirits. It began to open up an agenda for government that implied an ongoing effort to augment economic activity, although the heyday for such politics was to come later. This kind of politics could certainly be described as delivering good government, but its preoccupations were quite distant from those conveyed by established doctrines of good government, which were less social, dynamic and activist in their implications.

It would be wrong to identify the last part of the century solely with the politics of economics. The emphasis upon improving the moral texture of society evident in the liberalism of Lord John Russell was highly apparent in that of William Gladstone.[70] The flowering of what Jonathan Parry has called a 'democratic humanitarianism' held together a broad alliance on the left of British politics in the last third of the nineteenth century. This approach was intensely concerned with morality in politics, and could be firmly populist in assessing where in society good morals were to be found. Both domestic and foreign politics were embraced within this ethical vision, which imbued free trade with so much meaning beyond calculations of felicity.[71] It inspired a discourse of mission and crusade, of liberalism as a living faith, anchored in righteousness. The more modest idiom of good government was not the best instrument to communicate such grand designs.

While the early twentieth century has often been seen as an era of sectional conflict in British politics, it was, as G.D.H. Cole noted, a period in which organic and holistic visions of society had great resonance.[72] Models of society as an integrated whole, were widespread across much of the political spectrum, developing an existing consensus upon the significance of opinion and morality to emphasise the role of social consciousness.[73] Evolution and philosophical idealism, both of which achieved a currency well beyond the academy, were frequently held to demonstrate the existence of a social organism.[74] There was keen debate as to the exact meaning of the organic metaphor, and its political consequences could be interpreted in a number of ways, not least on the question of the appropriate extent of state intervention. The language of the social organism was certainly flexible, and could be linked to a variety of disparate political doctrines. Within the idealist tradition especially, a strong notion of the polity was present in which politics was deemed the highest expression of the communal spirit.[75] It is, though, notable that the more autonomous, and top-down sense of politics customarily associated with the trope of good government did not fit easily with the holistic language of the social organism that became fashionable at the close of the nineteenth century.

This chapter has sought to sketch the image of 'good government' over the long nineteenth century. The aim has been to recover a flexible ideal, with a complex range of associations, rather than a tightly specified theory of politics. Its examination provides a way into nineteenth-century assessments of what the ends of politics should be, but it scarcely exhausts them. Contemporaries deployed a range of ideas and languages in assessing, attacking and defending political action – some of which (patriotism and statesmanship, for example) are explored elsewhere in this book. By focusing, though, on the language of good government, it has been possible to trace important developments in British political culture over time.

The language of good government in late eighteenth-century Britain was shaped by classical and religious antecedents. It embraced virtuous leadership, directed towards the common good and committed to upholding justice. Its enemies were corruption, faction and the pursuit of private over public interests. It was strongly attached, especially in the Whig tradition, to an image of active and serious aristocratic leadership, rooted in the local community and committed to righteousness. This vision proved an important and enduring element of British politics in the nineteenth century. It was, though, a language that others could speak too. The republican tradition cast the vigilant citizenry as the guardians of good government. Some radicals similarly emphasised the role of the people. Philosophic radicals identified good government with maximising happiness, producing a highly consequentialist idiom that could be much less enamoured of aristocratic leadership. A focus on results, combined with an emphasis upon competence, was evident where the language of good government was deployed in the empire, though its associations with justice and securing the common good made it less useful for those imperial rulers who denied the existence of an indigenous community with a common good.

The middle of the nineteenth century witnessed many invocations of the man of business as the guarantor of good government. Administrative competence was a prime concern. As in the earlier period, however, this account was not uncontested. The virtues of landed leadership, and the dangers of moneyed rule, were also strongly asserted. Concern for the moral health of the nation continued for many to be a constitutive element of good government. The importance of national character and public opinion in shaping politics was widely asserted. It was increasingly common to see older arguments about the machinery of the constitution as reliant upon an outmoded conception of a fixed human nature. Analyses of the sources of good government laid greater stress upon its basis in the attributes of the citizenry, and tended to emphasise the need for policy to accord with national character and public opinion.

In the final years of the nineteenth and the early years of the twentieth century, the language of good government certainly did not disappear from politics. It could be mobilised against corruption, and contrasted with the vicissitudes and passions of mass mobilising party politics. It is, however, the case that the discursive terrain of politics was changing, with enhanced attention to wealth, welfare and social policy. Good government language could accommodate more populist forms of politics, but it was not as resonant as it had been. Debates about integrating the business elite in the 1880s, and about rejuvenating local politics in the 1890s, showed that older conceptions of who should provide political leadership were not extinguished. It was, however, perhaps in discussions of public service rather than in the heat of electoral battle that the language now proved most serviceable. In recent years, not least in comparative discussions of economic governance, considerable attention has been paid to good government, with an emphasis upon competence, the absence of corruption and the following of rules. These aims remain highly relevant in much of the world. In a context of considerable disenchantment about politics, they may appeal even in advanced economies. Charting, however, earlier discussion of good government, helps reveal both the meaningfulness of the long nineteenth century as a category, and the complex patterns of change and continuity, contained therein.

Notes

1. J. Vernon, *Politics and the People: A Study in English Political Culture, c. 1815–1867* (Cambridge, 1993); J. Vernon, *Re-reading the Constitution: New Narratives in the Political History of England's Long Nineteenth Century* (Cambridge, 1996); P. Joyce, *Democratic Subjects: The Self and the Social in Nineteenth-Century England* (Cambridge, 1994); C. Hall, K. McClelland and J. Rendall, *Defining the Victorian Nation: Class, Race, Gender and the Reform Act of 1867* (Cambridge, 2000).
2. G. Sutherland, *Studies in the Growth of Nineteenth Century Government* (London, 1972); S. Collini, *Liberalism and Sociology: L. T. Hobhouse and Political Argument in England 1880–1914* (Cambridge, 1979); J. Harris, *Private Lives, Public Spirit: Britain, 1870–1914* (Oxford, 1993); J. Meadowcroft, *Conceptualizing the State: Innovation and Dispute in British Political Thought 1880–1914* (Oxford, 1995).
3. Q. Skinner, *Visions of Politics II: Renaissance Virtues* (Cambridge, 2002), pp. 39–118.
4. H.S. Tremenheere, *How Good Government Grew Up and How to Preserve It* (London, 1893), pp. 3, 12, 19, 22.
5. C.A. Bayly, *The Birth of the Modern World, 1780–1914: Global Connections and Comparisons* (Oxford, 2004), pp. 285–6, 289–90, 296.
6. J. Newman, *The Character and Blessings of a Good Government* (London, 1714); B. Downing, *Religion, Good Government and Commerce United; or Christianity the Glory of England* (London, 1814).
7. For example, C.F. Dole, *City Government and the Churches: What a Private Citizen Can Do for Good City Government* (Philadelphia, 1895).
8. S. Collini, *Public Moralists: Political Thought and Intellectual Life in Britain, 1850–1930* (Oxford, 1993).
9. J.A. Hobson, *The Crisis of Liberalism: New Issues of Democracy* (London, 1909), p. 136.
10. This process was importantly treated in J. Harris, 'The Transition to High Politics in English Social Policy 1880–1914' in M. Bentley and J. Stevenson, eds., *High and Low Politics in Modern Britain* (Oxford, 1983).
11. G.R. Searle, *The Quest for National Efficiency: A Study in British Politics and Political Thought* (Oxford, 1971).
12. These trends are discussed at greater length in J. Thompson, 'Modern Liberty Redefined' in G. Claeys and G. Stedman Jones, eds., *The Cambridge History of Nineteenth-Century Political Thought* (Cambridge, 2011), pp. 720–47. See also H. S. Jones, *Victorian Political Thought* (Basingstoke, 2000).

13. J.P. Parry, *Democracy and Religion: Gladstone and the Liberal Party, 1867–1875* (Cambridge, 1986); J.P. Parry, *The Rise and Fall of Liberal Government in Victorian Britain* (New Haven, 1993); J.P. Parry, *The Politics of Patriotism: English Liberalism, National Identity and Europe, 1830–1886* (Cambridge, 2006).
14. J.P. Parry, 'Past and Future in the Later Career of Lord John Russell' in T.C.W. Blanning and D. Cannadine, eds., *History and Biography: Essays in Honour of Derek Beales* (Cambridge, 1996), pp. 142–72.
15. P. Mandler, *Aristocratic Government in the Age of Reform: Whigs and Liberals 1830–1852* (Oxford, 1990), pp. 37, 62, 39.
16. J. Mill, *Political Writings*, ed. T. Ball (Cambridge, 1992), pp. 3, 5, 21.
17. Ibid., pp. 40–2.
18. Jones, *Victorian Political Thought*, p. 36; A. Ryan, 'Mill in a Liberal Landscape' in J. Skorupski, ed., *The Cambridge Companion to Mill* (Cambridge, 1998), p. 509; N. Urbinati, *Mill on Democracy: From the Athenian Polis to Representative Government* (Chicago, 2002).
19. A.V. Dicey, *Lectures on the Relations between Law and Public Opinion in England during the Nineteenth Century*, intro. R. A. Cosgrove (New Brunswick, 1981), pp. 170, 173.
20. C. Buller, *Responsible Government for Colonies* 2nd edn (London, 1840), pp. iv, 4, 66.
21. On this theme, see P. Harling, *The Waning of 'Old Corruption': The Politics of Economical Reform, 1779–1846* (Oxford, 1996).
22. M. Taylor, *The Decline of British Radicalism 1847–1860* (Oxford, 1995).
23. On the general theme of popular anti-aristocratic sentiment, see A. Taylor, *Lords of Misrule: Hostility to Aristocracy in Late-Nineteenth and Early-Twentieth Century Britain* (Basingstoke, 2004).
24. G. Stedman Jones, *Languages of Class: Studies in English Working Class History, 1832–1982* (Cambridge, 1983), ch. 3; J.P. Parry, 'The Decline of Institutional Reform in Nineteenth-Century Britain' in J. Lawrence and D. Feldman, eds., *Structures and Transformations in Modern British History* (Cambridge, 2011), pp. 164–86; Taylor, *Decline of British Radicalism*.
25. J. Thompson, 'The Genesis of the 1906 Trade Disputes Act: Liberalism, Trade Unions and the Law, *Twentieth Century British History* 9 (1998), 175–200.
26. *The Collected Works of Walter Bagehot*, ed. N. St John Stevas, 15 vols (London, 1965–86), VI, pp. 85, 81, 82, 84.
27. Ibid., p. 110–11.
28. Ibid., p. 149.
29. Ibid., p. 130.
30. D.M. Craig, 'Bagehot's Republicanism' in A. Olechnowicz, ed., *The Monarchy and the British Nation* (Cambridge, 2007), pp. 139–62.
31. H.C.G. Matthew, 'Disraeli, Gladstone and the Politics of Mid-Victorian Budgets', *Historical Journal* 22 (1979), 615–43; M.J. Daunton, *Trusting Leviathan: The Politics of Taxation in Britain, 1799–1914* (Cambridge, 2001).
32. P. Johnson, *Making the Market: Victorian Origins of Corporate Capitalism* (Cambridge, 2010).
33. Debates about justice are addressed in J Thompson, 'Modern Liberty Redefined' and J. Thompson, 'The Great Labour Unrest and Political Thought in Britain, 1911–14', *Labour History Review* (forthcoming, 2014).
34. J. Toulmin Smith, *Local Government and Centralization: The Characteristics of Each; and its Practical Tendencies, as Affecting Social, Moral, and Political*

Welfare and Progress including Comprehensive Outlines of the English Constitution (London, 1851), p. 29.

35. Ibid., pp. 7, 33, 49, 69.
36. Parry, *Rise and Fall of Liberal Government*, passim.
37. On the Administrative Reform Association, see Taylor, *Decline of British Radicalism*, pp. 249–52. On the relationship between business and politics, see G. R. Searle, *Entrepreneurial Politics in Mid-Victorian Britain* (Oxford, 1993).
38. *Collected Works of Bagehot*, III, pp. 241–71.
39. Searle, *The Quest For National Efficiency*.
40. On Palmerston, see D. Brown and M. Taylor eds., *Palmerston Studies I* (Southampton, 2007); D. Brown and M. Taylor, eds., *Palmerston Studies II* (Southampton, 2007).
41. Collini, *Public Moralists*, ch. 3.
42. J.S. Mill, *Considerations on Representative Government* (London, 1861), p. 389.
43. *Bradshaw's Journal: A Miscellany of Literature, Science, and Art* 14 (1842), p. 224.
44. M. Francis and J. Morrow, *A History of Political Thought in the Nineteenth Century* (London, 1994).
45. John Stuart Mill reflected on this tendency, which he saw as overblown in his autobiography. See John Stuart Mill, *Autobiography* (London, 1989), p. 130.
46. J.W. Burrow, *A Liberal Descent: Victorian Historians and the English Past* (Cambridge, 1981).
47. G.C. Brodrick, *Political Studies* (London, 1879), pp. 19–20.
48. L.T. Hobhouse, *Liberalism* (London, 1911), p. 229.
49. Ibid., p. 46.
50. L.T. Hobhouse, *Social Evolution and Political Theory* (New York, 1911), p. 183.
51. Hobson, *The Crisis of Liberalism*, p. 136.
52. K. Feiling, *Toryism: A Political Dialogue* (London, 1913), pp. 34, 39, 40–1.
53. F.E. Smith, *Unionist Policy and Other Essays* (London, 1913), pp. 24, 31.
54. Feiling, *Toryism*, p. 67.
55. Dicey, *Lectures on the Relations between Law and Public Opinion*, p. 463, 213.
56. E.H.H. Green, *The Crisis of Conservatism: The Politics, Economics and Ideology of the Conservative Party* (London, 1995).
57. J. Harris, *Unemployment and Politics: A Study in English Social Policy 1886–1914* (Oxford, 1972).
58. This process was far from simple or universally welcomed. A useful introduction remains M. Pugh, *The Making of Modern British Politics* (Oxford, 2002). See also J. Lawrence, *Speaking for the People: Party, Language and Popular Politics in England, 1867–1914* (Cambridge, 1998) and E.F. Biagini, *British Democracy and Irish Nationalism 1876–1906* (Cambridge, 2007).
59. A.V. Dicey, 'Memorandum on Party Government' (July 1898) in *General Characteristics of English Constitutionalism: Six Unpublished Lectures*, ed. P. Raina (Oxford, 2009), pp. 141–2.
60. H. Maine, *Popular Government: Four Essays* (London, 1885).
61. Tremenheere, *How Good Government Grew Up*, pp. 19, 22.
62. J. Thompson, *British Political Culture and the Idea of 'Public Opinion'* (Cambridge, 2013).
63. Tremenheere, *How Good Government Grew Up*, pp. 12, 4.
64. Ibid., p. 3.

65. Green, *Crisis of Conservatism*; R. Middleton, *Government versus the Market: The Growth of the Public Sector, Economic Management and British Economic Performance, c. 1890–1979* (Cheltenham, 1996).

66. G. Stedman Jones, *Outcast London: A Study in the Relation Between Classes in Victorian Society* (Oxford, 1971); S. Koven, *Slumming: Sexual and Social Politics in Victorian London* (Princeton, 2004); Harris, *Unemployment and Politics*.

67. M. Freeden, *Liberal Languages: Ideological Imaginations and Twentieth Century Progressive Thought* (Princeton, 2005).

68. I. Packer, 'Religion and the New Liberalism: the Rowntree Family, Quakerism, and Social Reform', *Journal of British Studies* 42 (2003), 236–57; C. Walsh, 'The Incarnation and the Christian Socialist Conscience in the Victorian Church of England,' *Journal of British Studies* 34 (1995), 351–74.

69. A.C. Howe, *Free Trade and Liberal England, 1846–1946* (Oxford, 1997); F. Trentmann, *Free Trade Nation: Commerce, Consumption and Civil Society in Modern Britain* (Oxford, 2009).

70. H.C.G. Matthew, *Gladstone 1809–1898* (Oxford, 1997); E. F. Biagini, *Liberty, Retrenchment and Reform: Popular Liberalism in the Age of Gladstone, 1860–80* (Cambridge, 1992); Parry, *Democracy and Religion*.

71. Parry, *The Politics of Patriotism, passim*.

72. G.D.H. Cole. *The World of Labour: A Discussion of the Present and Future of Trade Unionism* (London, 1913), pp. 20–1.

73. J. Harris, 'Political Thought and the Welfare State 1870–1940: an Intellectual Framework for British Social Policy', *Past and Present* 35 (1992), 116–41; J. Harris, 'Platonism, Positivism and Progressivism: Aspects of British Sociological Thought in the Early Twentieth Century' in E.F. Biagini, ed., *Citizenship and Community: Liberals, Radicals and Collective Identities in the British Isles, 1865–1931* (Cambridge, 1996), pp. 343–60.

74. On evolutionary organicism see M. Freeden, *The New Liberalism: An Ideology of Social Reform* (Oxford, 1978).

75. On philosophical idealism, see especially P.P. Nicholson, *The Political Philosophy of the British Idealists: Selected Studies* (Cambridge, 1990).

2

Statesmanship

David Craig

In 1921 James Bryce observed in *Modern Democracies* how 'extremely small is the number of persons by whom the world is governed' and that free government was always 'an Oligarchy within a Democracy'.[1] Accordingly, a major theme in the historiography of Britain has been whether 'modernisation' was helped or hindered by its largely aristocratic elite, and how that elite adapted itself to the process.[2] This concern has led in two directions: assessments of the economic and political power of the elite, and studies of how far political decisions were impervious to democratic pressure. The latter trend has, in recent years, turned its attention to the role of 'ideals' and 'values' in the behaviour of politicians.[3] There are now important works examining, for instance, the way that leaders tried to mobilise and manipulate wider bodies of opinion; the heroic or tragic narratives of national history in which they located their political personas; and the deeper – sometimes anxious – gendered assumptions about the status of 'public men'.[4] What, generally, has not been explored was how leadership itself was understood at the time.[5] A political leader existed within a network of assumptions of what leadership was – these could be resources to draw upon, but they were also constraints which constituted an ideal and a form of evaluation. This chapter considers five aspects of statesmanship, beginning with its relationship to governance. It then explores the essential requirements of statesmen, that they possess both principles and judgement. The final section examines the important role of character, and also the necessity of communication skills – pre-eminently oratory. These were the elements of statesmanship: as Bryce argued, since the people themselves did not rule, 'a nation is tested and judged by the quality of those it chooses and supports as its leaders; and by their capacity it stands or falls'.[6]

Definitions

It may be useful to begin with terminology. While the word 'statesman' had an ancestry going back to the sixteenth century, 'statesmanship' was a recent coinage which appeared with increasing frequency from the 1830s and enjoyed its heyday between the 1880s and 1930s, before steeply declining thereafter.[7] The word referred to political leadership and the qualities by which it was marked. It was also a strongly idealised concept, as is apparent from the reaction to one of the few guides that explicitly addressed its scope and functions. First published in 1836, Henry Taylor's *The Statesman* argued that most writers on government were concerned with 'the structure of communities and the nature of political powers and institutions' and had little to say about the 'art of *exercising* political functions' unless – like Machiavelli, Bacon and Burke – they had themselves direct political experience.[8] The reception of the work was telling. While it was agreed that there was a real need for a work which delineated the ideal of a statesman, Taylor's book was not it. One reviewer thought it should have been called *The Minister* rather than *The Statesman*, and 'of the wide distinction which may exist between these terms, the world has had frequent and melancholy proof'.[9] The problem was that Taylor seemed more concerned with advising a politician how to get and keep office – 'the arts of rising' – than with teaching him the performance of his duty.[10] Such a man was 'destitute of all principle' except the 'love of place and power', and, inevitably, this led to Taylor being charged with Machiavellianism.[11] While this was not a fair account of the work, it does show that, first, anxiety about unmerited privilege remained strong in the 1830s, and second, that the concept of 'statesman' was widely conceived in idealised terms that required it to be distinguished from the mundane ambition and pragmatism of ordinary politicians.

In addition, there was also a revealing tension between the 'statesman-as-hero' and the 'statesman-as-common man'. This can best be seen by comparing Carlyle and Bagehot. Carlyle wanted a hero who could transcend the limits of his time and to whom 'our wills are to be subordinated'. Such a man was the key to 'perfect government' and 'no ballot-box, parliamentary eloquence, voting, constitution-building, or other machinery whatsoever can improve it a whit'.[12] To some degree this chimed with the mood of crisis in the early 1840s – both Gladstone and Disraeli, in differing ways, can be found hankering for a deeper sense of leadership and government.[13] Yet by 1850, when the *Latter-Day Pamphlets* were published, it seemed out-of-place. This tirade against parliamentary government insisted it was foolish to expect 'heroic wisdom' in parliamentarians, and that the best hope was a statesman who could 'shape the dim tendencies of Parliament, and guide them wisely to the goal'.[14] The fact that Carlyle believed Peel was such a man should not disguise how idiosyncratic the position had become. A safer guide is Bagehot, not least because he understood that statesmen had to work within the constraints of parliamentary government. In the mid-1850s he noted the persistent calls for a 'great statesman' to replace the Aberdeen coalition, but argued that while men like Alexander and Napoleon might suit nations with an 'imperial disposition' they would be out of place in Britain except at times of genuine emergency.[15] What was needed were statesmen in tune with the ordinary man on the omnibus and who understood the nature of parliamentary government. Carlyle might hate the 'jangling, talking, and arguing' of Parliament, but these were in fact its lifeblood: 'a dictator will not save us – we require discussion, explanation, controversy'.[16] When Disraeli lambasted a previous generation as 'arch mediocrities', Bagehot thought it something of a compliment.[17]

We must look to the various commentaries on leading politicians in order to tease out the assumptions that underlay the language of statesmanship. It was widely thought that biography was a peculiarly instructive literary form, a belief that culminated in the *Dictionary of National Biography* at the end of the century. Samuel Smiles's popular oeuvre of works almost entirely depended on biographical portraits of worthies, and even J.R. Seeley conceded that while the 'real subject' of history was the state, not the individual, nevertheless 'useful knowledge' was best diffused to the wider populace through biographies of famous men.[18] Various series such as 'Twelve English Statesman' and 'The Queen's Prime Ministers' were only the tip of an enormous iceberg of sketches, portraits, essays, obituaries and biographies which took interest in the 'characters of public men'.[19] For the purposes of this chapter, it does not matter whether these works succumbed to hagiography, nor whether their judgments of political successes and failures were accurate – indeed, it is striking how quickly reputations were born which have subsequently taken considerable historical effort to dislodge.[20] The aim here is not to judge statesmen but rather to illuminate the terms by which they were judged, and the ideals to which they ought to have aspired.

Governance

The nineteenth century saw a dramatic growth in government: the range of responsibility and complexity of business of the state grew with increasing rapidity, and placed pressures on a creaking bureaucracy and its departmental heads. Inevitably this meant more attention was focused on the duties of statesmanship. In the main, to be a statesman required effective holding of office. The definition of the term could slip: supporters of Fox always claimed he was a statesman, though others wondered whether he had ever really proven himself as a leader in office. Melbourne was commonly judged to have had 'little aptitude for public business' and hence, some concluded, could not be esteemed a great statesman. Lord Aberdeen, similarly, was blamed for an 'administrative incapacity' that impaired his reputation.[21] Bright represents an important case: a first-rate orator, and, by his death, recognised as a powerful politician, it was still agreed that he was an inferior administrator whose brief tenures in office were largely unsuccessful. Hence, as *The Standard* put it, he was not 'and did not profess to be, a great Statesman'. Such a person had to have 'the power of governing, of conducting administrative and legislative affairs, and of getting people to act under him, and with him'.[22] These abilities were central to the statesman. Doubts, for instance, were expressed about Disraeli. Bagehot commented that he would himself 'smile' to have been called a successful administrator, and his majority government seemed to show he had no real sense of what to do with power. That part of his mind intended for business and detail – 'the solid part' – was under-developed.[23] Even otherwise eulogistic obituaries conceded this point, and Froude, one of his biographers, concluded that few of his measures had lasted, and in that respect he could not claim to be a great statesman.[24]

The poor quality of statesmanship was a recurring theme in the first half of the century which the arrival of Reform – and with it aristocratic Whiggery – did not entirely address. As the scope of the state increased there was mounting suspicion that the traditional elite was not up to the task. If in the 1770s Burke's linking of good government with aristocratic families seemed plausible, by the 1830s it was under challenge: Reform might have prevented executive dominance of Parliament, but it did not seem to have eradicated aristocratic patronage or infused government with a more vigorous sense of its potential.[25] These concerns – waxing and waning, but never disappearing – continued into the 1850s, and came to a head during the Crimean crisis.[26] Ironically, it was the Whig governments that particularly attracted criticism, whether it was Melbourne's indolence in the 1830s or Russell's exclusiveness in the 1840s and early 1850s. The idea that government remained a nest of incompetence – and an aristocratic racket besides – was close to the heart of various forms of middle-class reformism in the 1850s.

Broadly speaking, there were two connected lines of criticism. The first was the radical argument that, while the aristocracy had a 'paralyzing grasp' over statesmanship, it had shown time and again that it was not up to the task. The reforms of the 1830s had only gone a little way to addressing the problem.[27] Although radicals continued to press this point in the 1840s and 1850s, they were not alone in raising question marks over the adequacy of the aristocracy. Bagehot, for instance, made the interesting argument that in reality the 'heavy lifting' had for a long time *not* been performed by the landed elite: they 'will rarely do the work, and can rarely do the work'. The daily grind of government was 'too much for refined habits, delicate administration, anxious judgment' which their style of life nurtured.[28] One solution – for instance in Taylor's *Statesman* – was to give more attention to the training of rising politicians. They should be settled in office as early as possible, in order to acquire a 'capacity for taking decisions', and to learn that drudgery was essential to teach patience and application.[29] In this, at least, the *Westminster Review* agreed, thinking an improvement in the 'character' and 'abilities' of politicians a start, to which should be added knowledge of political economy and moral philosophy.[30] More generally it was argued that there needed to be more middle-class men in Parliament, and radicals sought various measure of administrative and constitutional reform to that end.

This led into the second line of criticism which focused less on character and class than on the inherited structures of government. Taylor thought that there was something 'fatally amiss in the very idea of statesmanship' because constant parliamentary pressure on ministerial activity undermined incentives to implement constructive reform: it was invariably more trouble than it was worth. His solution was to increase the number of permanent under-secretaries in a department, and transfer to them as much routine business as possible, and so freeing the parliamentary heads to become 'efficient statesmen'.[31] Nearly two decades later W.R. Greg – a leading member of the industrial elite in Manchester – reflected on the apparently poor 'Prospects of British Statesmanship'. While it was customary to blame this on the exclusivity of the aristocracy, he doubted whether simply increasing the number of middle-class men in Parliament would be effective, because too few of them really had the skills requisite of a statesman. The problem ultimately lay in the way that Parliament had evolved. As it ceased to be a body designed to represent grievances and defend liberties, so it had less need of 'orators and legislators'. Instead it needed 'capable administrators' who could counteract its 'tedious, ponderous, and inefficient'

tendencies.[32] One solution was to enable the sovereign to choose ministers from any rank and profession of life: they would have parliamentary seats but not votes. In effect administration would be revived by
circumventing parliamentary government. Greg also adapted Taylor's
proposals about bureaucratic reform, and argued for more active departmental committees to consider plans and to advise ministers.

While such criticisms seemed fraught during times of crisis, they
tended to recede once the panic had passed. Palmerston's confident
charm seemed to beguile the nation over the next ten years. In any case,
some commentators argued that the lineaments of a solution could be
seen in the statesmanship of Peel. Despite – as we shall see – intense
criticism of his career as a whole, it was widely agreed that he was an
exemplary administrator. If he lacked the 'grandeur of the patriot-hero'
he more than made up for it by being a man of business.[33] This was the
nub of Bagehot's argument as well. Since the late eighteenth century the
landed elite realised it was temperamentally ill-suited to administration
and came to rely on 'men of a somewhat lower grade' whose ambition
and aptitude suited them to government, but who were still sufficiently
gentlemanly not to offend that elite. As the middle classes grew in
strength and demanded government in accordance with notions they
were familiar with, they found in Peel the 'plain sense' they required.
Hence he switched from being the 'the nominee of a nobility' to the
'representative of a transacting and trading multitude'.[34] In a different
way even Palmerston seemed to show that aristocrats were capable of
leadership. If in private some politicians had their doubts ('not a good
man for general business'), by the time of his death he was being depicted
as an 'energetic statesman' who had a 'business-like' talent for administration without the pedantry.[35] Whether or not these claims convinced,
it is striking that they could be applied to Palmerston without incurring
ridicule, and that the 'business-faculty' could be found in an aristocratic
dandy.

The second half of the century saw a shift of anxiety. Bagehot signalled
this in various criticisms of administrative reformers. While he agreed
that businessmen had a greater capacity for 'action and work' than most
country gentlemen, therein lay a problem: they often lacked the breadth
of judgement to know when to act and when not to act. Accustomed
to directing affairs for themselves, they disliked sharing power with a
permanent official, and could not see that their job was largely one of
co-ordinating the office. In parliamentary government 'excessive action
is almost as great an evil as gross incompetence', and there was something, therefore, to be said for 'aristocratic *laissez-aller*'.[36] This theme is

illuminated clearly by a comparison between Gladstone and Salisbury. The former, it was agreed, had an enormous capacity for administration: he could combine the largest of principles with the trickiest of details, and deftly oversee a torrent of legislation.[37] Yet he was often seen as 'unsafe'.[38] By the early 1870s some judged him incapable of 'calm and moderation', and various writers put this down to his business background – he was 'interested too much' in everything that came across his path.[39] Unsurprisingly this unease matured in the following decade, and later assessments frequently noted that his 'boundless energy' could sometimes over-ripen into autocratic will.[40] Salisbury's style was very different. He lacked the visionary ideals of his opponent, and deliberately buried himself at the Foreign Office in order to detach himself from popular enthusiasms. Yet 'he possessed that capacity for government and guidance which is … the most indispensable quality in a statesman'. Indeed his skill was in calming and controlling the very passions his antagonist had unleashed. *The Times* concluded that he exemplified aristocratic virtues and that 'in the aristocracy and gentry of England are preserved incomparable resources for the guidance and government of the nation. The more democratic a Constitution becomes, the more essential to it are leadership and guidance, authority and control'.[41] The reputation of aristocrats as statesmen had not come full circle, but it is notable that the arrival of populism and democracy provided the space in which aristocratic indifference could be repackaged as statesmanlike detachment.

Principles and judgement

The central question, of course, was what statesmen wanted to do with their leadership. Here the ideal of a principled political career in the service of the nation was always being threatened by the suspicion that selfish ends and nefarious means might lay behind a facade. The shadow cast by early modern raison d'état was a very long one, and the statesmanship pioneered by Richelieu and Olivares – with its justification of deceit and cunning – hardly sat easily in an age of religious seriousness. Indeed it was widely thought that the preceding two centuries had manifested fairly low standards of political morality.[42] The question of consistency of principle was therefore a central one which touched on the broader concerns of honesty and hypocrisy in politics.[43] Macaulay argued that for the mass of the populace 'the test of integrity in a public man is consistency' and while not a perfect barometer of character, it was a good one.[44] Similarly, Smiles insisted that honesty of purpose needed to be linked to 'sound principles' and that a man lacking them was like a ship without compass or rudder. Indeed, he feared that democratic pressures were encouraging politicians to pander to the public and loosen their consciences. All around him he saw 'diplomacy, expediency, and moral reservation... equivocation or moral dodging – twisting and so stating the things as to convey a false impression'.[45] The statesman had to find a way to balance his principles with the flexibility his situation required.

The estimate of statesmen always included some discussion of principle and integrity. Some were particularly commended in this regard: all obituarists commented on Grey's 'boasted consistency' and that he would have sacrificed objects of ambition if they clashed with his principles.[46] Russell, similarly, was viewed as consistent, though there was a danger that he could be 'intolerant as well as unbending'.[47] Conversely, some politicians were presumed to fall short of the ideal. Palmerston was accused of 'indifference to principles' – evident in his switching of parties – and yet this could be explained away in terms of his patriotism.[48] Disraeli was less fortunate, and the charge of being unprincipled never went away – an adventurer 'without fixed principles', he 'never had a political faith'.[49] Trollope did not even accuse him of hypocrisy, because that at least implied there were *some* private beliefs being concealed.[50]

The more complex cases were those where politicians made a point of having principles and yet seemed to change them at particular moments. Peel was perhaps the most notorious case because of his change of stance on both Catholic emancipation in 1829, and Corn Law repeal in 1846. Lengthy discussions tried to prove he was in reality totally devoid of principles, and that his policy was simply whatever was convenient for himself, a man whose 'idol was power'.[51] As Greg noted in Peel's defence, the charge of 'treachery and tergiversation' was always thought damning because inconsistency was presumed fatal to the character of a politician.[52] The supporters of Peel instead made the case that these changes of policy were proof that he served the needs of the nation even at the cost of his own career (though some thought questions of honour to his party were at stake in remaining in office to repeal the Corn Laws).[53] Yet this was not entirely easy to swallow: *The Times* was not alone in suggesting that Peel had inaugurated the 'unpalatable truth' that principle must 'give way to what he called "expediency"'.[54] The question was, expedient for whom – his own ambition or the whole nation? Similar problems pervaded Gladstone's career, but he tried to pre-empt critics by explaining his changed positions at some length, for instance in two separate autobiographical publications.[55] It was a common observation that his style of argument was oblique, subtle, tortured. As early as 1859 one perceptive critic argued that on any given question 'Mr Gladstone's former self' was always his strongest adversary and that a career of such 'instability' would have led to ridicule had not the intellect been so impressive: a mind 'so forcible in its faculties' and yet 'so facile in conversion' was worthy of study.[56] Bagehot noted that Gladstone's temperamental intensity, which attracted him to strong statements of principle, coupled with a scholastic intellect, meant he was forever proliferating arguments and splitting hairs to make the evolution of his positions seem consistent.[57] The point was affirmed in obituaries: the *Daily News* commented on the painful struggles Gladstone went through to avoid the charge of acting from 'interested motives'. 'It was not that he was inconsistent; he himself said and believed that a painful consistency had been the characteristic feature of his life.'[58] The danger, as Bryce suggested, was that because he could both respond to critics, and persuade himself of anything, he could to opponents and followers alike, seem dangerously erratic.[59]

Even the highest-minded statesmen struggled to reconcile the expectation of principle with the reality of politics. Some commentators therefore asked their readers to judge whether it was possible for any politician never to have changed their position. Ritchie, responding to the criticism that Disraeli lacked principles, asked 'Well, what eminent MP has? ... The best statesman in modern times is he who is least hampered by principles, and is free to follow the leading of public opinion.'[60] A point commonly made was that the very structure of parliamentary government made pure consistency, if not impossible, then certainly ineffective. Burke had famously castigated the independent member who preserved his conscience at the expense of achieving nothing, and instead defended the essential nature of party.[61] A related issue concerned cabinet unity: surely it was impossible to believe that a comparatively large number of men could agree wholeheartedly on any given issue, and so it was inevitable that individuals would need to set aside their personal beliefs from time to time.[62] Taking this idea further, Bagehot argued that office placed so many conflicting demands on politicians that 'those subject to it have no opinions' beyond the most general of views. Again and again statesmen had not only to make arguments that they did not think conclusive, but 'to defend opinions which they do not believe to be true'. Ironically, the need to seem convinced of a policy at one time, and then, at a later time, to embrace its opposite gave the impression of 'great apparent changes of opinion'.[63] The pressure of cabinet unity therefore created graver problems of inconsistency than were really the case. Greg argued that the reason why this seemed a problem was that in the eighteenth century Parliament had been a forum where politicians contended for mastery and in which changes of party arose from dubious motives, and so inconsistency was seen as a question of personal honour. Since then, however, Parliament had become a body of legislators designed to serve the needs of the nation. Yes, politicians needed to demonstrate a form of constancy – steadiness of purpose, largeness of vision – but not at the cost of flexibility. The very system required that politicians have an 'open and earnest convincability'.[64]

These structural explanations, however, did not dissolve the ethical anxieties. Taylor contrasted those who thought the virtues of private life must be carried into politics with those who deemed 'Necessity' – or expediency – to be justified. His solution was to argue that in terms of beneficial consequences it was better to relax the 'law of truth' in politics than to insist on it. Moralists must permit statesmen 'a free judgment ... though a most responsible one, in the weighing of specific against general evil'.[65] This did not satisfy reviewers. Some thought this little different from Machiavellianism and insisted that private morality must be the basis for political conduct, while others were puzzled why Taylor seemed to support utilitarianism in public but not private life.[66] A comparison of the 'Ethics of Statesmanship', as exemplified by the careers of Peel and Palmerston, also revealed some of these anxieties. Peel's seeming abandonment of principles led to the charge of expediency, and yet Palmerston's popularity did not suffer when he boasted that expediency was 'the one actuating motive of his public policy'. While the author agreed that the private life of a politician was no reflection of his public ability, he could not endorse Buckle's argument that the business of a statesman was to act 'not according to his own principles, but according to the wishes of the people'. The conscience should not be over-ridden by the public will, and a statesman who simply took instructions 'should not call his proceedings statesmanship nor should object if others call them "unprincipled"'.[67] Without a strong faith in expediency, and yet aware that pure consistency was unrealistic, the public was ultimately expected to put its trust in the judgment of politicians.

Although widely seen as a central aspect of successful statesmanship, political judgement was not easy to define. It may be helpful to look first at those politicians thought lacking in this quality. A telling example was Bagehot's study of Lord Bolingbroke. Here was a man 'exceedingly defective in cool and plain judgment' largely because his style of life, coupled with a warm nature and excitable imagination tended to make him 'erratic not only in conduct but in judgment'.[68] Such flaws were evident in the nineteenth century as well. Canning was occasionally thought too excitable, and Derby was often criticised for impatience and impulsiveness. Indeed one biographer thought him similar to Bolingbroke in this regard. Certainly it was thought to have impaired his statesmanship.[69] To a lesser degree, Gladstone seemed sometimes to show similar failings: he too was thought 'impulsive' and 'imprudent', although this was the result of the intensity of his convictions – whatever they happened to be.[70] By contrast, the ideal statesman – according to Taylor – needed to acquire calmness, order and equanimity as the necessary basis of judgement.[71] In particular, there needed to be the right mixture of decisiveness of reason and decisiveness of temperament. The 'reasoning and contemplative faculty' was obviously essential, and in the case of a complex question, the statesman needed to begin with a fairly open mind, and be able to suspend his judgement until he had got a good sense of its 'proportions and relations'. The man incapable of deliberation tended to make erroneous decisions. But, on its own, reason tended to multiply doubts, and so a temperament suited to making decisions was needed to 'abbreviate the operations of reason and close up the distances, thereby enabling the mind, where many things are doubtful, to seize decisively those which are least so'. So, in the early stages of a political issue, the statesman was permitted 'patience and circumspection' before striking with 'energy' towards the end.[72]

In broad strokes, this was the template for judging real statesmen. First, they needed to be able to access relevant knowledge. Of course, much attention was given to the education of statesmen, and – as we have seen – to the importance of mastering office. In addition, an understanding of the state of public opinion was a useful asset. While Wellington was a failure in this respect, Peel, it was thought, had a 'quick and instinctive' perception of the state of opinion and an unrivalled ability to tell which popular leaders mattered.[73] Similarly, Palmerston was credited with an understanding of the feelings of 'England', while Disraeli, conversely, was thought to be rather weak in assessing opinion outside Parliament. Gladstone – whether seen as a follower or leader of opinion – was at least credited with being open to fresh ideas.[74] Second, statesmen needed to consider a question appropriately. Peel was commended for being a practical statesman, rather than a 'star-gazer', who could assess every difficulty and foresee every objection.[75] Palmerston, also, took little interest in speculations about the future and had 'a head cool enough to weigh cautiously and accurately even his own political projects'.[76] He had a 'lucid, well-balanced, rapid grasp' of all aspects of a subject which enabled him to focus on the matter in hand.[77] Gladstone's ability to see all sides of a question was also frequently commented on, though – as W.E. Forster once said – since he could persuade himself of nearly anything this skill could also be put to perilous use. By contrast – for *The Times* at least – Lord Salisbury provided a steady hand and a clear vision as prime minister.[78]

When it came to acting on a decision, there appears to have been a balance between extremes. On the one hand, a measure of caution and moderation was always desirable and routinely praised. Once again, Peel was exemplary: his caution was the consequence 'not of timidity, but of prudence'; he was 'moderate by taste, his instinctive preference was always for a middle course: he disliked rashness and shrank from risk'. He was a '*tentative*' politician who always felt his way forward step-by-step.[79] But this virtue could be seen as a vice. Lord Aberdeen's caution meant that his nature was 'critical rather than practical, more capable of seeing what it was wrong, than of resolving what it was right do'. While Gladstone credited him with a strong 'deliberative faculty', critics thought him 'not a good driver, and when the horses grew restive and kicked over the trace, he lacked nerve, hesitated, and was lost'.[80] On the other hand, statesmen were also praised for their courage. Peel showed 'boldness, tempered by sagacity', and Palmerston was commonly lauded for his 'will', 'fortitude' and 'determination'.[81] Disraeli's entire career had shown 'high courage', though some wondered whether this had been more for party advantage than national interest.[82] But courage also had its vices: Russell's widely acknowledged fearlessness meant that he was often unwilling to take advice, and became increasingly liable to lapses of judgment in the 1850s. The dangers of recklessness were all too apparent in Derby – as we have seen – and Gladstone had something of, if not 'the rashness' then 'the boldness' of the Liverpudlian.[83] Even Lord Salisbury was thought prone to impulsiveness until his leadership in the 1880s proved otherwise. A further danger was vacillation – politicians who lurched from one extreme position to another. James Graham was thought as 'unstable as water', a man who 'oddly blended' both rashness and timidity in his nature.[84]

The final aspect of judgement worth considering is foresight. While highly desirable, it was unclear whether this was a quality which could be acquired or whether it was, ultimately, the result of good fortune. Peel, according to one critic, lacked 'sagacious foresight', but, conversely, a supporter argued that while he did not have a 'prophetic mind' that could see far into the future – as, perhaps, the elder Pitt had – he still qualified as a statesman.[85] Derby, by contrast, was largely lacking in prescience, while the verdict on Disraeli was mixed. Bagehot thought him prone to 'stupendous blunders' because of recklessness, but Reid disagreed: 'he *does* possess in a very high degree the foresight and the accuracy of judgment which are necessary to make a man a really great statesman'. When the leading Liberal ministers were tempted to support the South in the American Civil War, he had the prescience to see that the North must win.[86] He was also credited him with recognising that parliamentary reform might help rather than hinder the progress of Conservatism.[87] In the case of Gladstone, some – such as the *Pall Mall Gazette* – diagnosed a 'want of prescience': he might gauge the moment accurately, but he could not succeed in 'forecasting the future'.[88] In an otherwise positive account, Bryce agreed that he showed 'less than was needed of that prescience which is, after integrity and courage, the highest gifts of a statesman'.[89] An accurate calculation of the consequences of any line of action was therefore a central component of effective statesmanship.

Character and communication

Whether that calculation was successful was often only apparent in hindsight. To know whether to trust the judgment of politicians required that they possess something else: character. This referred both to 'the mental and moral qualities' of an individual as well as to 'moral qualities strongly developed' and was distinct from the eighteenth-century ideal of 'politeness' which stressed merely the outer forms of sociability.[90] By contrast a 'man of character' was supposed to demonstrate the coherence of qualities across private and public domains. Smiles's *Character* explained the importance of will in overcoming the impulses of the lower self, and unpacked the constellation of ideals that exemplified character: duty, honesty, courage, work, energy, restraint and so on. Many of these were expected of public just as much as private individuals. Russell, for instance, spoke in 1854 of how the character of rulers 'is a matter of utmost interest to the people of this country'. 'It is, in fact, on the confidence reposed by people in the character of public men, that the security of this country in a great degree depends.'[91] There were times when this idea seemed to be under attack, especially if the exponents of statesmanlike character seemed to be using it as cover for class governance. In a discussion of Earl Grey's life, the *Morning Chronicle* in 1845 suggested that rulers were increasingly being judged by their legislative achievements: 'If the ends be good...what matters it what this man is...if he will effect some palpable utility.' The reality, it went on, was that the character of public men lifted the character of the nation ('patriotism is awakened, ambition purified, and the national character invigorated and ennobled') and that this was more important than any specific financial or commercial reform.[92] At times it was argued that such weight should not be placed on character – do we judge the quality of military leadership by the morals of a general?[93] – but it was not displaced until the twentieth century. Morley's biography of Walpole, for instance, concluded that he could not be ranked among the highest of statesmen because 'in the world's final estimation character goes farther than act, imagination than utility, and its leaders strike us as much by what they were as by what they did'.[94] Whether Morley shared 'the world's estimation' is not entirely clear, but it does show that character still counted for a good deal.

Accordingly, great importance was attached to personality. As Bagehot explained, 'political business, like all others, is not transacted by machines, but by living and breathing men, of various and generally strong characters, of various and often strong passions'.[95] Since it was central to the idea of 'character' that the lower self could be disciplined, the balance of elements in personality was crucial. Smiles insisted that temper mattered more than talent, and he outlined the ideal of an estimable man: cheerful, kind, patient, sympathetic. Such a person could cope easily with the trials life threw at him. Other characteristics needed to be guarded against. A man of strong temper, for instance, should take care to control and direct it in order to avoid 'fitful outbreaks of passion'. Similarly, manners mattered: a rude man may be good at heart, but he would be more 'agreeable' and 'probably a much more useful' man if he adopted 'suavity of disposition and courtesy of manner'.[96] These maxims applied equally to public as to private life, and political biography frequently indulged in speculations about how personal character had affected political fortune.

There were recurring criticisms applied to leading politicians. Surprisingly, a common complaint was coldness. Pitt had a touch of this, but the exemplary cases were two leading Whigs. A gentle man in private, in public Grey had a 'cold, harsh, arrogant bearing'.[97] This reputation outlived the man, with later writers noting 'stately manners...aloof...somewhat cold', and summing up his character as 'cold, reserved, and proud'.[98] Russell fared little better. If there was 'Tropical warmth' in his political beliefs, there was 'Arctic temperature in his manners'.[99] He was incapable of the geniality necessary to popularity: 'There is an icy tone in his voice and glitter in his eye'.[100] His 'cold *hauteur*' was frequently commented on, and it was argued that his pride made his relations with other politicians fraught, especially from the 1850s.[101] Peel was also a difficult character, marked by pride and sensitivity, and 'impenetrable reserve'.[102] He rarely employed humour, and his aloofness from fellow MPs – 'a freezing bow' – was recorded anecdotally. One explanation was extreme shyness which he combated with 'an artificial manner, haughtily stiff, or exuberantly bland'.[103] Peel's diffidence was not to be confused with patrician reserve, which, it was thought, hampered Salisbury's popularity. Indeed his 'impersonality' led some to accuse him of lacking knowledge of other men.[104]

But class and character were not indivisible. Melbourne and Palmerston were both exemplars of aristocratic affability, and if in the former case 'thorough manliness' and 'easy temperament' were insufficient to rescue his reputation, in the latter they seemed integral.[105] Palmerston's '*bonhommie*' was crucial because 'a good-tempered, jolly man can never be unpopular'.[106] Numerous commentators fixated on his geniality, humour and sociability – it was his personality which had at times enabled his government to survive when in other hands it would have fallen.[107] This social tact, however, did not mean he was a weak statesman. While Melbourne had taken 'the *light* treatment' of politics too far, Palmerston got the balance right. The public saw a 'manly and masculine hardness of grain' that enjoyed a good fight, and stood up for friends.[108] Disraeli tried to pose in the same garments. He could deal with bores or avoid difficult questions 'with one of those happy phrases or pleasant jests which Lord Palmerston loved so dearly'.[109] Later writers spoke of his patience, temper, cheerfulness and above all wit.[110] Even the *Daily News*, which reprobated his policies, spoke warmly of his 'indomitable courage, the unflagging energy, the marvellous tact and skill and knowledge of mankind'.[111] Nevertheless, the themes of class and race were never far from the surface when, perhaps more than other politicians, he was criticised for artificiality and theatricality, and for constructing a personality which appealed to the Commons, and enabled his ambition to soar.[112]

The fact that there were no narrow set of traits which enabled or prevented political success is evident in the case of Gladstone. In the 1850s he was judged to have a 'delicate and fine' mind with a 'subtle and refining' temperament which would make him unsuitable for leadership.[113] Moreover, in comparison to Peel or Palmerston, he did not seem 'safe': he had a 'fluctuating' temperament which could be 'hot and hasty' but also sometimes 'indecisive'.[114] In opposition he was prone to take the controversial side of a question, thereby revealing an 'enthusiastic' and 'impulsive' character. His supporters lived in fear of where his 'eccentricity' might take them: his overbearing – even arrogant – style rarely condescended to explain to his rank and file.[115] Indeed, he knew little about how to conciliate, and so was a failure in managing individuals. The fact that he seemed largely incapable of humour and adopted a solemn tone only seemed to make this worse. Even amid all the panegyrics in 1898, it was felt that he had struggled to contain a hot temper to the point that he could easily be goaded by his opponents.[116] Given the centrality of the idea of Disraeli as 'alien', it is striking that Gladstone – for all his oratorical brilliance and administrative achievement – could also be seen as uncomfortably strange. Certainly a number of writers thought his 'serious failings' of temperament and character were indicative of a lack of the manliness required of politicians.[117]

The final quality required of statesmen was the ability to persuade the audiences that mattered. This was largely understood in terms of oratory.[118] James Mackintosh explained that as the power of public opinion grew so the 'faculty of persuading men to support or oppose political measures' became central, and so excellent debating skills were actually a rather good test of political ability.[119] Macaulay, similarly, argued that while early modern politicians oriented themselves to the court, since the Restoration the talent for speaking had developed: 'It has stood in the place of all other acquirements. It has covered ignorance, weakness, rashness, the most fatal maladministration.'[120] To develop the discussion further, three themes may be stressed. First, the nature and success of particular styles of speaking; second, the implications of emerging audiences; and third, controversy about the effects of oratory.

Oratory was typically evaluated – especially in the first half of the century – according to classical models. An exemplary speaker might be praised for his command of language, the use of 'ornament', and the arrangement of the argument. Considerable attention was paid to the manner of delivery: it should be graceful, easy, 'unaffected and unforced', and the speaker should be in control of his 'action, gesture, expression and elocution'.[121] Certain styles once favoured – for instance the 'theatrical effect' of the elder Pitt – were thought to be old-fashioned by the 1830s.[122] Similarly, Disraeli's maiden speech was drowned out in laughter because its 'exaggerated attitude and diction' seemed to be idiosyncratic.[123] What really mattered, however, was that a speaker was persuasive. For this reason, prepared speeches would not get one far. They might demonstrate the powers of reason and imagination, but not a talent for political leadership.[124] Macaulay himself, according to the *Morning Chronicle*, was all 'simulated fervour and laboured spontaneity' which looked hollow compared to Peel's style.[125] A much better ideal was Gladstone who, according to Bryce, could speak effectively with very limited notice, and was also able – unlike even excellent orators such as Pitt and Fox – both to open and close a debate.

Significant attention was given to the emotional power of a speech. Pitt 'transported' his audience, and Fox could sway and enthuse them.[126] In an early essay on Gladstone, Bagehot accepted that he was a fine speaker with superb command of language, but, he asked, 'Did the audience feel? were they excited? did they cheer?'[127] By the time of his death no one doubted the answers to these questions, and the almost 'magical' quality of his effects on audiences was widely noted. It was frequently argued that the root of Gladstone's appeal was the power and depth of his earnestness, and indeed this was an important quality for a speaker.[128] Canning, for example, made very effective use of wit, but his lightness and fancy sometimes became 'too exuberant' and the audience assumed he was not being earnest.[129] Disraeli's success as a speaker was also achieved at some cost to his reputation as an orator. He was certainly skilful, and knew how to perform a variety of roles – defiant, surprising, savage – and even though one could tell it *was* a performance, it nevertheless often worked on his parliamentary audience.[130] He could charm them, and his use of humour, and especially sarcasm, was thought a crucial ingredient of his success. But, as *The Times* argued, 'If earnestness is the soul of oratory, it would be strange indeed if we could bestow higher praise than brilliancy on most of the speeches of Mr Disraeli'.[131] Bryce developed the point, arguing that his failure in the true index of eloquence – 'the power of touching the emotions' – was evident in that while he could make men laugh, he could not make them cry.[132]

Less accomplished speakers could still prove effective. Melbourne, for example, was the target of considerable abuse – even on his death – for his indistinct, halting, and stumbling delivery. Yet his defenders turned this to his advantage – he was not capable of 'sustained flights of eloquence' because he disliked rhetoric and exaggeration. Instead he was commended for simplicity and truthfulness which spoke directly and powerfully to an audience. 'To gain a political character, it is not always necessary to be speech-making' – such arguments drew, as we shall see, on enduring suspicions about the dangers of oratorical display.[133] Perhaps the best instance of a comparatively poor speaker who excelled as a politician was Palmerston. He was not 'graceful' and to the end of his life there was 'hesitancy' while he searched for the right word.[134] He had never 'scaled the heights of oratory'; there was no 'dazzling light' – he was 'skilful at fence' but no more.[135] Sometimes he offended because of excessive vulgarity, but in general he was clever enough rarely to open himself to dangerous positions, and he employed ridicule and diversion effectively. He could make the House laugh and cheer and when necessary adopt a 'sham enthusiasm' that gave the impression of conviction. He was a partisan, a debater who could manage the House, but never aspired – when 'appealing to the passions or developing the policy of the hour' – to be an orator who could transcend the practicality of the moment.[136]

By mid-century it was widely agreed that the style of oratory had evolved to suit the needs of the age. In an essay on Gladstone, Ritchie noted the comparative absence of wit, and suggested that 'oratorical display' was less sought after in the Commons. That era had culminated in Canning, but was now over: the Commons had become 'a business assembly'.[137] The lodestone for this argument was Peel. In 1845 G. H. Francis argued that the traditional purposes of oratory – to excite passions, to sway judgment, to delight mankind – were being supplanted because since 1832 the Commons had become more 'business-like', and so powerful speakers attended more to 'immediate utility' than to lasting beauty. Peel was adept at this, and hence will be classed 'among the statesmen than among the orators'. This type of leader had to be ready with facts and figures, able to understand all shades of opinion, and capable of explaining himself clearly, or concealing himself effectively, as appropriate. The speeches of Peel were typified by 'common sense' rather than being marked for 'vivid imagination or profound thought'.[138] Obituarists agreed that Peel's speeches were 'like himself, practical' and that their eloquence 'consisted in their persuasiveness'.[139] Bagehot developed these points into a central argument. In an age of business there was no need to awaken deep passions, and so Peel's oratory was perfect for the time because he aimed to explain rather than to charm or amuse. Ironically he was better suited to the reformed Commons – a style more appropriate to its unreformed incarnation was Canning's 'easy fluency...nice wit...passing from topic to topic, like the raconteur of the dinner table'.[140] The idea that Peel represented a transition was repeatedly affirmed by later writers. Justin McCarthy saw in him the passing away of the eloquence of Pitt and Fox, and that from thereon any speaker needed 'a good deal of business-precision and practicality'.[141] In this respect Gladstone managed to combine the command and elevation of an orator, with the mastery of detail needed for a business age.

The second point about oratory is related: discussion of the opportunities and effects of new audiences. As Macaulay argued, at the time of the elder Pitt the fame of a speaker depended entirely on those who heard him in Parliament and so his style and manner were crucial. Since then the reporting of speeches gave the politician two separate audiences. The one in Parliament might be 'pleased or disgusted' by his voice and action, but over the breakfast table shrill tones and uncouth gestures became irrelevant.[142] A successful politician in the 1830s and 1840s tried to transcend this division. Within a generation, the problem became more marked as politicians took to the platform. Bagehot, in a review of Gladstone's speech at Greenwich in 1871, argued that it inaugurated an era when one of the prime minister's 'most important qualifications' would be 'to exert a direct control over the masses'. A statesman who could do this would have a 'vast' advantage, and while parliamentarians might be uneasy about these trends, they would soon understand the need to become popular orators and to deal in 'the broad, easy, and animated style' which touches the people rather than the 'subtle flavours' of parliamentary oratory.[143] Gladstone became the master of 'this branch of rhetoric', and few others were judged to be nearly as successful.[144] Disraeli's influence was restricted to Parliament, and he actively disliked speaking to large audiences.[145] Salisbury, similarly, was thought to be less effective outdoors. He had a strong aversion to the 'arts of the demagogue' and was not one to 'conjure' with the country.[146] His speeches were 'models of polished irony and effective declamation', but they excited no enthusiasm from wide audiences.[147] Yet, as Bryce noted in an essay on Northcote, it was the 'power of moving crowds' that the younger generation of politicians seemed especially to value.[148]

The third theme was both old and new, as the rise of the platform gave a more pronounced edge to some traditional criticisms of the art of oratory. Three connected points should be highlighted. First was the concern – especially among the high-minded – that the stress on public speaking in an adversarial system tended to undermine interest in and pursuit of the truth. Bagehot frequently articulated this anxiety, and cited Macaulay's argument that popular government encouraged eager young minds to mount arguments that no man of sense would ever make.[149] The net effect over time was to debase the reasoning faculties. The art of debating was very quickly separated from the capacity for belief, and this pressure was merely exacerbated by the widespread expectation that cabinet ministers had a 'ready, producible, defensible view of all great questions'.[150] A second anxiety was whether oratory actually undermined the conditions of statesmanship. Since politicians were trained to excel in speechifying and debating, they could sometimes be constitutionally unfit to manage a department and lead the nation. Carlyle, as we have seen, expressed these doubts in extreme form, but Greg in the 1850s could also be found wondering whether 'the talking and acting faculties' were really compatible.[151] The third theme was nicely expressed by Bryce: if Parliament was 'not a good place' for the pursuit of truth, 'the platform is still less favourable to that quest'.[152] This was the old problem of demagoguery. An ambitious man might use 'mean arts and unreasonable clamours' – the phrase was Macaulay's[153] – to rouse popular passions for his own factious ends. In the first half of the century Henry Hunt, O'Connell, and Bright were frequently painted in this light. They were routinely called demagogues and their style of speaking contrasted with the parliamentary art required of a true statesman. With the rise of the platform, however, the two realms blended, and it became easier to accuse established politicians of succumbing to demagoguery. Opponents of Gladstone found this a compelling line of argument. One such pamphleteer went so far as to argue that 'first-class oratory is only a theatrical entertainment' and that 'really great statesmen' were generally merely good speakers rather than exemplary orators.[154] By the end of the century, then, oratory was still assumed to be an essential ingredient of leadership, but it now also attracted anxiety – a statesman could not avoid speaking to the people, but he had to take care how he went about it.

In 'British Statesmanship in 1905' F.W. Raffety argued that the recent death of Harcourt marked a 'severance' in parliamentary tradition: 'with him departed nearly the last of a school of statesmanship which seems to be passing away before there is discovered any clear evidence of one that is to take its place'. Certainly, Edwardian leaders were of a much younger generation than the Victorian titans they had so recently replaced. Still, one does not need to share Raffety's partisan criticisms of Conservative failings to recognise that the terms he used were very familiar. He criticised the government for a lack of settled convictions and administrative ability. There was little sign of earnestness: expediency and opportunism ruled the roost. Some might argue for an infusion of business skills, but this missed the point – there ought to be 'an elevation of thought and object' that lifted the statesman above the level of the merchant. A particular anxiety – increasingly common in the Edwardian era – has been a central theme of this chapter. 'It is not assiduity in public service', demonstrated by 'long observation and study of public affairs or acquaintance with the history and constitution of the country', that was rewarded, but personal popularity. This, Raffety lamented, was often achieved through, among other things, exploiting sporting connections. Bryce, as we have seen, thought the voting nation was tested and proven by the leaders it chose. Raffety feared that at present the 'character and pretensions' of parliamentary aspirants were unlikely to change until 'the electors recognise that they require and must have a class of men...quite different to the president of a football club'.[155]

Notes

1. J. Bryce, *Modern Democracies*, 2 vols (New York, 1921), II, pp. 542, 550.
2. P. Anderson, 'Origins of the Present Crisis', *New Left Review* 23 (1964), 19–45.
3. D.M. Craig, '"High Politics" and the "New Political History"', *Historical Journal* 53 (2010), 453–75.
4. e.g. J. Parry, *The Politics of Patriotism: English Liberalism, National Identity and Europe, 1830–1886* (Cambridge, 2006); P. Joyce, *Democratic Subjects: the Self and the Social in Nineteenth-Century England* (Cambridge, 1994); M. McCormack, ed., *Public Men: Masculinity and Politics in Modern Britain* (Basingstoke, 2007).
5. A little-known exception is J.H. Grainger, *Character and Style in English Politics* (Cambridge, 1969).
6. Bryce, *Modern Democracies*, II, p. 551.
7. Based on an electronic search of *The Times*.
8. H. Taylor, *The Statesman* (London, 1836), p. vi.
9. *The Examiner*, 29 May 1836.
10. For example, see *Edinburgh Review* 64 (1836), p. 215.
11. *Fraser's Magazine* 14 (1836), p. 393.
12. T. Carlyle, *On Heroes, Hero-Worship, and the Heroic in History* (London, 1841), pp. 316, 317.
13. B. Disraeli, *Coningsby* (London, 1881), pp. 117–21; R. Shannon, *Gladstone 1809–1865* (London, 1982), p. 127. See also J. Parry, 'Disraeli and England', *Historical Journal* 43 (2000), 699–728.
14. T. Carlyle, *Latter-Day Pamphlets: Downing Street* (London, 1850), pp. 28, 30.
15. *The Collected Works of Walter Bagehot*, ed. N. St John Stevas, 15 vols (London, 1965–86) [hereafter CWB], VI, p. 86.
16. CWB, VI, pp. 83, 86.
17. Ibid., pp. 88–9.
18. J.R. Seeley, *The Life and Adventures of E.M. Arndt* (London, 1879), p. v.
19. CWB, III, p. 415.
20. See the sophisticated analysis of Russell's reputation in J.P. Parry, 'Past and Future in the Later Career of Lord John Russell' in T. Blanning and D. Cannadine, eds, *History and Biography: Essays in Honour of Derek Beales* (Cambridge, 1996), pp. 142–72.
21. *The Times*, 25 November 1848, 15 December 1860.
22. *Standard*, 28 March 1889; *Economist*, 30 March 1889.

23. CWB, VI, p. 151; III, p. 504.
24. J.A. Froude, *Lord Beaconsfield* (London, 1890), p. 260.
25. For example, see *Westminster Review* 5 (1837), pp. 1–31.
26. See O. Anderson, *A Liberal State at War: English Politics and Economics during the Crimean War* (London, 1967).
27. *Westminster Review* 5 (1837), p. 8.
28. CWB, III, p. 248.
29. Taylor, *Statesman*, p. 9.
30. *Westminster Review* 5 (1837), pp. 8–9.
31. Taylor, *Statesman*, pp. 160, 161.
32. W.R. Greg, *Essays on Political and Social Science*, 2 vols (London, 1853), II, pp. 394, 396.
33. Ibid., pp. 323, 327.
34. CWB, III, p. 251.
35. Lord Clarendon cited in Anderson, *Liberal State*, p. 35; *Daily News*; CWB, III, p. 276.
36. CWB, VI, pp. 209, 140, 92.
37. For example, T.W. Reid, *Cabinet Portraits. Sketches of Statesmen* (London, 1872), p. 23.
38. *The Times*, 20 May 1898.
39. CWB, III, pp. 469, 418.
40. J. Bryce, *Studies in Contemporary Biography* (London, 1903), p. 411. See also G.W.E. Russell, *The Right Honourable W.E. Gladstone* (London, 1891), p. 272.
41. *The Times*, 24 August 1903.
42. For example, T. Macaulay, *Critical and Historical Essays*, 2 vols (London, 1907), I, pp. 197–200.
43. See D. Runciman, *Political Hypocrisy: the Mask of Power, from Hobbes to Orwell and Beyond* (Princeton, 2008).
44. Macaulay, *Essays*, I, p. 201.
45. S. Smiles, *Character* (London, 1876), pp. 6, 137, 207.
46. *The Times, Morning Chronicle*, 21 July 1845.
47. *The Times*, 29 May 1878.
48. *The Times*, 19 October 1865; see also *Daily News* which explained that Palmerston carried the 'sneer' of the eighteenth century into the nineteenth.
49. Greg, *Essays*, II, p. 374; CWB, III, p. 486.
50. Runciman, *Political Hypocrisy*, p. 148. See D. M. Craig, 'Advanced Conservative Liberalism: Party and Principle in Trollope's Parliamentary Novels', *Victorian Literature and Culture* 38 (2010), 355–71.
51. J. Symons, *Sir Robert Peel as a type of Statesmanship* (London, 1856), p. 189, and *passim*.
52. Greg, *Essays*, II, p. 323.
53. D.O. Maddyn, *Chiefs of Parties, Past and Present*, 2 vols (London, 1856), II, pp. 34–5.
54. *The Times*, 4 July 1850; see also *Morning Chronicle*, 3 July 1850.
55. *A Chapter of Autobiography* (1868); *The Irish Question* (1886).
56. Maddyn, *Chiefs*, II, p. 259.
57. CWB, III, pp. 426–33. See also J. Ewing Ritchie, *Modern Statesmen, or Sketches from the Strangers' Gallery of the House of Commons* (London, 1861), pp. 76–8.

58. *Daily News*, 20 May 1898.
59. Bryce, *Studies*, pp. 416–17.
60. Ritchie, *Modern Statesmen*, p. 65; see also Greg, *Essays*, II, p. 332.
61. See D. Craig, 'Burke and the Constitution' in D. Dwan and C. Insole, eds., *The Cambridge Companion to Edmund Burke* (Cambridge, 2012), pp. 113–15.
62. Taylor, *Statesman*, pp. 112–13.
63. CWB, III, pp. 255, 258, 260.
64. Greg, *Essays*, II, p. 334.
65. Taylor, *Statesman*, pp. 109, 112, 119.
66. *Blackwood's* 40 (1836), pp. 218–27; *Westminster Review* 5 (1837), pp. 22–6.
67. *Fortnightly Review* 3 (1865), pp. 323, 324, 326.
68. CWB, III, p. 68.
69. G. Saintsbury, *The Earl of Derby* (London, 1906), pp. 202, 210–12. See *The Times*, *Morning Post*, *Pall Mall Gazette*, 25 October 1869.
70. Reid, *Cabinet Portraits*, p. 18.
71. Taylor, *Statesman*, pp. 76–81.
72. Ibid., pp. 141–3.
73. Greg, *Essays*, II, pp. 325, 327.
74. Bryce, *Studies*, pp. 413, 417.
75. J. McCarthy, *Sir Robert Peel* (London, 1891), p. 51; Greg, *Essays*, II, p. 327.
76. *Pall Mall Gazette*, 19 October 1865.
77. J.D.S.C. Lorne, *Viscount Palmerston* (London, 1906), p. 234.
78. *The Times*, 20 May 1898 and 24 August 1903.
79. *Morning Chronicle*, 3 July 1850; Greg, *Essays*, II, pp. 323, 355.
80. *The Times*, 15 December 1860; Gladstone cited in A. Stanmore, *The Earl of Aberdeen* (London, 1905), p. 308; Stuart J. Reid, *Lord John Russell* (London, 1895), p. 209.
81. CWB, III, p. 277; *Morning Post*, 19 October 1865; Lorne, *Palmerston*, p. 234.
82. *The Times*, 20 April 1881.
83. CWB, III, p. 419.
84. Maddyn, *Chiefs*, II, p. 256; Reid, *Russell*, p. 232.
85. Symons, *Peel*, p. 70; Greg, *Essays*, II, p. 358.
86. CWB, III, p. 492; Reid, *Cabinet Portraits*, p. 12.
87. Bryce, *Studies*, p. 57.
88. *Pall Mall Gazette*, 19 May 1898.
89. Bryce, *Studies*, p. 416.
90. S. Collini, *Public Moralists: Political Thought and Intellectual Life in Britain 1850–1930* (Oxford, 1991), p. 96.
91. Russell, *Hansard's Parliamentary Debates* CXXXI 305, 3 March 1854. See Ritchie, *Modern Statesmen*, p. 34 for the criticism that 'character' could mean just about anything.
92. *Morning Chronicle*, 21 July 1845.
93. *Fortnightly Review* 3 (1865), p. 322.
94. J. Morley, *Walpole* (London, 1889), p. 114.
95. CWB, VI, p. 56.
96. Smiles, *Character*, pp. 165, 236, 238.
97. *The Times*, 21 July 1845.
98. Reid, *Russell*, p. 65; H. Dunckley, *Lord Melbourne* (London, 1906), p. 166.
99. Maddyn, *Chiefs*, II, p. 214.

100. Ritchie, *Modern Statesmen*, p. 20.
101. Reid, *Cabinet Portraits*, p. 117.
102. *The Times*, 4 July 1850.
103. Maddyn, *Chiefs*, II, pp. 50, 48. See also McCarthy, *Peel*, pp. 2–4, 37.
104. *The Times*, 24 August 1903.
105. Dunckley, *Melbourne*, pp. 124, 152.
106. Ritchie, *Modern Statesmen*, p. 8.
107. See *The Times*, 19 October 1865.
108. *Pall Mall Gazette*, 19 October 1865.
109. Reid, *Cabinet Portraits*, p. 8.
110. For example, see F. Hitchman, *The Public Life of the Right Honourable the Earl of Beaconsfield* 2 vols (London, 1879), pp. ix–x; *Morning Post*, 20 April 1881.
111. *Daily News*, 20 April 1881.
112. See e.g. Bryce, *Studies*, pp. 21–6.
113. Greg, *Essays*, II, p. 371.
114. Maddyn, *Chiefs*, II, pp. 267, 270.
115. Ritchie, *Modern Statesmen*, p. 79; Reid, *Cabinet Portraits*, pp. 18, 19.
116. See Reid, *Cabinet Portraits*, p. 21; Russell, *Gladstone*, pp. 228–9; *Standard*, *Pall Mall Gazette*, 19 May 1898; *Daily News*, 20 May 1898; Bryce, *Studies*, pp. 420–2, 461.
117. Reid, *Cabinet Portraits*, p. 27.
118. See J. Meisel, *Public Speech and the Culture of Public Life in the Age of Gladstone* (New York, 2001).
119. J. Mackintosh, *Miscellaneous Works* (New York, 1871), p. 240.
120. Macaulay, *Essays*, I, p 243.
121. *Fraser's Magazine* 10 (1874), p. 513; J. Mill, *Disraeli, the Author, Orator, and Statesman* (London, 1863), p. 240.
122. Macaulay, *Essays*, I, p. 378.
123. Ritchie, *Modern Statesmen*, p. 57.
124. Mackintosh, *Works*, p. 240.
125. *Morning Chronicle*, 3 July 1850.
126. *Gentleman's Magazine* (February 1806), p. 129.
127. CWB, III, p. 419.
128. *Standard*, 19 May 1898; *The Times*, 20 May 1898.
129. Mackintosh, *Works*, p. 241.
130. See Reid, *Cabinet Portraits*, pp. 7–10; Ritchie, *Modern Statesmen*, pp. 60–4; CWB, III, p. 503.
131. *The Times*, 20 April 1881.
132. Bryce, *Studies*, p. 46.
133. *Morning Chronicle*, 27 November 1848.
134. *Standard*, 19 October 1865.
135. Ritchie, *Modern Statesmen*, pp. 9–10.
136. G. H. Francis, *Orators of the Age* (New York, 1847), pp. 104, 106.
137. Ritchie, *Modern Statesmen*, p. 71.
138. Francis, *Orators*, pp. 30–1, 35–6.
139. *Morning Chronicle*, 3 July 1850.
140. CWB, III, p. 268.
141. McCarthy, *Peel*, p. 11.
142. Macaulay, *Essays*, I, p. 377.

143. CWB, III, pp. 461, 462.
144. *Standard*, 19 May 1898.
145. CWB, III, p. 504; Bryce, *Studies*, p. 47.
146. H. D. Traill, *The Marquis of Salisbury* (London, 1891), p. 216; *Illustrated London News*, 29 August 1903.
147. *Statesmen Past and Future* (London, 1894), p. 10.
148. Bryce, *Studies*, p. 226.
149. CWB, III, pp. 257–8.
150. CWB, VI, p. 94.
151. Greg, *Essays*, II, p. 394.
152. Bryce, *Studies*, p. 214.
153. T. Macaulay, *The History of England*, 4 vols (London, 1906), I, p. 183
154. H. Strickland Constable, *On Certain Hindrances to Wisdom in Statesmanship* (London, 1887), p. 8.
155. *Westminster Review* 163 (1905), pp. 496, 499.

3
Patriotism

Jonathan Parry

This chapter considers the career of the concept of patriotism in parliamentary and elite politics after 1830. It aims to complement Hugh Cunningham's pioneering discussion of radical and popular patriotism 30 years ago.[1] In the space available it is only possible to study the use of the words 'patriotism' and 'patriot' themselves, rather than to survey the innumerable policy approaches that might or might not be deemed to be in the national interest. However, this seems justifiable, since the concept of patriotism had been integral to eighteenth-century politics, which is why it is worth exploring its later history.

In the eighteenth century, as is well known, patriotism involved the defence of popular and parliamentary rights in opposition to heavy taxation, patronage, public debt and other government misbehaviour – which, it was complained, infringed widely understood constraints on the exercise of executive power. The focus of patriotic language was always primarily domestic, but its preference for a 'blue water' naval and community-based defence policy and its dislike of a standing army implied certain positions on foreign affairs, as did its assumption that many corruptions of the body politic had arrived from abroad. For most of the century it was associated mainly with opposition groups, but it claimed to be above party. Then the American and French revolutions allowed Pitt the Younger – a famous patriot's son – and his supporters in government to rework many traditional patriot ideas into a vigorous defence of the constitution against what they presented as theory-driven foreign radicalism – but these events also encouraged radicals to claim that only 'patriotic' opposition could defeat Pitt's 'old corruption'. Both sides of this debate claimed a concern for the national interest as a whole against various sectional, selfish vested interests by which men were tempted; both, in different ways, thus upheld the old patriot ideal of independence and distrust of faction. So by the 1790s it was clear that patriotism involved a defence of constitutional freedoms against corrupting influences, that it condemned factions, cliques and parties, and that it upheld historic national political values against perceived threats from abroad. It was also clear that in practice these desiderata could be interpreted so variously that no political group any longer had a monopoly on the word, if they ever had.[2]

This study makes four main arguments about the political use of patriotism in the nineteenth century. The first is that the tendency for *different* groups to identify with patriotic rhetoric was exacerbated by the reform of Parliament during the century, and this weakened its impact. As the regime became less exclusive, it became more difficult to argue that patriotism was confined to clusters of virtuous individuals fighting against an entrenched system of powerful vested interests. It seemed increasingly generally shared in politics, but also therefore less worth boasting about. Those who made a particular claim to be patriots were often accused of empty posturing and cant.

Secondly, this tendency to ridicule patriotic hyperbole intensified as the party system became more widely accepted after 1832. Parties necessarily had different images of the nation and different interpretations of national interests, and so could easily be satirised if they tried to boast about the uniqueness of their patriotism. When the party system functioned well, it was clear that neither side monopolised the concept. The story is not as simple as this, however, since party was by no means fully accepted, and there was still mileage in arguing that patriotism was incompatible with party spirit; the opposition between the two remained the most standard of tropes.[3] The most effective Victorian governments were those that succeeded in suggesting that they rose above mere party and could indeed invoke a more patriotic, national spirit. Yet this was achieved rarely. Disquiet about the sectionalism and narrow-mindedness of parties drove a lot of patriotic talk, and the resurgence of the cry at the end of nineteenth century reflects renewed anxiety about the inadequacy of the political system.

Thirdly, though foreign elements of the patriotic appeal could be attractive, its domestic connotations continued to be most crucial to its meaning and success. Popularity could not be achieved merely by talking up the strength of Britain abroad; as the *Daily News* wrote in 1874, it was a 'medieval' interpretation of patriotism for a politician to worry about 'the predominant position of a country among surrounding nations' rather than 'its intellectual and political development at home'.[4] Throughout the century no political movement could succeed for long if it did not uphold domestic constitutional ideals that eighteenth-century patriots would have recognised: vigorous representative government and scrutiny of government expenditure. High defence spending was rarely popular; low taxes seemed likely to conserve national economic vigour best. Moreover, definitions of strength abroad, and of the purpose of foreign activity, were affected by perceptions of the strength of the political nation at home. The most important development in the whole century was the sense, from about 1850, that the nation was broadly united as a political community – that patriotism had real depth and strength. This allowed politicians like Palmerston the chance to develop powerful appeals to shared values in opposition to foreign challenges, though this worked well only when the threats had some plausibility to them or the values enjoyed clear success abroad. Conversely, governments which appeared weak at home were doubly vulnerable because they might more easily jeopardise the nation's standing overseas. Wellington's government in 1829–30 was criticised for its out-of-touch effeteness, imperilling Britain's strength against continental rivals at the same time as it failed to reassure the public at home; so were Gladstone's governments between 1880 and 1886.[5]

One reason why foreign events had a relatively limited effect on patriotic rhetoric was that the external threats to Britain were often not clearly defined. Despite occasional menaces from France or Russia, Britain had no permanent foreign enemies. Therefore, fourthly, for very many British people the most persistent and alarming threats to the patria could be found, instead, lurking on that endlessly unsettling frontier between the internal and the external: in other words, the Irish. In the years after 1848, 1870 and 1881 the strongest expressions of patriotism included a manifest hostility to Irish agitation. Weakness in dealing with Irish clamour frequently seemed a sign of lack of patriotic vigour. But Ireland could not simply be an 'other', since some of the most vocal 'patriots' within the Commons were themselves Irish MPs. So they criticised intensely any attempt to repress their claim to defend the rights of their constituents. It was therefore in Irish debates that some of the greatest clashes about patriotism occurred.

Patriotism was at its most effective as a cry when domestic, foreign and Irish themes could be worked together, preferably in a way that rose above narrow party lines. But most of the time, this was difficult; indeed sometimes patriotic language could appear absurd. Patriotism remained a contested term which was used more in condemnation than in celebration, not only to attack those who seemed to lack it, but also to mock the hypocrisy of many of those who swore by it. The chapter looks at these themes within each of three chronological sections, which consider the problem in the two decades after 1830, 1850 and 1870, respectively.

Before 1850

Throughout the first half of the nineteenth century, political appeals to patriotism remained couched in ways that eighteenth-century orators would have found familiar. Within Parliament, a patriotic course of action involved defending the independence and vigour of the House of Commons, particularly in opposing acts of tyranny, extravagance, corruption or sectionalism on the part of government. Excessive taxation and other measures which threatened the prosperity of the country were still seen as prime examples of dubiously patriotic behaviour. So too was anything factional: anything that benefited the few, not the many, anything that helped one interest, section, class or party at the expense of the whole. The core appeal of patriotism was domestic, in that the primary function of the Commons was to scrutinise government proposals to tax and legislate for the people, but it was connected to foreign affairs in two ways. There was a general presumption that low and fair taxation, combined with rational defence spending, best preserved the strength and sinews of the country and thus its real international power. Secondly, a country that was well governed at home had greater power, and also greater right, to encourage the spread of its principles abroad. There were many movements abroad with which British commentators tended to sympathise because they seemed patriotic movements of peoples in favour of representative institutions and against oppression by a small class, often military-clerical and often foreign or foreign-backed. Between the 1810s and 1830s the focus of this patriotic concern was on Portugal, Spain and Greece; from the 1830s until the 1860s it moved to Italy, Poland and Hungary.

The potency of these various 'patriotic' assumptions was particularly evident during the Reform crisis of 1829–32. The Reformers successfully presented themselves as channelling popular grievances against the old order into a noble and virtuous tide of patriotic fervour that must carry all before it. In early 1830 Brougham suggested that the old patterns of party loyalty were breaking up and that MPs were coming over to 'the patriot list of that House'.[6] The new Reform coalition of November 1830 had three great patriotic merits: it appeared to have listened to the people's legitimate demands expressed over the past year; it had committed to the general principles of parliamentary reform and expenditure reduction; and it had done so in an explicitly non-partisan spirit. The radical

Hobhouse, believing that the unreformed system had 'sapped the foundation of all legitimate patriotism', expressed his delight at hearing something he had never expected, 'the language of patriotism from men in office'.[7] The combination of a pro-Reform government and an apparently supportive new monarch quickly gave William IV the sobriquet of 'the patriot king'.[8] A crucial element of the government's argument was that Reform was not so much a concession to popular pressure as a means of legitimating government and strengthening its authority to act for the nation as a whole. Public acquiescence in it would bolster its power to pass major national legislation (such as the New Poor Law) and to take firm steps to discipline over-mighty vested interests (such as in abolishing slavery and reforming municipal corporations). A Reformed state would reduce expenditure but also act more vigorously to support British interests and representative liberal movements in Ireland and the Iberian peninsula, in contrast to Wellington's perceived feebleness and reactiveness in both areas. Thus a patriotic agenda would be followed in every sense.[9]

These arguments were not as virtuous and non-partisan as they seemed; one major purpose of them was to place the Tory opposition in the worst possible light. The more patriotic, consensual and disinterested Reform appeared to be, the more the opponents of it seemed to be miserable vested interests, and this was a great problem for Peel and his Commons followers. Frederick Shaw admitted that 'those who opposed this measure were charged with want of liberality, of disinterestedness, and of patriotism' but contended that the defence of the constitution, law, justice and property was the properly disinterested and patriotic course. Peel taunted those 'who manifested [their] patriotism by exerting all [their] powers to excite the people to discontent with the existing Constitution'.[10]

After 1832 Tories could not afford to continue to be hostile to the Reform Act. They accepted the new political settlement and acquiesced in the assumption that, whether or not the unreformed Commons had represented a broad array of national interests, it certainly did so now. The battle of the 1830s was instead over how best to define and defend the national interest, and this battle led to the rapid growth of party; the coalition spirit of 1830 was replaced by sharp divisions between Liberals and Conservatives on Church, Irish and then commercial policy issues. The Whigs sought to incorporate traditional outsiders – Irish Catholics and British Dissenters – into a broader political nation, and to reach out to commercial, urban and radical opinion. The Conservatives organised their party in defence of the interests that these initiatives seemed to threaten. Was it more patriotic to defend the national Protestant religion against Catholicism or to try a union of hearts between Britain and Ireland? Was the proposal to reduce tariffs on imported corn a bribe and a class policy or an overdue attack on an overmighty monopoly that would advance national prosperity? The disputes were intensely partisan, though each side claimed to speak for the real nation, and in 1841 the pro-Conservative *Times* claimed that they formed a 'new NATIONAL PARTY'.[11]

In fact, explicit references to patriotism were less frequent than during the heady debates of 1830–2. The growth of party spirit contributed to that: it was much easier for each side to accuse the other of specific betrayals of the national interest than to boast a simple patriotism oneself. Most Whigs believed strongly in party as a mechanism for disseminating and protecting great principles, and indeed in the legitimacy of patronage in ensuring good government by right-minded men in Britain and the better integration of Catholics in Ireland. Critics thought this active deployment of patronage showed 'a desperate devotedness to pelf'.[12] There was similar condemnation of their willingness to spend taxpayers' money on civilising projects such as education and the arts, and their explicit approval of a reformed Church Establishment. Some radicals thought their support for the Church inconsistent with their former patriotic rhetoric, while their opposition to further parliamentary reform and the ballot led many to doubt that Whigs were still 'sincere and ardent patriots'.[13] However, radicals who claimed to rise above faction or selfishness were equally satirised, particularly by sceptical Conservatives. In 1836 George Sinclair attacked 'pseudo patriots' whose fevered rhetoric disguised their 'selfishness': to ensure that army and navy jobs went to their own party supporters.[14]

Similarly, any Conservative use of overtly patriotic language risked accusations of hypocrisy disguising partisan and class-based objectives.[15] Both at the 1841 election and during the later debates about Corn Law repeal, Protectionists consciously asserted their patriotism, in order to counter the torrent of abuse from free trade campaigners that agriculturalists formed the ultimate vested interest. In a widely admired speech, McNeile at Liverpool in 1841 called on voters to 'cultivate patriotism in wheat' and to rely on domestic production rather than to be deceived by 'the new-fangled cant of cosmopolitan liberalism'.[16] But opponents ridiculed Protectionists as a monopoly interest trying to scare voters about foreigners' intentions to sabotage British food supply, when in fact free trade would benefit both the country and the world, thus in Morpeth's view revealing the Creator's benevolent intention that 'our patriotism and our philanthropy should be the same'. In 1844 Milner Gibson quoted Byron's jibe of 1823 against 'country patriots' whose sole purpose was 'to hunt and vote, and raise the price of corn'.[17] Notwithstanding this, in the heady climate of 1846 the Protectionist leader Bentinck theatrically claimed that he and his friends were a 'patriotic band', while Newdegate saw them as charged with 'a great and a patriotic cause' in resisting repeal.[18] In 1849 Protectionists used similar rhetoric against the Navigation Bill.[19]

One group of MPs were particularly fond of explicitly patriotic rhetoric and were particularly abused for its inappropriateness. These were the Irish MPs under the leadership of O'Connell, who portrayed themselves as patriots of their country in the tradition of Grattan. For them, 'patriot' implied a determination to represent the downtrodden people of Ireland against oppression, and a disdain for the narrow partisanship of Westminster politics. There were frequent arguments about the legitimacy of this claim. The issue was particularly complicated for the Whigs, who began by accepting the genuineness and patriotism of Irish grievances, but then split badly over it in 1834–5. Many thought, like Henry Ward in 1833, that while Parliament would support any sober requests from O'Connell to remedy clear Irish grievances, he would lose its confidence if 'a factious disposition assumed the garb of patriotism' and he agitated for 'private' benefit.[20] Ward meant here to warn O'Connell against adopting Repeal, but less ambitious O'Connellite campaigns seemed no less factional and disruptive to more unsympathetic British politicians. Peel attacked the posturing self-indulgence of 'flaming patriots' who automatically condemned measures of law and order as 'tyranny and oppression towards Ireland'. Burdett, the former radical, now anti-Catholic Tory convert, claimed that patriotism, formerly noble, now involved 'exciting in the people the most hostile passions against the lawful authorities and government of the country'.[21] For Burdett, the foundation of patriotism was the disavowal of personal gain, and he had great fun with the 'annual tribute' that Irishmen paid to compensate O'Connell for the loss of his legal earnings. O'Connell had to admit that he was indeed a 'paid patriot'.[22] But the more common charge against Irish MPs was that, in Stanley's words, they made 'their patriotism the means of barter for place or pension'. They were only kept loyal by 'golden and most copious showers of honors and emoluments', and were thus holding the country to ransom.[23]

These allegations were made throughout the O'Connell era by Conservatives, but after 1848 they became more widespread than ever. The attempted Irish rebellion stirred up hostility in Britain; after

O'Connell's death no successor could compete with his generally high national standing; the Irish MPs were more prone to faction; then in 1852 the leaders of the Independent Irish Party, Keogh and Sadleir, overthrew their pledge not to take office within months of making it, by joining the Aberdeen coalition. Sadleir's name soon became a byword for corruption, and when ruined he committed suicide in 1856, while Keogh became a rich but unpopular judge. By the early 1850s the reputation of the 'Irish patriots' was at a low. Their 'great show[s] of patriotism' were generally seen by other MPs as disguising partisan, irresponsible or venal objectives.[24]

In short, there were many problems in reconciling patriotic rhetoric to post-Reform Act politics. Parties claimed to promote the national interest but differed strongly about how this was best done, and could not avoid acting as self-serving patronage machines. On the other hand, Parliament could claim more plausibly than before 1832 to represent the nation, and the legislative reforms and expenditure, tax and tariff reductions that governments implemented between 1830 and 1850 demonstrated some responsiveness to popular grievances and to many elements of the old patriotic agenda. Thus that agenda was bound to lose its urgency. It is impossible to be categorical about the precise timing of its decline, since individuals had such different perspectives on how exclusive the state remained and how genuine the spirit of reform was. There remained significant scope for old-style British radicals to criticise party as factional and exclusive and to demand further tax reductions and more open government, and such men were particularly vocal during the depression and international turbulence of the late 1840s, and briefly during the Crimean War. Even so, they were increasingly criticised for an outdated rhetoric unsuited to the era of the Reformed Parliament and sober Peelite finance. In attacking one such figure, Lord Dudley Stuart, in 1852, the Conservative Captain Harris suggested that the era of the 'ranting speech' from 'popular orators' was over, and that the people now expected 'more solid qualities' in their representatives. The Irish Conservative Whiteside attacked the administrative reformers of 1855 on similar grounds, quoting Cowper's verse that people had grown 'too wise to trust' patriots; they raised agitations about crotchety principles to get applause, but they were unwilling to address practical questions in a sober spirit.[25]

Though individuals continued to exemplify this radical patriot politics throughout the 1850s and 1860s, and indeed beyond that, the fundamental legitimacy of the political system was broadly accepted by the early 1850s, and there was a greater disposition to accept that the state could mediate fairly between economic, social and even religious interests. There was less scope for individuals to parade their superior virtue without appearing either ridiculous or subversive of the Victorian constitutional settlement. The 'cant of patriotism' seemed relevant on fewer occasions.[26] There was particularly little willingness to accept its legitimacy for Ireland. Patriotic struggles were admired in opposition to feudal, military, clerical regimes on the continent, but few MPs now wished to claim that the same abuses operated in the United Kingdom.

1850–1867

Between 1848 and 1859 one dramatic new fact was added to the discussions about patriotism: the evidence, repeated and unmistakeable, that there was a real, broad and deep patriotic sentiment in the country. Before 1848 one might hazard a guess about this, but there was no particular reason for it to manifest itself. This changed, firstly with the mobilisation of special constables against the Chartist and Irish threat in 1848, then with the no-popery agitation of 1850–1, then with the enthusiasm for enrolment in the militia in response to the invasion scare of 1852. Following this there was no doubting the support for the Crimean War from 1854, the enthusiasm for patriotic entertainments and publications, the increased respect for British soldiers fighting it, and the popular backing for the Patriotic Fund which was set up to provide help for soldiers' widows and orphans. The decade was capped by the extraordinary success, across all classes, of the volunteer movement which began in response to the next invasion scare of 1859. Few of these events were kindled by political action; they were in varying degrees spontaneous. Their collective message seemed obvious, all the more so given the continuing belief that almost no continental states had achieved the British combination of stability and liberty. For Carlisle, nothing was 'more calculated to excite feelings of patriotic though I trust humbled pride' than the mature British response to the Europe-wide crisis of 1848–9. Palmerston was quick to suggest that enthusiasm for the militia revealed the 'patriotic spirit and feeling of the English people' and their 'contempt' for peace-at-any-price principles.[27] The large number of enrolments into it at the beginning of the Crimean War made these sentiments commonplace.[28] The class solidarity of the volunteer movement was particularly widely praised as demonstrating popular loyalty to the constitution, while Lovaine thought that volunteers' 'spirit, energy, and patriotism have completely altered the opinion formerly entertained by continental nations of the want of military spirit' among the English people.[29]

This patriotism was not a rallying cry for domestic purification but a celebration and mobilisation of national virtue against perceived external threats. The prevalence of these sentiments strengthened the hands of those politicians who called for a strong attention to defence policy and a vigorous resistance to invasion – feared from France – or to Russian and Austrian aggression in Turkey, Italy or Hungary which threatened to consolidate power in Europe in the hands of enemies of constitutional liberty and British values. Though stimulated by foreign events, these opinions were fundamentally chauvinist, concerned far less with the merits of Turks or Italians than with the superiority of the British and their duty to defend their noblest values against assault. Press commentary encouraged the view that these sentiments, mixing enthusiasm for military defence with constitutional libertarianism, were broadly shared in the nation.

Palmerston was the elite politician who was most identified with both elements of this appeal.[30] He retained the premiership for most of the decade 1855–65 because he was better able than his rivals to reconcile parliamentary and national needs, by commanding a largely party majority in the House yet bolstering it with a supra-party authority derived from outside. He was less of a party zealot than most of his rivals; his concentration on foreign and defence matters rather than domestic reform helped to reduce partisan division, in tune with traditional patriotic sentiment. Conversely the mood of the 1850s weakened the Manchester school radicalism of Cobden and Bright, which appeared too concerned with materialism – with private profit and tax reductions – rather than with the broader public interest – with Britain's mission to safeguard world progress. The old antagonism between love of gold and patriotic love of country was expressed by a number of commentators in the run-up to the Crimean War, in a deliberate attack on the spirit of selfish money-grubbing which they felt had come to dominate commercial society and undermine national morals.[31]

For all that, the best way to play the patriotic card was to understand that, just as in years gone by, patriotism and low taxation were complementary rather than at odds. Palmerston and the Liberal governments which he dominated from 1852 to 1865 were at their strongest when they combined a vigorous defence and foreign policy with an awareness of the attractiveness of low and fair taxes. Mere boasting about Britain's greatness – to which Palmerston, like many others in this period, was susceptible – could easily appear empty gesturing, indeed cant. The Liberals commanded the political centre to the extent that they seemed to square the circle between strong defence, a patriotic support of constitutionalism against autocracy abroad, and prudent tax cuts for both middle and working classes at home. Though Palmerston and his Chancellor Gladstone did not always see eye-to-eye during the 1859 government, their alliance suggested that sober Peelite finance was compatible with a successful foreign and defence policy – though this balancing act, the apogee of patriotic politics, was only achieved, and briefly, because of unprecedented national prosperity and the apparent ascendancy of liberalism in Europe.[32] By the end of the Crimean War there was little parliamentary appetite for paying for an extended war for the 'principle of nationalities' across Europe, and Palmerston was wise enough to hope that Britain would not need to fight another war in the life of the youngest MP.[33] The unification of Italy was so widely welcomed because it seemed a true liberal victory – one of opinion and moral suasion. Britain's continental enemies – Russia, Austria, France, the Pope – had been defeated without British blood or taxes being spent. One of the major attractions of the volunteer movement, at least for radicals, was that its popularity opened up the possibility of cutting expenditure on the regular army, and thus the tax burden on the ordinary people whose patriotism was underpinning the movement.[34] This was a sentiment that eighteenth-century patriot admirers of the militia would have understood.

Broadly speaking, the Palmerstonian consensus about Britain's beneficial world role held until his death in 1865, though it was fast losing its political potency. The apparent victory of liberalism in Europe in 1856 and 1859–60 undermined Russia's bogey status, while Palmerston's ironclad and fortification policy drove Napoleon III of France to abandon his gestures against England after 1862 in favour of ambitions on the Rhine. The withdrawal of these external threats reduced the intensity of patriotic feeling from the early 1860s, while the realisation that European politics was now more complex than a black-and-white struggle between liberalism and autocracy, and likely to be influenced by continental armies more than Mediterranean fleets, revealed the embarrassing fact that the British no longer had a clear continental mission. In the absence of direct threats to the country, the government found itself faced with demands from both the Cobdenite radicals and the Conservative opposition to cut taxes faster.[35]

This more uncertain mood of the 1860s did not disguise the manifest working-class patriotic loyalty to the broad outlines of the constitution (even if it might still need reform). Palmerston had some sense of how to invoke and exploit this loyalty, but the leading opposition politician Disraeli did not. It is remarkable how slowly Disraeli stumbled towards an effective patriotic politics. He had always talked about patriotism a lot, but could not resist a sarcastic treatment of it, in the sense of belittling those who claimed lofty motives. He bitterly and repeatedly attacked the 'highly-gifted patriots' of the Aberdeen coalition for clinging to place despite their differences of principles, even to the extent in 1854–5 of appearing to undermine the war effort; Russell complained that one speech of his lacked 'a single gleam of patriotism'.[36] Gladstone, similarly, claimed that Disraeli's 'dishonourable' motion of 1864 against the government's Schleswig-Holstein policy showed an unprecedented delight in belittling the standing of the country.[37] These criticisms aimed to exploit Disraeli's perceived lack of principle; they were also, perhaps, coded allusions to his 'unEnglish' racial inheritance and ideas. In fact, Disraeli approached politics from a strong sense of English history: his attacks on coalitions were grounded in his reading of the Fox-North affair, while his sarcasm about patriots rested on his belief that patronage was essential to an effective politics.[38] However, his position in opposition meant that he could not make the political weather, and his taste for trying to reconcile high ideals and low manoeuvre led him into creative but problematic strategies such as his alliance with Irish Catholicism for the defence of religion against atheism and cosmopolitan liberalism in the 1860s.

Nonetheless Disraeli must have noticed the public demonstrations of patriotic sentiment from which Palmerston benefited throughout the 1850s and early 1860s. Perhaps this explains why he – and many of his party – were relaxed about a substantial extension of the franchise in 1867. He foretold in April 1868 that as a result of the 1867 Reform Act 'you will have a Parliament returned to this House full of patriotic feeling and national sentiment'.[39] It was logical for him to think that the frequent expressions of popular patriotism since 1848 were at least as representative of popular opinion as the sporadic agitation for Reform. Meanwhile the standard Liberal argument for extending the franchise was that patriotism, in the sense of a capacity to think about the public interest as well as private ones, was widespread among non-voters and that they were more likely to behave on class or sectional lines if excluded from the franchise than if included.[40] Politicians had several tactical and strategic reasons for opposing, delaying or amending particular Reform measures in the late 1850s, but, after the patriotic ebullitions of the 1850s, perhaps we should believe those who claimed that they nonetheless 'trust[ed]' working-class 'loyalty and patriotism'.[41] By 1867, at any rate, neither party leader wished to deny the patriotism of a wide electorate.

After 1867

The 1867 Reform Act made it more difficult than ever to argue that the political system was not representative, and made grand claims of superior patriotic virtue by individuals even more open to ridicule. As late as 1868 the old radical John Bright boasted his superiority over Disraeli, by claiming that he, at least, had never endeavoured 'to claim the ladder of parliamentary promotion and notoriety' – a show of 'patriotism' that was promptly satirised by Disraeli's old friend Manners.[42] Even Bright accepted cabinet office a mere seven months after this noble outburst, while the leading administrative reformers of 1855 had all become ministers by 1863. One of them, Layard, carried on giving frank speeches to his constituents, prompting the *Daily Telegraph*'s pleasure that it was now possible to be 'at once a placeman and a patriot'.[43] Only a few radicals like Charles Dilke and, more consistently, Joseph Cowen continued to talk the language of patriotism and popular rights in opposition to party and faction well beyond 1867.[44]

The most important political theme of the post-Reform period was the growth of party organisation in order to politicise the expanded electorate, with the result that the legitimacy of party was more broadly accepted than ever. Naturally, both parties were capable of impugning the patriotism of their opponents. In 1874, for example, Conservative newspapers implied that Gladstone lacked patriotism, accusing him of a combination of materialism at home and feebleness abroad, given his proposal to abolish the income tax and his low-key foreign policy.[45] But patriotism itself was not a leading issue at the election, and shifts of political opinion were driven mainly by the perception that explicit class, economic and religious interests were threatened. The *Daily News* spoke for many when it said that both parties were now recognised to be patriotic but that neither could claim to be the sole preserver of national institutions, a healthy situation.[46] As in 1841, the Conservatives benefited in 1874 from the defensive reaction by propertied and Anglican voters against perceived radical pressures since the Reform Act. Party spirit was intense, and the degree of party organisation unprecedented – despite an occasional willingness by some Liberal-leaning moralists to prefer 'patriotism to party' by voting for candidates representing single-issue pressure groups instead of party men who would not commit to their cause (whether temperance, disestablishment or Contagious Diseases Acts repeal).[47]

At the next election in 1880, however, patriotism was an enormously contested term, but the nature of the contest was very instructive. After some initial consolidatory social policy, the Conservative government had focused on foreign policy in pursuit of Disraeli's desire to restore Britain's weight in Europe and the nation's sense of self-confidence. He claimed to have defeated the Russian threat to Turkey, to have made Britain central to the new international settlement at Berlin in 1878 and to have reinvigorated domestic appreciation of the empire. In a speech in November 1879 he asserted that his creed was 'Imperium et Libertas'; he stood for re-election in 1880 on the basis that 'the power of England' would rest on the result. For good measure, he claimed that Irish MPs were seeking to undermine the union and that Liberals might ally with them to challenge 'the imperial character of the realm'.[48] There is no doubt that the Conservative Party's main electoral claim was that they would defend the national interest abroad. An enthusiastic supporter of the Conservative candidate in Huddersfield claimed that the election vote would decide whether 'England or Russia be ascendant'.[49] It is at this point, according to Hugh Cunningham, that we can see patriotism becoming mainly a right-wing cry. In 1877–8 raucous popular support for Disraeli's threat to go to war against Russia was christened 'jingoism'. Though Cunningham presents suggestive evidence of popular patriotism at this time, even he makes some valuable qualifications: that much of the jingo spirit was in fact domestic and partisan in nature, and that much of the rest of it reflected the popularity of music hall and theatrical re-enactments of dramatic events, which were often politically ambivalent rather than simplistically nationalist.[50] In fact the events of 1880 reveal that there was little mileage in an idea of patriotism which did not connect foreign policy with good government at home, and that Disraeli failed to read the English political mindset.

The Conservative attack made two fundamental errors. The first was the failure to appreciate the continuing potency of the Liberal claim that the essence of patriotism was fair, responsive, economical and representative domestic government. This fitted naturally with the patient spread of these same values abroad wherever they could be encouraged effectively, but that was the reverse of jingoism. Anyone who claimed 'to foster a spirit of patriotism and morality' should be judged on their domestic record, but Disraeli had presided over a betrayal of sober finance.[51] Goschen defined Liberal patriotism as reducing the burdens of the people, stimulating trade by reviving confidence, exorcising the baneful military spirit on the continent and spreading education and freedom.[52] Disraeli offered the reverse: income tax increased from 2d to 6d, crippling deficits which made an economic depression worse, and a failure of domestic reform while seeking to distract voters with the false glitter of a continental 'imperialism'. He was embracing 'the principles of Continental absolutism', which were variously interpreted as 'the worst excesses of the Second Empire', 'Russian Imperialism' or a reliance on 'Austro-German testimonials'. This was 'comedy patriotism', 'patriotism in swagger and brag'.[53] Foljambe claimed for Liberals 'a holier, and a truer, and a loftier patriotism' based on 'the prosperity and contentment of her inhabitants' while his co-speaker denied that the true patriot was 'the bully ... seeking somebody to leather' or the party of 'secret treaties' which sought to degrade Parliament. Or as Whitwill more pithily put it, true patriots were those who carried the flag of commerce everywhere, rather than 'blowing out the brains of your customers'.[54] Hostility to 'Beaconsfieldism' was so intense that old Whigs who had no time at all for Gladstone still rallied enthusiastically to the party.

The second Conservative error was their shrillness in claiming that they were a national government and that Liberals should put 'patriotism before party'. This was a reference back to Liberal divisions on foreign policy discussions in 1877–8, at which point many of the party's MPs had baulked at following Gladstone in arguing against an assertive policy towards Russia. Conservatives urged them now to do the same, to 'rise above the spirit of party and say they are for England', and praised a few anti-Russian Liberals, such as Walter, Hoare and Cowen, for doing that.[55] Leading Conservatives were among the boldest in taking this line: Northcote praised Liberals who had abandoned 'faction ... for the support of a national Government', while W.H. Smith claimed that the 'interest of party' should 'always give way to the vital interests of the empire', and, astonishingly, that Disraeli's government had 'not been a party government' because some of the best Liberals had supported (some of) its foreign policy. The *Derby Mercury* even referred to the 'fast-fading tradition of party'.[56] It was ridiculous to disavow party after the intense organisational activity by both sides since 1867, and during one of the most partisan elections ever fought, which saw a record number of contested seats. It was, after all, Gladstone's effigy, not the Tsar's, that the jingo mobs burned in 1878.[57] The relative weakness of Conservative Party organisation at this election has often been noted, and perhaps this supra-party rhetoric helps to explain this; certainly Disraeli took little interest in it. Such arguments also added fuel to Liberal arguments that 'imperial' or 'continental' Conservatives did not appreciate the safeguards that party offered for popular liberties and values. Demands that Liberal MPs should vote with the government rather than their party were demands that they should ignore the wishes of those who had elected them in 1874.[58] Party was 'merely the means we have in this and in every other free country for furthering the welfare of the State.... It is a mark of our freedom'. The Tory attack on party was 'of a piece with imperialism, with the slighting and undervaluing of Parliamentary control' as in the French Second Empire. A nation not organised into parties could be taken in any direction by a despot.[59]

The Liberals won the 1880 election because the economic depression and their superior party organisation added to the innate advantages that they already possessed; when united by a common threat to core Liberal principles, they could expect a majority as at most elections since 1832. Disraeli was outdated in claiming to offer national leadership, above party, for a policy directed at one particular country – Russia – and that boasted about imperial grandeur in abstract terms, but that offered little of substance to a domestic audience.

His failure was all the more striking since after 1886 the Conservatives made a much better fist of constructing a patriotic politics. This was partly because in the early 1880s a series of external events increased the sense of threat to Britain's global position. There was a defence scare and a demand to spend more on the navy; there was great tension with France over Egypt and an escalating threat from Germany in southern Africa; above all the Gordon affair demonstrated how failure in far-flung parts could generate a sense of national humiliation in an age of media sensationalism and international rivalry. The principal effect of these tensions was to convince most leading younger Liberals, as well as Conservatives, of the need to show greater vigour in defence of the national interest abroad. Thus by 1885 there was something approaching a new consensus about the need to protect Britain's imperial territory and global influence against any threats to it, though it was a consensus which Gladstone and a significant number of his party explicitly rejected.[60] However, the most crucial change from 1886 was that Conservatives fused defence of empire and opposition to Irish Nationalism into a political crusade which also in some sense rose above party through their alliance with Liberal Unionists. Defence of the national interest abroad fitted with a firm opposition to perceived enemies within and a governing approach that while based on Conservative Party organisation claimed to transcend narrow party interest.

Conservatives and Liberal Unionists united to claim that Gladstone's new alliance with Parnell's Irish Nationalists in pursuit of Home Rule marked a grave threat to Britain's global position, and was an inappropriate reward for the unpatriotic behaviour of Nationalist MPs, incendiary republican gangs and Romanist priests. For some years, the boycotting and other violence in Ireland, culminating in the Phoenix Park murders of May 1882, had appalled British opinion. Home Rule was even more contentious at a moment when Britain's world power seemed generally threatened by rival powers and by economic uncertainty. Indeed in 1882 the press had made frequent comparisons between Egyptian and Irish violence, and tended to justify repression of both in terms of Britain's global role to uphold law and justice.[61] Many former Liberals thought that Home Rule risked undermining British world power at a time when it needed to be consolidated.

Both political groups also presented their informal coalition against Home Rule as a national necessity, and occasionally as placing 'patriotism before party' or creating a 'national party'; Chamberlain particularly identified with this language.[62] In practice, however, Unionism relied on party organisation; the Liberal Unionists were strong in a few particular areas (such as Chamberlain's Midlands), while the Conservatives developed an increasingly impressive structure across the country in order to reach out to new voters after the 1884–5 Reform settlement. They also had the great benefit of the Primrose League, whose membership grew from 11,366 to 550,508 in the two years after March 1885.[63] It emphasised loyalty to hierarchy, monarchy, empire and Church, and in November 1885 Lord Henniker declared at one meeting: 'Our first principle is patriotism ... our second principle is patriotism, and our third principle is patriotism. Patriotism pervades ... all we do', because the word incorporated the defence of the constitution, the empire and organised religion.[64] The Unionist appeal was not just based on old Tory principles, though the monarchy, the Church and the army all became more widely admired as national institutions, as opposed to vested interests, from the 1870s.[65] The alliance with Liberals made it easier for Conservatives to invoke the language of justice, liberty and progress than they had in the age of Disraeli, and to acknowledge the achievement of Palmerston for his vigorous yet on the whole peaceful and economical foreign policy. Conservatives claimed to continue that tradition better than modern-day Liberals, who, not seeing the importance of national prestige, lowered Britain's reputation abroad and then had to spend more money to recover it.[66] Unionist emphasis on economy was facilitated further because after 1885 radicals increasingly urged more government expenditure at central and local level and indeed tax redistribution, thus allowing their opponents to take up the former Liberal banner of low taxes and laissez-faire. The emerging criticism of Liberals' 'socialism' was a patriot cry in more than one sense.[67] Meanwhile, perceived 'faddism' within the Liberal Party in the late 1880s added to the sense that it was a group of vested interests, not a national party. In all these ways, the alliance of 1886 was in general much more successful in commanding the centre ground of politics, in a way redolent of the traditional patriotic agenda, than Disraeli had been in 1880.

The Unionist identification with the various meanings of patriotism that this chapter has highlighted served the alliance well at various points after 1886, such as in the 'khaki' election of 1900.[68] Indeed in 1887 the *Economist* found it alarming that for the first time one party might have 'a monopoly of ability and patriotism'.[69] However, the benefit to Unionists was less permanent than it appeared in the immediate aftermath of the Home Rule crisis. If the Liberals suffered particularly for their factionalism and Little Englandism, the political system in general was being widely criticised for its failings by the late 1890s. The 'National Efficiency' movement that emerged from the Boer War crisis was inspired by several old 'patriot' sentiments. It was a cry of anguish at a regime that seemed complacent, sclerotic and poor value for money at home while unable to ward off serious threats from abroad. The most vigorous critics of the system – Rosebery, Milner, Chamberlain – all took issue, in various ways, with the narrowness and conventionalism of both political parties and their agendas. All wanted a rearrangement of politics around a reinvigorating supra-party national effort.[70] As in the past, patriotism had particular resonance at times of apparent threat to national interests. However this did not mean that it could be tapped for a productive purpose. All these 'Efficiency' movements failed, leaving most of their advocates politically marginalised, while Chamberlain's attempt to rebrand the Unionist party around imperial tariff reform proved a spectacular political miscalculation. The party system, unromantic and mundane, trundled on, and in 1906 the Liberals managed to present their own policies as within the patriotic tradition, once again reflecting its flexibility.[71] As Chamberlain himself had remarked in 1886: 'The party tie is the strongest sentiment in this country – stronger than patriotism or even self-interest'.[72]

In conclusion, the tradition of patriotic argument helps to illuminate a good deal about Victorian politics. Most nineteenth-century politicians wanted to identify with constitutional and economical government that avoided overt partisanship as between classes and interest groups. Most of them, indeed, recognised that the regime's claim to offer such government had contributed a lot to political stability at home and to Britain's attractiveness as a constitutional model to other peoples. Sometimes a particular government or opposition might succeed in mounting an appeal that married the traditional domestic, foreign and (superficially) non-partisan elements of patriotic language unusually well, and this could pay substantial political dividends. However, these dividends rarely lasted long. The flexibility of the concept of patriotism, together with the growth of the party system, ensured that politicians could always be accused of falling short of the ideal in some way or other. Moreover, lack of patriotism could be defined so variously – as a preference for class, for party, for money, for ambition, for power – that the word was increasingly used as a cover for other more material criticisms.[73] Though one can trace continuities of appeal through the century, it is also clear that, as the system became more democratic and party became more established, electoral language became more mundane and also more concerned with specific domestic policy on its own terms. Even Unionists made foreign policy a low priority in 1895, for example.[74] Patriotism could appeal in many circumstances, but equally it could easily be ridiculed as an abstraction and an unjustified claim of individual or group superiority.

This flexibility and slipperiness suggest problems with Cunningham's argument that the patriotic cry transferred in any very straightforward way to the Conservative cause in the late nineteenth century. What his material indicates, perhaps, is that the crucial change was not so much in the meaning of patriotism as of radicalism. The old radicalism that defined itself against the political establishment and its vested interests was necessarily weakened and eventually all but killed by the extension of the franchise and the cleansing of 'old corruption'. The radicalism that falteringly took its place discussed using the power of the state to correct economic and social abuses, and this made it intermittently possible for old radicals as well as Conservatives to criticise these newer ideas using similar libertarian, fiscal, constitutional and patriotic arguments to those that had been used against the *ancien régime*.

Another major part of the Conservative appeal after 1886, as it had been at some previous points of the century, was hostility to Irish nationalism and Catholicism. Many Unionists combined opposition to Home Rule with defence of empire in a rhetorical package emphasising the maintenance of British global greatness. This naturally appealed to parts of the traditional patriotic agenda. However Liberal supporters of Home Rule could also claim to be true patriots, defending the principle of representative government and popular rights. This required some sort of cooperation with Irish MPs who vigorously claimed the title of patriot, a claim that was now more bitterly contested than ever.

It was in discussing Ireland, therefore, that the problem of patriotism was most intense. By the 1880s, the Irish patriot tradition was very strong – imprisonment and exile had created not just past heroes but also new ones like Michael Davitt (elected to Parliament while in prison in 1882). Some Liberal MPs in particular were increasingly troubled by the evidence that Irish nationalism was a genuinely popular and irreversible movement, something that the 1885 election results brought into sharp relief. Parnell learned from history, recognising the importance of avoiding the charge that his MPs, like Keogh and Sadleir, were out for personal gain; he explicitly refused to allow them to trade in patronage, at least as a general rule.[75] Moreover, from the late 1870s the Nationalists' signature policy in Parliament was the long declamatory Commons speech, a deliberately historical initiative, taken to the extreme of obstructing government legislation. They claimed that this use of parliamentary privilege was necessary in order to protest against executive tyranny, particularly the coercive legislation of the early 1880s to repress Irish protest.[76] Patriotic obstruction was their answer to *ancien régime*-style repression of popular rights. British MPs retorted that a proper patriot should support 'law, order, and peace'.[77] In 1882, Gladstone's government was forced to propose and eventually carry unprecedented measures to limit the duration of parliamentary discussions, as well as far-reaching coercion legislation, but this revealed its constitutional illiberality on both grounds, something that mischievous opponents like Churchill were not slow to point out.[78] As in the 1830s, and after 1886, British Liberalism, historically so keen on the language of patriotic constitutionalism, could not speak with one voice on its suitability for Ireland.

Ireland created the biggest political problem of the second half of the nineteenth century, because an indigenous patriotism confronted British self-satisfaction about her own constitutional achievement. There were many animated discussions about whether and how Ireland could or should be governed on 'British' principles, and how to deal with Irishmen who were discontented with British rule. Some British political groups sympathised with some aspects of Irish complaints, but it was impossible for any government to treat Irish grievances as indulgently as many of them treated continental patriot movements. Various strategies were employed to demonise, ridicule or ignore Irish patriotism. However, it could not be ignored, because the battle of patriotisms took place on the floor of the most crucial symbol of the British polity, the Westminster Parliament itself. From time to time, Irish MPs held the balance of power and then exercised great influence. Even when they did not, their presence was a constant reminder that repression was not a straightforward policy for an institution which claimed to have laid the foundations of British greatness by defending the liberties of its people.

Notes

1. H. Cunningham, 'The Language of Patriotism, 1750–1914', *History Workshop Journal* 12 (1981), 8–33.
2. These arguments are drawn from the following essential works on the topic, though their authors might not quite present them in these terms, since all except Grainger seem keener than I would be to suggest significant changes in the identity of patriotism over time: B. Kemp, 'Patriotism, Pledges, and the People', in M. Gilbert, ed., *A Century of Conflict 1850–1950: Essays for A.J.P. Taylor* (London, 1966), pp. 37–46; Cunningham, 'Language of Patriotism'; L. Colley, 'Radical Patriotism in Eighteenth-Century England', in R. Samuel, ed., *Patriotism: the Making and Unmaking of British National Identity: I: History and Politics* (London and New York, 1989), pp. 169–87; J.H. Grainger, *Patriotisms: Britain 1900–1939* (London, 1986), pp. 13–20.
3. See e.g. Gladstone, *Hansard's Parliamentary Debates* [hereafter H] LXI 373, 9 March 1842; Walrond, *Trewman's Flying Exeter Post*, 10 March 1880; Hamilton, *Aberdeen Weekly Journal*, 17 March 1880; A.V. Dicey in 1909, quoted in Grainger, *Patriotisms*, p. 174; and several examples quoted below.
4. *Daily News*, 21 January 1874, criticising Bismarck for resurrecting the old view.
5. I explore the interaction of these foreign and domestic arguments further in *The Politics of Patriotism: English Liberalism, National Identity and Europe, 1830–1886* (Cambridge, 2006).
6. H XXII 723, 18 February 1830.
7. H XXIV 1237, 28 May 1830; H I 1084, 13 December 1830; see also Harvey, H I 939, 9 December 1830.
8. From Hunt, H VI 1202, 6 September 1831, Macaulay, H VII 311, 20 September 1831, Hume, H VIII 425, 10 October 1831. See John Watkins, *The Life and Times of England's Patriot King: William IV* (1831); J.S. Knowles, *Alfred the Great or the Patriot King: Dedicated to William IV* (1831) and D. Armitage, 'A Patriot for Whom? The Afterlives of Bolingbroke's Patriot King', *Journal of British Studies* 36 (1997), 415–16.
9. Parry, *Politics of Patriotism*, pp. 49–54, 150–1.
10. Shaw, H XIII 141, 25 May 1832; Peel, H II 1337, 3 March 1831; see also Croker, H VII 352, 20 September 1831.
11. *The Times*, 28 June 1841.
12. *The Era*, 27 June 1841.
13. Duncombe, H XXXV 360, 19 July 1836; Roebuck, H XXXVI 31, 31 January 1837.
14. H XXXIV 1177, 4 July 1836; see also Graham on Duncombe, H LXV 668, 26 July 1842.
15. See Hume, H LVIII 376, 13 May 1841.
16. *Hull Packet*, 25 June 1841; *Derby Mercury*, 30 June 1841; see also Chamberlayne in *Hampshire Advertiser*, 10 July 1841.
17. Morpeth in *Sheffield and Rotherham Independent*, 26 June 1841; Gibson, H LXXV 1501, 26 June 1844, quoting from *The Age of Bronze* (1823); see also Wakley, H LX 786, 21 February 1842.

18. H LXXXIV 1321, 20 March 1846; LXXXIII 1295, 20 February 1846.
19. See Willcox, H CIII 590, 12 March 1849, criticising them for 'effusions of patriotism' which made it necessary to retain outdated manning restrictions in the new legislation; these were abolished in 1853.
20. H XV 542–3, 11 February 1833.
21. Peel, H LXXVI 1047, 18 July 1844; see also idem, H XCVIII 464, 18 April 1848; Burdett, H LI 403, 21 January 1840.
22. See H XXXIX 782, 796, 7 December 1837; see also Shaw, H XXXIV 283, 9 June 1836 and Disraeli on the 'professional patriots of Ireland', H CII 541, 9 February 1849.
23. Stanley, H XCVI 1247, 24 February 1848; Sinclair, H LIV 338, 19 May 1840; see also Shaw's satire on Sheil's patriotism, quoting Cowper's famous verse of 1785 on human changeability: H LVI 1070, 25 February 1841.
24. Hamilton, H CXXI, 5 May 1852; Lucas, H CXXX 332–3, 7 February 1854; Bowyer, H CXXXII 542, 6 April 1854.
25. Harris, H CXIX 316–17, 9 February 1852; Whiteside (on Layard), H CXLI 1901–2, 1 May 1856.
26. This phrase was famously used by the Conservative convert Burdett in 1837, criticising Dissenters. He meant by it 'jargon' rather than 'hypocrisy'. It prompted Russell's devastating retort to the former radical orator, that 'the recant of patriotism was infinitely more disgusting': H XXXVIII, 965, 1070, 22 & 23 May 1837. See also Baillie, quoting Merivale on patriots' hypocrisy: H CII 940, 20 February 1849.
27. Carlisle, H CVII 655, 20 July 1849; Palmerston, CXXIV 360, 21 February 1853.
28. Newcastle, H CXXXI 182, 2 March 1854; Hildyard, CXXXVI 476, 18 December 1854; Denman, ibid. 718, 21 December 1854; Palmerston, CXXXIX 2153, 14 August 1855.
29. St Aubyn, H CLVI 79, 24 January 1860; Lovaine, CLXX 1693, 14 May 1863.
30. Opinions differ as to quite how popular he was in the country: D. Brown, *Palmerston and the Politics of Foreign Policy, 1846–55* (Manchester, 2002), pp. 36–7; A. Taylor, 'Palmerston and Radicalism, 1847–1865', *Journal of British Studies* 33 (1994), 157–79; Cunningham, 'Language of Patriotism', 19–20.
31. Parry, *Politics of Patriotism*, pp. 209, 218–19.
32. Ibid., pp. 210–11, 233–6.
33. H CXLII 134–6, 6 May 1856.
34. Parry, *Politics of Patriotism*, pp. 70–1, 78, 223–36.
35. See Cobden's defences of his patriotism: H CLV 717, 29 July 1859, CLXVII 1557–8, 7 July 1862; and Conservative demands for lower taxes and a peace policy: Derby, H CLXI 32–3, 5 February 1861, Disraeli, CLXIII 257, 30 May 1861 & CLXVII 957, 23 June 1862; Lennox, CLXVI 1856, 16 May 1862. More generally, see Parry, *Politics of Patriotism*, pp. 237–41.
36. H CXXXI 303, 3 March 1854, CXXXV 229, 13 July 1854, CXXXVI 1852, 23 February 1855; Russell, CXXXVI 216, 12 December 1854.
37. H CLXXVI 775–7, 4 July 1864.
38. In 1855 he mocked the patriot cant that patronage distribution was not a major role of a prime minister: H CXXXVIII 2200, 18 June 1855. I have discussed the general theme of Disraeli's patriotic politics in 'Disraeli and England', *Historical Journal* 43 (2000), 699–728.

39. H CXCI 900, 3 April 1868. See also H CLXXXVIII 1604, 15 July 1867 that a broader franchise would make it easier to arrive 'at the more patriotic and national feelings of the country'.

40. J. Parry, *The Rise and Fall of Liberal Government in Victorian Britain* (New Haven, 1993), pp. 207–10.

41. Cairns, H CLIII 612, 22 March 1859. See also Hibbert's acknowledgment of Conservative patriotism in recognising the strength of public support for Reform: H CLXXXVII 273, 9 May 1867.

42. H CXCI 1942–3, 7 May 1868.

43. *Daily Telegraph*, 5 December 1864.

44. For Dilke, see e.g. his speech at Chelsea, *Lloyd's Weekly Newspaper*, 11 January 1874.

45. *Standard*, 27 January 1874; *Hampshire Advertiser*, 28 January 1874.

46. 11 February 1874.

47. See e.g. the United Kingdom Alliance election address, in the *Glasgow Herald* and *Liverpool Mercury*, 28 January 1874. I have discussed how far these moral-istic campaigns obstructed the growth of party loyalty in 'The Disciplining of the Religious Conscience in Nineteenth-Century British Politics', in I. Katznelson and G. Stedman Jones, eds., *Religion and the Political Imagination* (Cambridge, 2010), pp. 214–34.

48. J. Parry, *Benjamin Disraeli* (Oxford, 2007), pp. 112–15.

49. *Standard*, 20 March 1880; poem, *Huddersfield Daily Chronicle*, 26 March 1880.

50. Cunningham, 'Language of Patriotism', 23–6; idem, 'Jingoism in 1877–78', *Victorian Studies* 14 (1971), 429–53.

51. Parry, *Politics of Patriotism*, pp. 333–41. Quotation is from a letter from an 'old miner' to *Sheffield and Rotherham Independent*, 4 March 1880.

52. *Leeds Mercury*, 24 March 1880.

53. 'Occasional notes', *York Herald*, 25 March 1880; *Daily Gazette (Middlesborough)*, 20 March 1880; *Sheffield and Rotherham Independent*, 1 April 1880; Robert Leader, ibid., 5 March 1880; Adam, *Daily News*, 23 March 1880.

54. Foljambe and Falding, *Sheffield and Rotherham Independent*, 11 March 1880; Whitwill, *Bristol Mercury*, 30 March 1880.

55. *Derby Mercury*, 10 March 1880; Lascelles, *Leeds Mercury*, 8 March 1880; Miles, *Bristol Mercury*, 11 March 1880; Arkwright, *Derby Mercury*, 17 March 1880; Bruce and Compton, *Hampshire Telegraph*, 20 and 24 March 1880.

56. Northcote, *Glasgow Herald*, 1 April 1880; Smith, *Morning Post*, 18 March 1880, and *Hampshire Advertiser*, 20 March 1880; also R.A. Cross, *Standard*, 30 March 1880; *Derby Mercury* quotation is from 24 March 1880.

57. Cunningham, 'Jingoism', 448. See T. Lloyd, 'Uncontested seats 1852–1910', *Historical Journal* 8 (1965), 260–5.

58. Chamberlain, *Birmingham Daily Post*, 26 March 1880.

59. *Sheffield and Rotherham Independent*, 29 March 1880.

60. Parry, *Politics of Patriotism*, pp. 341–73.

61. Ibid., p. 351.

62. Chamberlain, *Times*, 8 July 1895, 11 July 1895; see also St John Brodrick, ibid., 2 July 1895. More generally, for Chamberlain, Frank Harris and Montague Crackanthorpe on the idea of a national party in the later 1880s, see G.R. Searle, *Country before Party: Coalition and the Idea of 'National Government' in Modern Britain, 1885–1987* (London, 1995), pp. 34–40.

63. M. Pugh, *The Tories and the people 1880–1935* (Oxford, 1985), p. 27.
64. At Diss, *Ipswich Journal*, 12 November 1885.
65. J. Parry, 'The Decline of Institutional Reform in Nineteenth-Century Britain', in D. Feldman and J. Lawrence, eds., *Structures and Transformations in Modern British History* (Cambridge, 2011), pp. 179–80.
66. *Reasons why you should vote for the Conservative candidate* (1885), pp. 16–17, 21.
67. See P.A. Readman, 'The 1895 General Election and Political Change in Late Victorian Britain', *Historical Journal* 42 (1999), 479–81 on this libertarianism in 1895.
68. See P. Readman, 'The Conservative Party, Patriotism, and British Politics: the Case of the General Election of 1900', *Journal of British Studies* 40 (2001), 107–45.
69. June 1887, quoted in Searle, *Country before Party*, p. 31.
70. Grainger, *Patriotisms*, pp. 173–9; G.R. Searle, *The Quest for National Efficiency: a Study in British Politics and Political Thought, 1899–1914* (Oxford, 1971).
71. P. Readman, 'The Liberal Party and Patriotism in Early Twentieth-Century Britain', *Twentieth Century British History* 12 (2001), 269–302.
72. To Churchill, quoted in Searle, *Country before Party*, p. 1.
73. See, for example, John Tyndall used it in a Carlylean sense as the opposite of materialism, money-worship and 'the mere husks and rinds of good': 'Local and General', *Leeds Mercury*, 20 January 1874.
74. Readman, '1895 General Election', 492.
75. J. McConnel, '"Jobbing with Tory and Liberal": Irish Nationalists and the Politics of Patronage, 1880–1914', *Past and Present* 188 (2005), 107–12.
76. See Sullivan, H CCLXVII 620, 10 March 1882, Power, CCLXX 1802, 20 June 1882, O'Donnell, CCLXXI 147–8, 22 June 1882.
77. Wiggin, H CCLXXI 117, 22 June 1882; TE Smith, CCLXX 1385, 15 June 1882.
78. See e.g. Harcourt's jibe about Irish patriots and Churchill's response: H CCLXXIV 1339, 1364, 13 November 1882.

4

Religion

Simon Skinner

Given that even the crudest renderings of nineteenth-century Britain recognise the inherence of religion in 'Victorian values', and that caricatures of the age – starting famously with Lytton Strachey's – fasten onto the piety and prudery of its manners and morals, it may seem odd to assert the need to rehabilitate religion in any aspect of the historiography of nineteenth-century Britain. But the dialogue particularly between its political and religious historians has, until fairly recently, lacked intimacy. Much deeper into the century than is typically appreciated, religion and politics – though often separable analytical categories for the historian – were for many coterminous: if the repeal of the Test Acts and Catholic emancipation were central to the passing of an *ancien régime*, successive issues, such as Irish Church reform, the Ecclesiastical Commission, the Maynooth grant, Jewish relief, the universities, church rates, disestablishment, burials, education and in some senses ultimately Bradlaugh, were the pith and marrow of political debate. For much of the century, the language of politics was freighted with commonplace, dog-whistle associations between church, state, property and hierarchy – a Burkean 'wisdom of ancestors'[1] – on the one side, and dissent, emancipation, pluralism, and progress – the 'march of intellect'[2] – on the other. Late into the nineteenth century, Disraelian and Salisburyite Conservatism articulated constant appeals to the former, and Gladstonian Liberalism to the latter; moreover, idioms such as 'Adullamites' or 'Elijah's mantle' demonstrate that political discourse assumed a public familiarity with scripture. This chapter is divided into four sections which look, firstly, at the formative polemical legacies of the French revolutionary epoch; secondly, the neglected ecclesiastical dimensions of the age of reform; thirdly, the endurance of denominationalism as a determinant of political identity and of electoral alignment in late-Victorian party;

and, finally, the decline of a religious politics. The chapter ultimately suggests that it was at least as much the programmatic resolution of so many ecclesiastical questions, as the diminishing purchase of religious rhetoric itself in an age of declining confessionalism, which help to explain the relatively rapid superannuation of late-Victorian political agendas, and their effacement by a socio-economics which has often been back-projected onto an earlier period.

For much of the twentieth century the survey literature of nineteenth-century Britain told us at least as much about its surrounding era: one which had only recently navigated major constitutional changes and the electoral reforms of class and sex, and whose transcendent issues duly concerned social class and economic systems, poverty and welfare. To an extraordinary degree, its historians treated the religious languages and preoccupations of this earlier politics as simply figurative and epiphenomenal to what were thought to be more salient socio-economic issues. The successive volumes in the *Oxford History of England* series, for example, E.L. Woodward's *The Age of Reform 1815–1870* and R.C.K. Ensor's *England 1870–1914*, embodied this form of secularised anachronism: books of well over 600 pages, they devoted respectively 26 and 15 pages discretely to the subject of 'religion'.[3] Woodward rendered political themes with major ecclesiastical dimensions – such as the reform programme of the 1830s, or the very character of political parties – essentially in constitutional and economic terms. Ensor strikingly affirmed that 'No one will ever understand Victorian England who does not appreciate that among highly civilized … countries it was one of the most religious that the world has known', and of an evangelical ethos in particular that 'After Melbourne's departure it inspired nearly every front-rank public man, save Palmerston, for four decades', and that 'to ignore its effect on outward life would be to render much of the period's history unintelligible'. But given its periodisation the book chose to register rather religion's 'first signs of decline', spotlighting Charles Bradlaugh and T.H. Huxley rather than recovering those broader phenomena.[4] The consistent emphasis of the literature is that the salient thing about Victorian religiosity was its decline.

In the later decades of the twentieth century scholars began to lower the disciplinary partitions between the political and religious histories of nineteenth-century Britain. The work of J.C.D. Clark and others, in extending the confessional political languages of a 'long' eighteenth century, parked such major issues as confessional difference, Protestant identity and ecclesiastical policy squarely in nineteenth-century view.[5] A trinity of important monographic studies also served to illuminate the religious languages which inflected some established episodes. Boyd Hilton argued that insofar as 'liberal tories' were touched by theoretical influences these had more to do with evangelical ethics than 'classical' political economy or utilitarianism.[6] In turn, Richard Brent argued that Whig reform politics in the 1830s derived not merely from the *rechauffé* constitutionalism of Holland House elders but the definite religious vision of a younger and more pious generation.[7] And Jonathan Parry, accepting that 'interventionism' and 'class' are 'tools of only limited utility to the historian of Victorian politics', sought to establish an alternative ideological context for politics after 1867 by concentrating primarily 'on arguments about religion', insisting that 'for most politicians, politics had a religious dimension; and that, for vast numbers of voters, it was conceived as an activity of significance mainly because religious issues were so prominent'.[8]

The impact of these studies on the broader introductory literature of the century (and certainly of the strictly Victorian period), however, remains limited. One reason is that they focus mostly on particular ministries, and on an apparently hegemonic progressive politics (much of it of course culminating in Gladstone). As Eileen Groth Lyon has noted, although – to our enormous historiographical profit – this 'framework recognizes the importance of religion in the socio-political debates of the day, it continues the almost exclusive association of religion with government policy'.[9] In consequence, there has been comparatively little attention to the tenacious religious languages of Victorian Conservatism. There is a basic need, therefore, to recover the enormous political impact of such issues as Irish Church reform in the 1830s, or the Maynooth grant in 1845, or the legislation provoked by the 'Papal Aggression' in 1852 or by high church ritualism in 1874. Moreover, this literature has taught us that to treat the religious and the socio-economic as separate categories of analysis would be to introduce another sort of anachronism: the point is not that we should duly relegate hitherto canonical nineteenth-century issues such as political economy, free trade or the poor laws; it is rather that such issues were themselves so often articulated and justified in conspicuously religious terms. We need therefore not only to comprehend the enduring political importance of religious questions, but also the religious dimensions of ostensibly secular ones.

Pulpits and politics after the French Revolution

Any survey of the language of politics and religion in the nineteenth century must briefly comprehend the polemical bequest of the French

Revolution and its aftermath. It is a commonplace that the Revolution, at a time of dissenting centenary celebration of the gains from the Glorious Revolution – it was the Unitarian Richard Price's jubilant address to the Revolution Society which provoked Burke's *Reflections on the Revolution in France* – and growing dissenting clamour for the repeal of the Test (1661) and Corporation (1673) Acts restricting government offices to Anglicans, catalysed the radical case against the establishment in all its aspects. Long-established battlelines between radicalism and dissent on one side, and conservatism and the Church on the other, were thus dynamically reinforced. The 'establishment' was not just a slang term for the status quo, or the ruling orders; it connoted in particular the establishment of the Church of England and the relationship between church and state, from politically motivated episcopal nominations down to the administration of local justice by clerical magistrates. It was a staple of the emerging radical programme – chiefly of course Paine's two parts of *The Rights of Man* – that a more representative Parliament would repeal Anglicanism's privileges: the Test Acts, tithes, church rates and the bishops in the House of Lords. If Paine himself was an atheist, there was a natural confluence of political and religious dissent over the dismantling of the *ancien régime*. Atheism itself was of course very rare; far more common was an alienation from orthodox religion which translated directly into religious and political dissent. The young Samuel Taylor Coleridge, himself the son of a Devon vicar, lectured in Unitarian chapels in Bristol in 1795 on the poverty of the apostles and spoke portentously of Christ as a reformer and Christianity as 'a religion for Democrats'.[10] If Elie Halévy and E.P. Thompson once famously posited Methodism's sedative effect on English would-be radicals,[11] much subsequent scholarship has demonstrated the manifold ways in which dissenting grievances in fact often incubated popular political self-organisation,[12] with Barbara Taylor and Anna Clark recovering the gendered dimensions of this process.[13] James Bradley, for example, has demonstrated how, throughout this period, 'Nonconformity functioned as a midwife to radical political behaviour among the artisans', with the corporations in such growing towns as Nottingham, Bristol, Newcastle and Coventry cleaving between Anglican loyalists and dissenting opponents.[14]

The popular identification of dissent with Jacobinism was fatal to Fox's Bill for the repeal of the Test and Corporation Acts in March 1790, in which debate Burke condemned Price in the same breath as an atheist and anarchist, and remarked that 'it was not a time to weaken the safeguards of the Established Church'.[15] Burke himself is of course the embodiment of the counter-axis: the relationship between conservative politics and religion, in whose service the Church performed obvious institutional and ideological functions. Institutionally, the church-state establishment had at its apex the royal supremacy, at its near apex de facto prime ministerial nomination of bishops, and along its lower ranks a wealth of cathedral and parochial patronage which, under Pitt, was used systematically to reward those loyalist clerical hacks who had spilled ink in the pamphlet wars from the 1790s.[16] The low-political dimension of establishment, moreover, was the institution of clerical magistracy: their proportion doubled between 1760 and 1830, to around 25 per cent – much higher in rural areas – and their status in radical demonology was assured after Peterloo, where a clergyman read the riot act, and where two of the three magistrates who called in the yeomanry, were clergymen.[17] The term 'establishment', therefore, connoted much more than a political connection between church and state. Early nineteenth-century anticlericalism was driven politically by resentment at 'that huge hideous and lubberly leviathan, the law church'.[18]

Ideologically, from Bishop Horsley's (in)famous and widely printed sermon at Westminster in 1793, which enjoined 'dutiful submission to government' as a Christian duty, and through thousands of provincial pulpits raining bromides on their congregations, radicalism met both barrels: legislation such as Pitt's Seditious Meetings and Treasonable Practices Acts pronounced sedition a crime, punishable by gaol; and parish clergymen the length and breadth of the land pronounced sedition a sin, punishable in hell. The contractual language employed by establishment's apologists underlines that church and state were held to be organically related: lose religion, and the whole sacred edifice of civil society would come tumbling down, so that in loyalist hands, religion became a synonym for order, irreligion for anarchy. Horsley directed his auditors to the example of France, its 'Altars overthrown', and in train 'Her riches, sacred and profane, given up to the pillage of sacrilege and rapine! Atheists directing her Councils! Desperadoes conducting her Armies! Wars of unjust and chimerical ambition consuming her Youth! Her Granaries exhausted! Her Fields uncultivated! Famine threatening her multitudes! Her streets swarming with Assassins, filled with violence, deluged with blood!'[19] The 'people of England', Burke wrote in the *Reflections*, in words which the young, confessional-state Tory Gladstone was fond of quoting,[20] 'do not consider their church establishment as convenient, but as essential to their state … They consider it as the foundation of their whole constitution, with which, and with every part of which, it holds an indissoluble union. Church and state are ideas inseparable in their minds, and scarcely is the one ever mentioned without mentioning the other.'[21] This language, as we shall see, could as easily have come from Salisbury a century later.

In the next generation, religious vocabulary was enlisted in a much broader defence of the established order than merely that of the Protestant constitution. In 1798 the Revd Thomas Malthus had postulated in his famous *Essay on the Principle of Population* that scarcity and therefore misery were ineradicable because population, capable of increasing exponentially, would always outrun the means of subsistence, only capable of increasing arithmetically. This divergence could only be reconciled by what he notoriously called the providential 'Checks to Population' of disease, pestilence, war and ultimately famine. At a time of giddying population growth Malthus's tract enjoyed obvious empirical purchase. But as Andrew Waterman has additionally observed, 'the ideological purpose of Christian Political Economy was to refute Jacobinism and to justify the *ancien régime*'.[22] Malthus's arguments were congenial to a propertied order anxious to frame a response to radical political demands, for they could be deployed to demonstrate that the social optimism of the British Jacobins – polemicists such as Paine and Cobbett, and theorists such as Thomas Spence – was fundamentally misplaced, since organic social improvement was ultimately unattainable: poverty was divinely ordained, this mortal life a vale of tears.

But in affording the conservatives of the revolutionary epoch an eschatological rejoinder to radical utopianiasm, Malthus bequeathed a theological hangover to his clerical brethren in the post-Jacobin generation: how this dismally pessimistic world-view might be reconciled with the existence of a benevolent Creator. This was the work of a coterie of clerical political-economists which included the Scottish evangelical Thomas Chalmers, who became a celebrated proponent to a worldwide readership of the reconcilability of Christianity with the fashionable precepts of political economy, the evangelical John Bird Sumner, later archbishop of Canterbury, and the Oriel 'Noetics' – principally John Davison, Richard Whately and Edward Copleston.[23] Purveyors of what has been dubbed by Boyd Hilton the 'Christian economics', they duly argued that a Malthusian cosmos was part of Design: contained in His system were the necessary checks and spurs to good conduct. Shortages were a clever contrivance of the Almighty, to ensure that in competing for the crumbs men were forced to be hard working, virtuous and sexually abstinent. Providential language was thus deployed not just in defence of political and social order but of economic order. The fashionable Christian economics gave a significant twist to orthodox political economy as expounded by Adam Smith and David Ricardo – and certainly as it is now understood. As Hilton stressed, it was preoccupied less with the growth of the economy than with the growth of morality; pessimistic about shortages and privation, it was optimistic about their moral dividends.[24] As Richard Whately was to put it, 'If good boys have a larger slice of cake than the rest, this does not indeed increase the amount of cake, but it may increase good conduct.'[25] Moral arguments for the market are a modern political commonplace, all the way to the 'greed-is-good' sado-capitalism of Thatcherism and Reaganomics in the 1980s. Any account of free trade's nineteenth-century hegemony needs to comprehend that its contemporary appeal was not simply that it was thought to be economically optimal but that it was thought to be Christian. 'Political economy', Chalmers wrote, reflected the 'Power, Wisdom, and goodness of God'; it was 'a grand exemplification of the alliance, which a God of righteousness hath enlisted, between prudence and moral principle on the one hand, and physical comfort on the other'.[26] In seeking to extend the divine scheme across the globe, Sir John Bowring, Unitarian, political economist, and governor of Hong Kong 1854–9, declared that 'Jesus Christ is free trade, and free trade is Jesus Christ'.[27] Of course, even where one religious discourse became hegemonic, the political inferences which might be claimed from scripture remained violently contested. Southcottian millenarians thought the French Revolution a Revelatory portent of far more than temporal change, evangelical paternalists and factory campaigners such as Shaftesbury insisted that Christian duty compelled legislative intervention rather than laissez-faire, and Anglican high churchmen scourged the dismal science as a 'philosophy of Antichrist' and mourned its consequences for 'Christ's little ones'.[28]

Religious politics in the age of reform

Ultra Tory and high church inheritors of a Burkean religious politics always dated the beginning of its end from 1828–9. Parliament's admission of dissenters and Roman Catholics invalidated almost at a stroke centuries of Anglican apologetic for Parliament as the lay synod of the Church, and rendered it instead, as Keble put it 'a body of laymen, any number of whom may be heretics', raising the spectre of 'profane intrusion' by 'an infidel Government'.[29] Yet when the government moved to capitulate to the long-standing dissenting campaign Protestant constitutionalism was the dog that failed to bark. This was partly for doctrinal reasons – in a period of growing Catholic nationalism in Ireland, the strategic boundaries between Anglicanism and Nonconformity might seem more porous – partly for the executive reason of seeking to harness respectable bourgeois Nonconformity, and partly for the practical reason that to a considerable extent the Acts were a dead letter, with so-called Dissenting Deputies in the Commons ever since Walpole's Indemnity Acts from 1727.[30] The dog, however, barked long and loud in 1829. Catholic emancipation was an emergency, ad hoc solution to an executive crisis in Ireland rather than considered policy, but its political fallout was much greater, with placards warning of Jesuit assassins and Judge Jeffreys, cartoons depicting Wellington and Peel carrying rosaries and kissing the Pope's toe, Peel thrown out of his seat at Oxford University, and Wellington duelling Lord Winchilsea in defence of his honour.[31] From few quarters was religious language ever as hysterical as that emanating from anti-Catholicism: the 'Address of the Grand Orange Lodge against Catholic Emancipation' warned that in its event 'The liberty of these realms, our religion, and our monarchy would again be placed under Papal darkness and despotic oppression.'[32]

Historiographical recovery of 'the autonomous importance of religion and politics' in the 'final demise'[33] of the *ancien régime* has helped to sensitise nineteenth-century historians to languages of religious politics thought to have been the remit of a preceding epoch. But it may inadvertently also have encouraged the notion that, after those twin torpedoes to the confessional state, religion receded from authentically central political status, as the other half of the constitution – the unreformed representative system – took front stage. This is misleading in two ways: it loses sight, firstly, of the prominence of anticlericalism in the reform agitation of 1831–2; and, secondly, of the centrality of ecclesiastical policy to the Whig administration of the 1830s. For a start, the concessions of 1828–9 did nothing to diminish radicals' hostility to the established Church itself. On 8 October 1831 the second Reform Bill was lost in the Lords by 41 votes. Reformers could therefore argue that if the 21 bishops who voted against the Bill had voted in favour it would have passed. In the debate Grey had darkly warned the bishops 'to set their house in order, and prepare to meet the coming storm',[34] and at a meeting in Regent's Park the radical MP Joseph Hume raised a placard which read 'Englishmen – remember it was the bishops, and the bishops only, whose vote decided the fate of the Reform Bill'. John Wade, a Unitarian journalist, issued *The Extraordinary Black Book* in the summer of 1831, selling over 50,000 copies. This was an attack through statistical exposé of the wealth of the establishment in its widest sense – Crown, civil list, aristocracy, Bank of England, East India Company – but the very first chapter was entitled 'Church of England', the second 'Church of Ireland'. The bishop's palace was the focal point of the worst riots, in Bristol in October 1831. Bishop Blomfield of London cancelled all his engagements out of fear; Archbishop Howley's carriage was chased from the streets of Canterbury; the rector of St Martin's, Birmingham, was beaten up in the street; the bishops of Carlisle, Lichfield and Coventry, Llandaff, Bath and Wells, and Durham were variously menaced, stoned and abused. On 5 November, dummies of Guy Fawkes and the Pope were replaced by effigies of bishops.[35] The Reform agitation figures prominently in debates over 'out-of-doors' politics and Britain's moments of insurrectionary potential; it was also the most serious wave of anticlerical sentiment in modern British history.

It was in this climate that Thomas Arnold pronounced that 'The Church, as it now stands, no human power can save.'[36] The extremes of the 1828–32 period, from Chaucerian anticlerical radicals to frothing high churchmen, demonstrated to centrist executive politicians the necessity of marginalising both, and did much to shape a degree of bipartisanship in the ecclesiastical agenda of the next few decades, with both legislative concessions to dissenters and administrative reform to the Church of England. That is not, of course, to say that there were not major flashpoints in religious politics – as we shall see shortly, there were – but rather that with Whiggery and Peelism competing for the centre ground, the denominationalism of party politics – or more precisely, of the parties' high commands – was subdued at least relative to the periods both before and after mid-century. This was not, however, before major divisions over the appropriation clauses of the Irish Church Temporalities Act of 1833, which proposed the suppression of two archbishoprics and eight bishoprics and the redirection of the revenues to an Ecclesiastical Commission. Grey's abandonment of clause 147, ensuring that clerical revenues would be internally redistributed rather than alienated, reconciled much parliamentary opposition but scandalised O'Connell and the Irish members, who had been encouraged to contemplate concurrent endowment of the Catholic church, and also utilitarian radicals such as Joseph Hume and James Mill, who regarded Church property as held on trust. Of course, there remained a compound of high-Anglican sentiment, to which the Bill – in any form – represented the burglary by an infidel state that the changes of 1828–9 had always portended: it was the Irish Church Bill which occasioned Keble's famous 'Assize Sermon' from which the Tractarian movement is conventionally dated.

The evisceration of the Irish Church Bill, however, set parameters on subsequent ecclesiastical legislation which made it possible to secure frequent Peelite support. Many contemporaries saw the unreformed Church in the same terms as the unreformed constitution: its non-resident parishes were the Church's rotten boroughs, while the redistribution of revenues such as the cathedral endowments, and the translation of bishoprics from anachronistic territories such as Sodor and Man to new areas of population such as Manchester seemed as necessary as the redistribution of parliamentary seats to the new industrial towns. Peel's minority administration of 1834–5 established an Ecclesiastical Commission for the Church of England which the Whigs retained and which generated three major pieces of legislation directed respectively at the bishops, the clergy and the cathedrals: the 1836 Established Church Act equalised stipends and authorised two new sees at Ripon and Manchester; the 1838 Pluralities and Residence Act regulated the number of livings a clergyman could hold; and the 1840 Ecclesiastical Duties and Revenues Act raided the cathedrals, suppressing most non-resident prebends and sinecure rectories and directing the income to the Ecclesiastical Commission; it also made all the bishops ex officio members of the Commission – an important concession to high church critics, since this ensured a clerical majority. The Tithe Commutation Act and Dissenters' Marriage Bills of 1836 were also bipartisan measures, proposed by Peel and executed by Melbourne. It was in the sphere of education, however, as Richard Brent has demonstrated, that a vein of 'liberal Anglicanism' conspicuous in the post-Foxite generation was most pronounced. These liberal Anglicans, unlike their sceptical Holland House forebears, pursued a programme of educational and ecclesiastical legislation aimed at transforming a confessional state into one which was more Christian because less sectarian. Their influence was felt in what Brent has called the 'constitutional moralism' of Lord John Russell, Althorp and Morpeth, who 'altered the conception of whiggery from an interest in the mechanics of the constitution to a consideration of its moral foundations'. In 1838 the Whigs had given the non-denominational University College, London authority to confer degrees, and Russell's proposals for a national system of non-sectarian elementary education in 1839 – the so-called Normal Schools proposals – marked, in Brent's words, 'the high point of liberal Anglicanism'.[37]

That the Normal Schools proposals were dropped due to Anglican opposition demonstrates the familiar denominational politics which endured behind front-bench collaboration over aspects of the ecclesiastical agenda of the 1830s. Moreover, it was the vexed issue of Irish Church reform which provoked the most important and pregnant realignment of parliamentary politics in the decade, with the 'Derby dilly' of four ministers – Stanley (later Lord Derby), Graham, Ripon and Richmond – all leaving the Whig cabinet in 1834 over the threat of further attacks on the Church of Ireland. All four migrated to Peel's Conservative ranks, the first three serving prominently in Peel's cabinet after 1841 and Derby of course later Conservative prime minister. Just as the Whigs' ecclesiastical programme has been marginal to accounts of a Whig decade conventionally framed by parliamentary reform, municipal corporations and the New Poor Law, so Peel's administration of 1841–6 is overwhelmingly remembered for its social and economic agenda: the free trade budgets of 1842 and 1845 with the reimposition of the income tax, railway acts, the 1844 Bank Charter Act, the 1842 Mines and 1844 Factory Acts, and of course – always ultimately – Corn-Law repeal. Yet there are good grounds for regarding an Irish religious matter – the Maynooth grant crisis – as fatal to Peel's administration, with repeal a mere epilogue. Neither Peel nor his legions of religious opponents would have recognised this legislative hierarchy: Protestant sentiment was successively provoked by the 1844 Charitable Bequests Act, which relaxed the law of mortmain in order to allow private endowment of Catholic chapels and benefices, a Catholic Relief Bill of the same year which repealed various enactments against Catholics dating from the reign of Edward VI and from the Elizabethan Act of Supremacy,[38] and the 1845 Academical Institutions Act, which established without religious tests or theological teaching the 'Queen's Colleges' – and therefore subsequently so-called 'godless colleges' – at Cork, Galway and Belfast, the first two in due course boycotted by the Irish Roman Catholic hierarchy.[39] Much the most explosive element of Peel's Irish strategy, however, was a bill introduced to the Commons on 3 April 1845, which proposed to triple and annualise the annual grant to the Roman Catholic seminary at Maynooth which had been inherited at Union.[40]

That the bill provoked one of the great anti-Catholic orgies of nineteenth-century Britain is well known and properly acknowledged in the survey literature of 'No Popery'.[41] But political historians, typically mesmerised by the Anti-Corn Law League and the economic split of 1846, have paid significantly less attention to the Anti-Maynooth Committee and the religious split of 1845.[42] The Protestant Association – originally founded 'in the Midst of the Tumults' of the Gordon Riots in 1780 – founded the Committee in the spring of 1845,[43] issued a grand 'Address' 'To the Protestants of the United Kingdom', proclaiming that 'To endow Popery once more in a land that has been rescued from its yoke, is a madness little short of high treason against heaven',[44] and distributed the petitions which, as Macaulay put it in the Commons, 'showered, thick as a snow-storm, on the Table of the House'. Between February and May 1845 10,204 petitions, containing 1,284,296 signatures, were presented to Parliament. 'The Orangeman raises his howl,' Macaulay observed, 'and Exeter-hall sets up its bray'.[45]

Where Maynooth's political importance is acknowledged it is invariably in terms which make it secondary to protectionism: Edward Norman, for example, while acknowledging the gravity of Conservative divisions over Maynooth, thought it 'a dress-rehearsal for the corn law split in the following year'.[46] In affirming an 'authenticity for "Maynooth" as the litmus of party', Michael Bentley is therefore one of the few historians to treat the grant controversy as more than the penultimate spike on a graph of mounting Tory disaffection.[47] Perhaps Gladstone's own storied somersault over Maynooth – he resigned from the cabinet because his support for the measure contradicted his stated opposition to the grant in 1838 – has obscured the wider political crisis it provoked. Peel himself was under no illusions as to the scale of the storm, writing to Gladstone, 'I think it will very probably be fatal to the Government',[48] while Graham observed in March 'that all our enemies, political and religious, may combine against us',[49] and Gladstone confided to his diary in April, reaching for classical rather than biblical allusion: 'It is a Trojan horse, full of armed men.'[50] On the third reading on 21 May, the Bill passed with 169 Liberal votes; of the Conservatives, 148 voted for, 149 against. As Graham had written presciently to Heytesbury: 'The Bill will pass, but our party is destroyed.'[51]

Another feature of the Maynooth grant crisis which is typically ascribed to the corn crisis a year later is the decisive emergence of Disraeli, who came out into the open against Peel in the course of the debate on the second reading in the Commons in April 1845. Disraeli famously spoke of Peel as 'a great Parliamentary middleman ... a man who bamboozles one party, and plunders the other', and called on the House to dethrone 'this dynasty of deception, by putting an end to the intolerable yoke of official despotism and Parliamentary imposture'.[52] Those words are better known than their context: it was over Maynooth, not agriculture, that the anti-Peel cause found, in Bentley's words, 'an advocate of deadly brilliance'.[53] Indeed, the issue itself explains Disraeli's need for a different platform from which to attack Peel, for Maynooth had proved fatal even to the parliamentary coterie with which he had hitherto associated, Disraeli himself recollecting 'that it was his opposition to the Maynooth Bill that had broken up Young England'.[54] Much of the other vituperation around the Conservative split derives from the grant controversy. The oft-quoted line, 'How wonderful is Peel! / He changeth with the Time / Turning and twisting like an eel / Ascending through the slime' preceded these lines: 'He gives whatever they want / To those who ask with Zeal / He yields the Maynooth Grant'.[55]

Protestantism, rather than protection, split the Conservative Party, such as it was. Nor did the issue of Maynooth end with the passage of the grant, but continued to resonate electorally. Gash, for example, recognised that the 'general election of 1847 – repeal of the Corn Laws notwithstanding – was fought on the religious rather than the economic records of the Peel and Russell ministries in so far as it was fought on any general issue at all'.[56] Richard Floyd's recent analysis of the role of religious politics in various sample constituencies has demonstrated the degree to which, for many local Conservatives, and despite the more recent passage and therefore fresher affront of Corn-Law repeal, the Maynooth grant was the transcendent electoral grievance.[57] Most arresting is the party manager F.R. Bonham's remark to Peel over the fortunes of the Peelites in the general election of 1847: 'Maynooth has certainly destroyed several of our friends', he wrote, adding, 'Free Trade hardly any.'[58]

Religious politics and late-Victorian party

Maynooth was formative to Gladstone's migration from 'the rising hope of those stern and unbending Tories'[59] to a committed pluralism which was formative to his later Liberalism. A measure of the pace of this transition was his principled position during the next spasm of popular Protestant protest, the 'Papal aggression' of 1850: when Russell's government yielded to public indignation over the restoration of the Roman Catholic hierarchy, framing an Ecclesiastical Titles Bill to proscribe the Catholic assumption of territorial titles to its sees, Gladstone's swaggering opposition to the bill marked a further breach with the Conservative ranks (as well as with those Nonconformists whose Protestantism transcended their voluntarism at such moments). 'We cannot turn back the tendencies of the age towards religious liberty', Gladstone declared to the Commons in March 1851. 'It is our business to forward them. To endeavour to turn them back is childish, and every effort you may make in that direction will recoil upon you with disaster and disgrace.'[60] At the time of Maynooth, recanting his confessionalism, he had written to Newman that '[t]he State cannot be said now to have a conscience' and – ever the politique – that 'When I have found myself the last man in the ship, I think that I am free to leave it.'[61]

Of course, Gladstone was not the last man in the ship, and a neglected aspect of party politics in this phase is the extent to which the Conservative rump left aboard sought to premise its identity on defence of the Anglican establishment in their struggle for self-definition between the fall of Peel (and protection) in 1846 and the death of Palmerston (and pragmatism) nearly two decades later in 1865. In 1861 Disraeli wrote to a colleague: 'The fact is, in internal politics there is only one question now, the maintenance of the Church.'[62] Salisbury too reflected in 1867 that beyond suffrage and the Church 'there is nothing, so far as I know, of which the Conservatives are in any special way the protectors'.[63] Throughout the 1850s and early 1860s, the Conservative leadership fastened onto two questions as a means of rallying morale: church rates and burials. Palmerstonian inertia in the face of dissenting demands for the abolition of church rates had escalated Liberation Society (formerly the Anti-State-Church Association) campaigning, affording Disraeli the opportunity to present the establishment as under threat equally from Whig infidelity and radical dissent. At a diocesan meeting at Amersham in his Buckinghamshire constituency in December 1860, Disraeli delivered a speech which amounted to a Church defence manifesto: he argued against any compromise on the rates issue and rejected the moderate Tory suggestion that Nonconformists should be allowed to claim exemption from the rate – on the ground that this would be a fatal admission that the Church was no longer the Church of the nation. In that year, 1860, he began to oppose annual bills for the abolition of church rates. These were a close-run thing: in 1861 there was a tie on the third reading in the Commons with the Bill only defeated when the Speaker cast his deciding vote against; in 1862 the Bill was defeated in the Commons by only 1 vote, and in 1863 by 10. Disraeli brushed aside Derby's anxieties over the electoral implications of this stand in the persistent calculation that it would help to build Conservative identity and support.[64] A second point of defence of the establishment was Disraeli's opposition to bills to remove the Nonconformist grievance over exclusion from burial in parish churchyards. At Aylesbury in November 1861 he offered a defence of the principles of Church establishment in language with obvious Burkean notes: the Church, he said, was 'a majestic corporation – wealthy, powerful, independent – with the sanctity of a long tradition, yet sympathising with authority and full of conciliation, even deference, to the civil power. Broadly and deeply planted in the land, mixed up with all our manners and customs … the Church of England is part of our history, part of our life, part of England itself.'[65] It was a summation of all this agitation that Disraeli made the defence of the Church the very first item in his general election address issued in the summer of 1865.

Thereafter, with Palmerston's death and with Gladstone ultimately able to take Liberalism in a more programmatically pluralist trajectory, the religious rhetoric which Conservatives had peddled with such futility in the wilderness years of opposition could gain much greater traction. Gladstone had supported the abolition of religious tests at Oxford in 1854, supported further measures of Roman Catholic relief in 1859 and 1867, and church-rate abolition in 1868. The inflammatorily messianic nature of his political language – epitomised in his apocryphal declaration, on receiving the Queen's commission in 1868, 'My mission is to pacify Ireland' – was of course realised in an agenda whose landmark was disestablishment of the Church of Ireland. For much of this programme Nonconformity was therefore a natural and obvious source of Liberal electoral support, as Disraeli's 'Church in danger' strategy in the 1860s had apprehended. Moreover a Nonconformist conscience, as is well known, went beyond a denominationally self-interested support for Gladstone's pluralist ecclesiastical legislation to a wider ethical alignment on such issues as temperance, international justice and probity in public life.

But the Gladstonian strategy of appeasing religious grievances, especially once it had developed into a respect for the 'religious nationality' of Irish Catholics and support for Home Rule after 1885,[66] afforded his Conservative opponents an opportunity to recast their religious language from one of narrowly Anglican defence to one of wider Protestant defence. While neither Disraeli nor Salisbury ever retreated from their vision of the Church of England as symbolically and even functionally central to nationhood,[67] and while Disraeli especially had always sympathised with the grievances of Irish Catholics, the Protestantism of 'low' toryism and its traction especially in areas of Irish immigration gave an opening to a broader anti-Liberal religious language than that narrowly of 'Church in danger'. This perhaps had especial appeal given the exigencies of an expanding electorate, and ancestral consciousness of the party's failures when in office to safeguard Protestant interests in 1829 and 1845. At Glasgow in 1873, Disraeli declared that England must maintain 'faith and freedom': her 'proud destiny' ought to be 'to guard civilization alike from the withering blast of atheism and from the simoom of sacerdotal usurpation'.[68] The first piece of legislative business in his ministry of 1874–80 was the Public Worship Regulation Act of 1874, aimed at the suppression of high church ritualist practices within the Church, framed by Archbishop Tait but with the assistance of the Conservative

Chancellor Lord Cairns, and steered through the Commons by Disraeli. As Parry has observed, 'In supporting the Public Worship Regulation Bill he reiterated his call for England to "rally on the broad platform of the Reformation" against the challenges brewing on the continent.'[69] A more than incidental political dividend of this strategy was that – just as in the Ecclesiastical Titles Bill controversy – the Liberal-Nonconformist axis was divided between its Protestant and pluralist impulses. His ferocious hostility to the Act had occasioned Gladstone's return to politics after the blow of the 1874 election. 'The course which I felt it my duty to take last Session with regard to the Public Worship Bill', Gladstone duly reflected in January 1875, 'unquestionably gave offence to some members of the Liberal party, and rendered it doubtful policy for me to reply upon the ties which have heretofore bound us together'.[70]

As a point about politics rather than party politics, the sheer scale of the national furore around these measures needs to be comprehended. In 1874 Parliament was in a tumult which everyone who could remember it compared to the Ecclesiastical Titles Bill controversy a quarter of a century earlier: Queen Victoria even urged Gladstone to stay away from the Commons, and with characteristic sobriety told the Dean of Windsor that had the Bill failed she would have abdicated in favour of the Stuarts.[71] Nowhere was this politico-religious distemper more demonstrable than in the course of the Bradlaugh affair, where the Commons was in a chronic state of distraction and occasionally uproar throughout the whole of the 1880–5 Parliament. Gladstone's speech on the second reading of his Affirmation Bill, in April 1883, made on behalf of a man whose morality he abhorred, with a section of the Liberal Party in open revolt, and a Nonconformist howl going up across the land, was the ultimate manifestation of his pluralist moorings. 'I am convinced', Gladstone declared, 'that upon every religious, as well as upon every political ground, the true and wise course is not to deal out religious liberty by halves, by quarters, and by fractions; but to deal it out entire'.[72] The spectacle of Gladstone defending the legal rights of an atheist advocate of freethought and contraception allowed reactionary Conservative elements, led in the Commons by Lord Randolph Churchill's 'Fourth Party', to rally Conservative morale. The Bill was duly lost (by three votes) after Churchill had conjured up Burkean phobias over the conjunction of irreligion and anarchy: 'Surely the horrors of the French Revolution should give some idea of the effect on the masses of the State recognition of Atheism.'[73]

Salisbury, too, always apprehended a simple endurance of the Manichean religious politics of the early nineteenth century. '[T]here is no more formidable obstacle than the Established Church', he had written in 1861, 'to the spirit of rash and theoretic change which we, almost alone among the nations, have escaped. Her atmosphere is poison to the revolutionary growths that flourish so rankly in other lands'.[74] Just as Gladstone's measures for the Irish Church permitted Disraeli to position the Conservatives as the party of reformed religion, Gladstone's principled support for Bradlaugh permitted a Conservative positioning in defence of religion itself. Home Rule marked a third and decisive recasting of religious politics: the infusion of often pluralist Liberal Unionists (led by a Unitarian, Joseph Chamberlain), and of overwhelmingly Nonconformist Presbyterian Ulster Unionists, into Conservative ranks, demonstrated that Conservative principles could be firmly held by dissenters from Salisbury's antediluvian confessional-state ideals. In their studies of electoral sociology, David Bebbington and more recently Jon Lawrence have both noted how the Nonconformist vote became less 'monolithic' in consequence.[75] Although, as we shall see, some recognisable aspects of denominational politics endured into the twentieth century – nationally, with ongoing Nonconformist animation over the education issue, and locally in Wales over disestablishment – the parties' language of religious politics was thus fundamentally recast in final third of the century. It ceased to connote specific denominational positions over such issues as church rates, burials and education, but increasingly spoke to wider values as conscience, reason and justice on one side, and property, order, and hierarchy on the other.

The decline of a religious politics

A recognisable denominational politics endured beyond the eras of Gladstone and Salisbury, and into the twentieth century, over the question of education. The Conservatives' 1902 Education Act had cheered Anglicans by permitting rate support to be given to denominational schools, where the Church was of course predominant. The Nonconformist reaction was predictably immense, manifested in a nationwide 'passive resistance' campaign with Nonconformist rate-payers refusing to pay the objectionable portion of the rates, and significant mobilisation in favour of the Liberal opposition in the general election of January 1906.[76] The umbrella Free Church Council issued a manifesto demanding amendment of the 1902 Act, while local Free Church councils established election funds and sought to obtain pledges from local candidates. Leading Liberals duly committed to educational reform, including Churchill at Manchester, and Asquith, who declared at Huddersfield that 'corrective' educational legislation would be the ministry's first task. On the other side, of course, Tory candidates played up the threat to the Church which an incoming Liberal administration would pose, Balfour's Conservative manifesto stating that the Liberals intended to carry 'Home Rule, disestablishment, [and] the destruction of voluntary schools'.[77] The upshot was the biggest Liberal majority since meaningful comparisons begin in 1832. With 400 seats (inclusive of the Lib-Labs) the Liberals had an overall majority of 132. The Conservatives won only 157 seats, even Balfour losing his. In Wales the Liberals won all 34 seats (with the exception of Hardie's where they stood aside under the pact); 25 of the 33 Welsh Liberal MPs were Nonconformists. In other less obvious areas of historic Nonconformity there were big swings towards the Liberals: in Suffolk four of the five seats, in Essex five of the eight and in the West Riding 15 of the 38 were Liberal gains.[78] Herbert Gladstone – congenitally attuned to denominational psephology – drew up a list of what he called historically 'probable loss' and 'certain loss' seats and tactically ran Free-Church candidates in them: 30 won.[79]

Kenneth Morgan has judged the 1906 election 'the greatest triumph of the chapels over the Church of England since the time of Cromwell'.[80] Eighty-three members of the Liberation Society alone won seats. The total number of Nonconformist MPs, which had previously reached a peak of 117 in 1892, was now 210. Of those, 200 were Liberal (strictly speaking, Lib-Lab – the split was 180/20): a third of the Commons was therefore Nonconformist. As they were quick to point out, there were more Nonconformist than Conservative MPs. Campbell-Bannerman's front bench, too, had more Nonconformists than any previous: he was a Scots United Free Churchman, Asquith formerly Congregationalist, Bryce and Lloyd George Baptist and Birrell and Haldane from Baptist backgrounds, and Fowler a Wesleyan Methodist. All parties were agreed on the religious psephology of 1906. 'We have been put into power by the Nonconformists', remarked Campbell-Bannerman,[81] while Balfour, the Conservative leader, wrote in *The Times* in May: 'I suppose that this is the first time in the history of our country since the Commonwealth when the great Nonconformist party, always powerful, always big…are, or conceive themselves to be, supreme.'[82]

If the story were stopped there, the analysis might therefore seem simple enough, with religious languages retaining their primal force, and religious questions remaining of paramount importance to electoral behaviour and party affiliation. In terms of low politics, Hugh McLeod has suggested, on the basis of a survey of the oral evidence of the three decades before 1914, that 67 per cent of churchgoers voted Conservative compared to 16 per cent of chapel-goers; and the political affiliations of the non-church- and chapel-going may be inferred from the Sunday schools attended by their children, where 64 per cent of non-churchgoers with children at Church of England Sunday schools voted Conservative, compared with 25 per cent of those with children at Nonconformist ones.[83] High politically, Edward VII himself was to lament the 1906 Education Bill's perpetuation of 'a kind of political-religious warfare'.[84]

Yet in many regards this was a last hurrah for such a language. This was partly because the Lords' rejection of the Liberals' ensuing 1906 Education Bill transformed the issue into a wider constitutional confrontation which, reinforced by the Home Rule and budget impasses, would dominate British politics in the next few years. More generally, the Liberal-Nonconformist electoral phalanx might be seen as a victim of its own success: so extensive had the pluralist programme been by the end of the century – with dissenting triumphs over tests, tithes, ecclesiastical reform, university admission, church rates, disestablishment and burials – that there was incrementally less to drive a purely denominational politics. The transformation of progressive politics in Wales in this generation exhibits this process in microcosm. In 1906, Welsh Church disestablishment had powerfully reinforced education grievances: Lloyd George had affirmed at the Welsh National Liberal Council that Welsh disestablishment was an essential part of the Liberal programme and, as we have seen, with the Liberation Society mobilising for Liberal candidates at the polls they swept the board. With the consequent Welsh Church Act of 1914 the political direction of Welsh Nonconformity might be thought to have largely expired. Although, plainly, the political allegiances of generations did not evaporate overnight, the relative pace at which Welsh Labourism effaced Welsh Liberalism can only be explained by a distinct shift in the relative priorities of voters, beyond a straightforward increase in their numbers or class preponderance in 1918. With wage reductions of 18.75 per cent in the south Wales coalfields in the years 1903–6,[85] a Methodist miner might have felt his socio-economic grievances as a miner transcending his denominational grievances as a Methodist; and have considered those grievances – especially when confronted with a Liberal employer caste – better pursued within the nascent Labour movement. It was in 1909 that the Miners' Federation decamped to the Labour Party and, by 1918, 25 of the 57 Labour MPs were from its ranks. A similar dynamic may have been in force within an Irish Catholic immigrant demographic, with the 1916 Easter Rising and the 1922 Free State taking Irish nationalism beyond its tactical concert with parliamentary Liberalism and thereby reordering the relative weight of religious-nationalist and material grievances felt by immigrant Irish Catholic voters. The electoral impact of any such mutations was of course to be hugely augmented by the franchise extension of 1918. Between 1918 and 1922 the number of Labour MPs in Glasgow, which was more than 20 per cent Irish, increased from 1 to 10.[86]

It should not be inferred from this that the nascent Labour movement was itself a secular alternative progressive credo. Labour's first Chancellor Philip Snowden, himself a Methodist, and co-author with Keir Hardie in 1903 of *The Christ That Is to Be*, was to recall that the Labour Party 'derived its inspiration far more from the Sermon on the Mount than from the teachings of the economists',[87] and the comparatively unideological character of the British Labour movement has of course excited much historical commentary. Kenneth Brown's close analysis of the religious commitment of Labour MPs in 1906, while clarifying regional variations in religiosity – Labour leaders in the West Riding, for example, abandoned their Church activity while miners and especially the Welsh did not – confirmed 'the existence of a strong free church influence on the general development of the British labor movement', and 'that socialism often appealed to moral sensibilities which had been largely molded by non-conformity',[88] and J.F. Glaser has pointed out that 'The early "Lib-Lab" MPs, such as Burt, Broadhurst, Arch, Abraham, and Pickard, were usually Dissenters and often lay preachers'.[89] Hardie came from a radical Morisonian-Congregationalist background, Arthur Henderson converted from Congregationalism to Methodism and became a lay preacher, Ramsay MacDonald was a Free-Church Presbyterian. That they so frequently deployed a religious rhetoric – that they should speak of the 'socialist gospel', or that when excoriated in 1914 Hardie could observe that he now knew 'what Christ suffered in Gethsemane'[90] – ensured that Liberal immigrants to Labourism need not have felt that they were adopting a less Christian political culture.

Religion therefore featured in the reconfiguration of late-Victorian and Edwardian politics – the establishment of a popular Conservatism, Liberalism's decline, and Labour's ascent – in three obvious ways. Firstly, Nonconformist anti-Catholicism generated a Unionist and therefore Conservative alignment which could not be premised on a narrowly Anglican affiliation. More generally, an expanding franchise permitted the cultivation of a populist Conservatism which stigmatised the Liberals as a movement of bourgeois puritans and which boisterously repudiated the pharisaical and sanctimonious tones which endured in its language. Secondly, the resolution of so many of the religious grievances which had forged the Nonconformist-Liberal axis exhausted the denominational politics of the nineteenth century and emancipated Nonconformists to pursue non-religious grievances potentially via other political affiliations. Thirdly, the overtly Christian and not merely ethical notes in much early Labourism and the conspicuous Nonconformist origins of much of its leadership must have done much to ensure that, as a spiritual environment, the Labour movement did not feel alien to chapelgoers hitherto harnessed to Liberal politics.

How far religiosity declined in the late-Victorian and Edwardian periods is a notoriously complex question; yet how far a denominational politics declined is a more tangible phenomenon. The decline of a religious politics, that is to say, was more abrupt than any decline of religion itself. Relatively quickly, such religiosity as endured was uncoupled from the stuff of public politics, party manifestos and general elections. The newly pluralist Gladstone had remarked in 1846 that 'the process which I am now actively engaged in carrying on is a process of lowering the religious tone of the State, letting it down, demoralizing it – *i.e.*, stripping it of its ethical character, and assisting its transition into one which is mechanical'.[91] So 'demoralized' were the affairs of state by the 1920s that it would have been hard to comprehend the nationwide political tumult over such questions as the sartorial dispositions of clergymen, or the admission to the Commons of an unbeliever, only a generation earlier. Religious languages became essentially figurative and metaphorical, deployed to connote social justice by New Liberals, ethical socialism by Labourites and patriotism and propertied order by Conservatives, but with ecclesiastical issues themselves ceasing either to dominate the legislative agenda, or to determine party affiliations as axiomatically as they had for so much of the nineteenth century.

Notes

1. E. Burke, *Thoughts on the Cause of the Present Discontents* (London, 1770), p. 49.
2. A phrase popularised by a 1828 satirical print by William Heath.
3. E.L. Woodward, *The Age of Reform 1815–1870* (Oxford, 1938), pp. 483–509; R.C.K. Ensor, *England 1870–1914* (Oxford, 1936), pp. 137–43, 305–10, 527–31.
4. Ensor, *England 1870–1914*, pp. 137, 139–40.
5. J.C.D. Clark, *English Society 1688–1832: Ideology, Social Structure and Political Practice during the Ancien Régime* (Cambridge, 1985).
6. B. Hilton, *Corn, Cash, Commerce: the Economic Policies of the Tory Governments 1815–1830* (Oxford, 1977); also *The Age of Atonement: the Influence of Evangelicalism on Social and Economic Thought, 1795–1865* (Oxford, 1991).

7. R. Brent, *Liberal Anglican Politics: Whiggery, Religion, and Reform 1830–1841* (Oxford, 1987).
8. J.P. Parry, *Democracy and Religion: Gladstone and the Liberal Party, 1867–1875* (Cambridge, 1986), pp. 2, 3, 5.
9. E.G. Lyon, *Politicians in the Pulpit: Christian Radicalism in Britain from the Fall of the Bastille to the Disintegration of Chartism* (Aldershot, 1999), p. 151.
10. P.J. Kitson, 'Coleridge's *Lectures 1795: On Politics and Religion*', in F. Burwick, *The Oxford Handbook of Samuel Taylor Coleridge* (Oxford, 2009), pp. 127–43.
11. E. Halévy, *The Birth of Methodism in England* (Chicago, 1971); E.P. Thompson, *The Making of the English Working Class* (Harmondsworth, 1968), esp. pp. 385–440.
12. J.F.C. Harrison, *The Second Coming: Popular Millenarianism 1780–1850* (London, 1979); I. McCalman, *Radical Underworld: Prophets, Revolutionaries and Pornographers in London, 1795–1840* (Cambridge, 1988); P. Lockley, *Visionary Religion and Radicalism in Early Industrial England: From Southcott to Socialism* (Oxford, 2012).
13. B. Taylor, *Eve and the New Jerusalem: Socialism and Feminism in the Nineteenth Century* (London, 1983); A. Clark, *The Struggle for the Breeches: Gender and the Making of the British Working Class* (Berkeley CA, 1995).
14. J.E. Bradley, *Religion, Revolution, and English Radicalism: Non-conformity in Eighteenth Century Politics and Society* (1990), p. 423.
15. Cited in J.H. Overton and F. Relton, *The English Church, From the Accession of George I to the end of the Eighteenth Century* (London, 1906), p. 220.
16. J.J. Sack, *From Jacobite to Conservative: Reaction and Orthodoxy in Britain, c. 1760–1832* (Cambridge, 1993), pp. 23–4.
17. E.J. Evans, 'Some Reasons for the Growth of English Rural Anti-Clericalism, c.1750-c.1830', *Past and Present* 66 (1975), 84, 101–6.
18. *Church Examiner*, cited in Evans, 'Some Reasons', 106.
19. S. Horsley, *A Sermon, Preached Before the Lords Spiritual and Temporal* (London, 1793), pp. 21–5.
20. W.E. Gladstone, *The State in its Relations with the Church*, 2 vols (London, 1838), I, p. 24.
21. E. Burke, *Reflections on the Revolution in France* (Harmondsworth, 1986), p. 96.
22. A.M.C. Waterman, *Revolution, Economics and Religion: Christian Political Economy, 1798–1833* (Cambridge, 1991), p. 255.
23. Hilton, *Corn, Cash, Commerce*, pp. 308–13; Hilton, 'Chalmers as Political Economist', in A.C. Cheyne, ed., *The Practical and the Pious: Essays on Thomas Chalmers (1780–1847)* (Edinburgh, 1985), pp. 141–56; Waterman, *Revolution, Economics and Religion*, pp. 150–70, 222–9; R. Brent, 'Note: The Oriel Noetics', in M.G. Brock and M.C. Curthoys, eds., *The History of the University of Oxford VI: Nineteenth-Century Oxford, Part 1* (Oxford, 1997), pp. 72–6.
24. Hilton, *Corn, Cash, Commerce*, pp. 309, 311.
25. E.J. Whately, *Life and Correspondence of Richard Whately*, 2 vols (London, 1866), I, p. 77.
26. T. Chalmers, *On the Power, Wisdom, and Goodness of God* (1833), cited in Hilton, *Corn, Cash, Commerce*, p. 310.
27. Cited in D. Todd, 'John Bowring and the Global Dissemination of Free Trade', *Historical Journal* 51 (2008), 385.

28. Lockley, *Visionary Religion*; Lyon, *Politicians in the Pulpit*; S.A. Skinner, *Tractarians and the 'Condition of England': the Social and Political Thought of the Oxford Movement* (Oxford, 2004).
29. *British Critic* 26 (1839), pp. 355, 387; J. Keble, *National Apostasy Considered in a Sermon* (Oxford, 1833), p. v.
30. G.F.A. Best, 'The Protestant Constitution and its Supporters, 1800–1829', *Transactions of the Royal Historical Society* 8 (1958), 105–27.
31. O. Chadwick, *The Victorian Church*, 2 vols (London, 1966–70), I, pp. 7–24.
32. Cited in E.R. Norman, *Anti-Catholicism in Victorian England* (London, 1968), pp. 129–30.
33. Clark, *English Society*, p. x.
34. *Hansard's Parliamentary Debates* [hereafter H] VII 968, 3 October 1831.
35. Chadwick, *Victorian Church*, I, pp. 25–8, 33–4.
36. A.P. Stanley, *The Life and Correspondence of Thomas Arnold* (London, 1846), p. 184.
37. Brent, *Liberal Anglican Politics*, pp. 1, 3.
38. G.I.T. Machin, *Politics and the Churches in Great Britain 1832–1868* (Oxford, 1977), p. 169.
39. T.A. Jenkins, *Sir Robert Peel* (London, 1999), pp. 120–2.
40. C.S. Parker, ed., *Sir Robert Peel: From His Private Papers*, 3 vols (London, 1891–9), III, pp. 101–2; Machin, *Politics and the Churches*, p. 172.
41. Norman, *Anti-Catholicism*, pp. 23–51; J. Wolffe, *The Protestant Crusade in Great Britain, 1829–1860* (Oxford, 1991), pp. 198–210; D.G. Paz, *Popular Anti-Catholicism in Mid-Victorian England* (Stanford, 1992), pp. 6, 36, 64, 198, 218; G.A. Cahill, 'The Protestant Association and the Anti-Maynooth Agitation of 1845', *Catholic Historical Review* 43 (1957), 273–308; also Machin, *Politics and the Churches*, pp. 169–77.
42. N. Gash's *Politics in the Age of Peel* (London, 1953) contains three perfunctory references.
43. Cahill, 'The Protestant Association', 276.
44. A.S. Thelwall, ed., *Proceedings of the Anti-Maynooth Conference of 1845* (London, 1845), p. vii.
45. T.B. Macaulay, *Speeches*, 2 vols (New York, 1853), II, p. 268.
46. E.R. Norman, 'The Maynooth Question of 1845', *Irish Historical Studies* 15 (1967), 407.
47. M. Bentley, *Politics without Democracy 1815–1914: Perception and Preoccupation in British Government* (London, 1984), pp. 125–6, 131.
48. M.R.D. Foot and H.C.G. Matthew, eds., *The Gladstone Diaries*, 14 vols (Oxford, 1968–94), III, p. 425.
49. C.S. Parker, *Life and Letters of Sir James Graham*, 2 vols (London, 1909), II, p. 8.
50. *Gladstone Diaries*, III, p. 456.
51. Parker, *Life of Graham*, II, p. 10.
52. H LXXIX 565–6, 11 April 1845.
53. Bentley, *Politics without Democracy*, p. 122.
54. G.E. Buckle and W.F. Moneypenny, eds., *The Life of Benjamin Disraeli, Earl of Beaconsfield*, 6 vols (London, 1910–20), II, p. 330; R. Faber, *Young England* (London, 1987), p. 156.
55. *Punch*, 3 May 1845.

56. N. Gash, *Reaction and Reconstruction in English Politics, 1832–1852* (Oxford, 1965), p. 98.
57. R.D. Floyd, *Church, Chapel and Party: Religious Dissent and Political Modernization in Nineteenth-Century England* (Basingstoke, 2008), pp. 30, 46–7, 85–7, 262.
58. Cited in N. Gash, *Sir Robert Peel* (London, 1972), p. 625.
59. T. B. Macaulay, *Critical and Historical Essays*, 3 vols (London, 1843), II, p. 430.
60. H CXV 579, 595, 25 March 1851.
61. D.C. Lathbury, ed., *Correspondence on Church and Religion of William Ewart Gladstone*, 2 vols (London, 1910), I, p. 72.
62. Earl of Malmesbury, *Memoirs of an Ex-Minister: An Autobiography*, 2 vols (London, 1884), II, p. 247.
63. G. Cecil, *Life of Robert, Marquis of Salisbury*, 4 vols (London, 1929–32), I, p. 264.
64. Machin, *Politics and the Churches*, pp. 311–19, idem, *Disraeli* (London, 1995), pp. 97–9.
65. Cited in R.J. White, *The Conservative Tradition* (London, 1950), p. 107.
66. D.G. Boyce and A. O'Day, eds., *Gladstone and Ireland: Politics, Religion and Nationality in the Victorian Age* (Basingstoke, 2011).
67. A. Warren, 'Disraeli, the Conservatives and the national church', *Parliamentary History* 19 (2000), 96–117.
68. Cited in J. Parry, 'Disraeli and England', *Historical Journal* 43 (2000), 714.
69. Ibid.
70. Gladstone Papers, British Library, Additional MS 44762, fo. 150, January 1875.
71. J. Bentley, *Ritualism and Politics in Victorian Britain: The Attempt to Legislate for Belief* (Oxford, 1978), p. 74.
72. H CCLXXVIII 1191, 26 April 1883.
73. H CCLXXVIII 1451, 30 April 1883.
74. *Quarterly Review* 110 (1861), pp. 544–5.
75. D. Bebbington, 'Nonconformist and Electoral Sociology, 1867–1918' *Historical Journal* 27 (1984), 648–52; J. Lawrence, *Speaking for the People: Party, Language and Popular Politics in England, 1867–1914* (Cambridge, 1998), pp. 198–9.
76. D. Bebbington, *The Nonconformist Conscience: Chapel and Politics, 1870–1914* (London, 2009), pp. 146–7.
77. G.I.T. Machin, *Politics and the Churches in Great Britain 1869–1921* (Oxford, 1987), pp. 275–6.
78. Ibid., pp. 277–8.
79. S. Koss, *Nonconformity in Modern British Politics* (London, 1975), pp. 73–4.
80. K.O. Morgan, '1906: "Blissful Dawn"?', *Journal of Liberal History* 51 (2006), 33.
81. Koss, *Nonconformity*, p. 73–4.
82. Cited in N.J. Richards, 'The Education Bill of 1906 and the Decline of Political Nonconformity', *Journal of Ecclesiastical History* 23 (1972), 51.
83. H. McLeod, 'New Perspectives on Victorian Class Religion: the Oral Evidence', *Oral History* 14 (1986), 31–49.
84. Richards, 'Education Bill', 58.
85. H. Pelling, *Popular Politics and Society in Late-Victorian Britain* (London, 1968), p. 113.

86. J.J. Smyth, 'Resisting Labour: Unionists, Liberals, and Moderates in Glasgow Between the Wars', *Historical Journal* 46 (2003), 379.
87. P. Snowden, *An Autobiography*, 2 vols (London, 1934), I, p. 63.
88. K.D. Brown, 'Non-Conformity and the British Labour Movement: A Case Study', *Journal of Social History* 8 (1975), 113–18.
89. J.F. Glaser, 'English Nonconformity and the Decline of Liberalism', *American Historical Review* 63 (1958), 357.
90. W. Stewart, *J. Keir Hardie: A Biography* (London, 1921), p. 346.
91. Lathbury, ed., *Correspondence*, II, p. 272.

5
Popular Political Economy
Anthony Howe

In a remarkable discursive revolution, a variety of economic languages (customary, mercantilist, protectionist, proto-socialist) which competed in the late eighteenth and early nineteenth centuries were replaced in early Victorian Britain by a 'hegemonic' language of liberal political economy at whose centre lay not an abstract concept of the market but a popular notion of free trade. This common language had largely united elite and popular political worlds by the second half of the nineteenth century, creating a powerful supra-party value, which remained uniquely dominant in British political culture before 1914, despite the emergence of powerful alternatives on both the right and the left.[1] In part this political language possessed a coherent content deriving from a canonical body of economic doctrine ('the laws of political economy') whose diffusion had in turn marginalised competing economic languages. Yet its appeal extended beyond its scientific authority, for it resonated with a whole range of different languages, ranging from those of religion, where free trade became part of a providential vision of order and redemption, to patriotism, for free trade was easily melded into the birthright of the 'free-born Englishman', as readily traceable in the Saxon realm of King Offa as it was in the pages of Smith's *Wealth of Nations*.[2] It also proved malleable, responsive to changing economic idioms, but also able to incorporate new languages such as that of Darwinism, whose intellectual genesis was intimately linked to that of political economy.[3]

The ideal of free trade

Nevertheless, what appears the easy nineteenth-century dominance of liberal political economy should not blind us to what was in many ways an abrupt and unexpected transition. For in early nineteenth-century

Britain the notion of moral economy remained strong and the traditional language of forestalling, engrossing and regrating had by no means disappeared.[4] By contrast, later in the century such terms survived simply as the test against which 'this free trade country' celebrated its emancipation.[5] The more formal language of mercantilism, including bounties, prohibitions and regulation, was arguably, despite the early impact of Smith's attack on the 'mercantile system', still the dominant (and patriotic) discourse, not least in a Parliament ready to impose the 1815 Corn Law and in which those proclaiming the laws of political economy felt themselves an isolated minority.[6] Oppositional languages of popular politics were still primarily pre-Smithian 'radical' ones deriving from the mid-eighteenth century resistance to oppression, and culminating in the public political language of Chartism.[7] This traditional language was increasingly challenged by a new 'socialist' discourse, building on Smith and Ricardo to incorporate notions of rent, labour value and 'exploitation'.[8] However, the early peak of such ideas under the influence of Robert Owen was all the more noticeable for the rapidity of their subsequent erosion, with co-operative stores the best known example of a potential socialist prototype absorbed within the culture of liberal political economy. Against this background, as Stedman Jones has shown, the early 1840s saw first the dethronement of the radical language of political oppression but also, this chapter will suggest, its effectual replacement by a new language of political economy, which sought equally to liberate the 'People' from oppression, and which became an integral part of popular liberalism. It was this language that was associated by Walter Bagehot with the rhetoric of the Anti-Corn Law League, which became the most effective vehicle for popularising the language of political economy, both through its huge effusion of popular printed literature, and through the immense number of speeches addressing the evils of the Corn Laws delivered under its aegis between 1838 and 1846.[9] Through the communication of its message in a variety of media, the League itself became a hugely successful tool of education, creating a 'national interest' in free trade.[10] 'The League', Harriet Martineau observed, 'is most effectually rousing the people's intellects, and training them to thought and action with a power and success to be found in no schools.'[11]

Undoubtedly the main purpose of the League's 'intellectual training' of the people was to reveal the laws of political economy, laws which were set against man-made intervention in the natural order. Thus, typically, George Moffatt, tea merchant and future Liberal MP, wrote, in a letter to *The League*, that the benefits of commercial freedom, long advocated by political economists, were scarcely understood by the people, until the advent of the League which was to 'simplify this foundation principle by its incontrovertible demonstration'.[12] This ability of the League to demonstrate 'the truths of political economy' was in turn related to its appeal to its own empirical or scientific authority based on 'facts' in order to disprove the claims of protectionist economic knowledge. When Mill's *System of Logic* appeared in 1843 the League endorsed its conclusions, for 'none are more concerned in the diffusion of correct principles of reasoning than the friends of Free Trade', while it went on: 'The whole occupation of the League, from its first formation has been the exposure of fallacies.'[13] In terms of substance rather than method, Kadish has carefully analysed the League's economics of high wages as the theoretical kernel of its claims for repeal, while political economy lay at the forefront of the propagandist efforts of the 'Napoleon of free trade', Thomas Perronet Thompson, who 'flooded the whole land with his arguments in pamphlets, in broadsides, in speeches, in letters, in addresses, in every one of the different forms of circulating literature, whereby the truths of political economy are made accessible even to the artisan in his workshop'.[14] The League saw as central to its mission the diffusion of the message of the benefits of free trade and a whole gamut of ideas linked to monopoly, the natural rights of labour and the overwhelming evidence of the 'evils of protection'. In part the best evidence for the success of this campaign came from the more combative yet ineffective articulation of protectionism, whose 'restorative political language' attempted to defend British agriculture within a balanced economy, supporting the home market, and its benefits in terms of social and political cohesion.[15] Whilst the League's language proved inclusive and expansive, that of protectionism was presented as exclusive and tied to narrow vested interests.

Thus, while Bagehot, editor of *The Economist*, reflecting in the tranquillity of the Age of Equipoise, identified a dominant secular language of economics in the 1840s, the League's rhetoric had frequently been intermingled with different languages, above all, that of religion. For, as is now well established, the first age of political economy had been primarily an age of Christian political economy;[16] this too was fully reflected in the League's linguistic weaponry, which put the emphasis on the beneficence of the divine order, hitherto frustrated by man's interference. Only the removal of the Corn Laws would lead to the self-working of the God-given natural order. As Winch has put it, 'Providentialist conceptions of a naturally harmonious world that needed to be purged of the artificial evils of feudal privilege and protectionism' supplied the League's sense of missionary zeal in a way that secular theories of economic growth and market freedom did not.[17] However, by and large, this was a far more optimistic view of the possibilities of economic growth, replacing the pessimism of earlier evangelicals with a stronger emphasis on the potential benefits of free trade to the people and the nation once the yoke of unscriptural monopoly was lifted. The League's optimism also helped lift the shadow of an earlier popular Malthusianism.[18] This suffusion of political economy within a religious language was also in part a carefully contrived strategy, not only with the League famously organising several meetings of ministers but, as one League orator recorded of his 'Prayer book appeals', 'our enemies can dispute our political economy but their mouths are shut up by our theology'.[19] Even so, it is interesting that he was eager not to alienate this audience by some of the League's cruder propaganda efforts, noting 'We are backed, here & elsewhere, by evangelical dissenters, who would be suspicious that they were supporting infidelity, if they saw us turning chapter & verse of the bible into anti-corn-law pellets.'[20] But religion infused many elements of the League's appeal, not only numerous meetings held in chapels, or the famous League membership certificate proclaiming 'Give us our daily bread', but also the exploitation of the link between the clergy and the Corn Laws introduced a restrained element of anti clericalism.[21] The use of scriptural vocabulary was widespread, with such extravagant metaphors as that of Lord Morpeth as the 'Moses' to conduct the people of Yorkshire out of the desert created by the Corn Laws.[22] Religious authorities were widely called upon to demonstrate the immorality of artificially raising the price of food; free trade too, as the League leader Cobden often emphasised, was part of the 'religion of the soul', while for Benjamin Parsons (of Stroud), one of many 'Friends of the People' who moved from Chartism to campaigning against the Corn Laws, the issue was simply one of 'justice and therefore of religion'.[23]

The association between the Corn Laws and justice opened up a further range of discursive linkages between free trade and moral reform. This was above all the case, as several historians have recently shown, with regard to slavery, as free trade became the principal language of slave emancipation, replacing a language dependent upon quasi-protectionist notions of restrictions, boycotts and imperial preference.[24] Secondly, free trade was linked through both secular and religious arguments to a more pacific view of the relations between states, extending at its extreme to a quasi-millenarian prospect of 'peace on earth'. Cobden, while no utopian, was keen to advertise the links between free trade and peace, so that free trade, the triumph of the Almighty, was also the triumph of pacific principles in the world, replacing territorial aggrandisement and empire.[25] Numerically we might think the audience for peace principles was a small one but for Cobden it became a successful means by which to attach many Nonconformists to the League bandwagon and it also derived support from a considerable body of secular friends of peace, including many Benthamites.[26] Thirdly, the moral language of the League appealed to the self-respecting artisan, the archetypal Gladstonians in the making, for example those active in the temperance movement. Thus Joseph Livesey's temperance newspaper *The Struggle* played an important part in the repeal campaign. It was intended chiefly for the working class but also agricultural labourers and farmers for whom it sought to 'illustrate and enforce the principles of free trade'. It achieved a regular circulation of 10,000 to 15,000 copies, almost as many as *The League* itself. According to John Bright, *The Struggle* 'told the story of the Corn Laws in pictures and language that could not be misunderstood'.[27]

The morality of free trade was however linked not only to the prospects of working-class reform but was presented above all in a constitutional language of emancipation from aristocratic governance. Here, as Joyce has emphasised,[28] the language of populism widely deployed the motif of Justice versus Privilege, but much of this language can be detected in the League's rhetoric, which brilliantly combined the economic and political concepts of monopoly in its attack on the aristocracy. Injustice was rife at all levels of society, for example, in wages, land distribution, voting power, while Privilege explained the war of town versus country, farmer versus manufacturer, landlord versus labourer. At its most extreme the League appealed to concepts of republican citizenship which would follow from the redistribution of the land in small freehold properties, but for most the emphasis was on the restoration of class harmony once the Corn Laws were removed.[29] Interestingly, as in the language of Chartism, the vocabulary of the Norman Yoke was widespread, with landlords equated with 'Norman despoilers', with free trade regularly identified with Magna Carta and Wat Tyler a campaigner for free markets against aristocratic monopoly;[30] Cobden himself later signed letters to the press as 'A South Saxon' while 'A' of the 'A. B. C.' of the League, Henry Ashworth, investigated the origins of the 'entrepreneurial' Saxon race in Lancashire.[31]

The rhetoric of the League, although understudied, also reveals sizeable inflections from other discourses, for example, those of phrenology and geology.[32] At no point did it descend simply into the doses of Gradgrindian economics imagined by its critics. On the contrary, it deployed its fair share of romantic and melodramatic devices. While these were not to the fore in the speeches of Cobden, known for their rationality, many considered W. J. Fox to be the League's most popular orator, with a rich vocabulary steeped in German metaphysics and romanticism. Typically, Fox, the self-styled 'Norwich Weaver Boy', sought to mobilise the people against the aristocracy, 'Here we are in our hired theatre and there the yare in their senatorial halls, and with yet statelier buildings erecting, and to be paid for by the nation's toil, and at the expense of the privations of thousands. Here we are with *right*, and they with *might*; we take up the gauntlet they have thrown down and we hurl defiance on tier teeth.'[33]

While the popularity of repeal of the Corn Laws may therefore have been greatly enhanced by the varieties of language deployed, the League also successfully addressed its message to women, including them among those with the rationality to grasp the truths of political economy. Such a project built on the success of the earlier women authors who had acted as important and influential exponents of popular political economy, above all, Jane Marcet's pioneering *Conversations on Political Economy*, a model of the more radical Martineau's writings popularising political economy.[34] This literature gave liberal political economy a feminine slant, which differentiated its tone from the more virile world of protectionism (with its predominantly masculine connotations of land, shipping and the empire) and which was then exemplified by the League's readiness to recruit women into its organisational and 'missionary' framework.[35] Later economists added some – but little – sophistication to the League's emphasis on the price of bread as central to working-class household consumption and free trade as the basis for economical household management.[36] By contrast, contemporary protectionist language focused far more upon the nation and the empire rather than on the 'homespun' and the self-sufficient household.[37] Hence the League not only embraced the well-being of women (and children) in its goals but, as Morgan has shown, looked to women as agents of social change.[38]

Overall, therefore, the Anti-Corn Law League had successfully built a 'totalising' language of political economy around a central core of 'free trade', although its success was in part the result of its successful integration of a variety of different languages, ranging from patriotism to proto-feminism. In this way the language of free trade did not become simply 'the frigid language of political economy', nor as in France was it tied to a narrower concept of 'free exchange';[39] rather its long-term success was deeply entwined with its avoiding becoming simply a market-based or laissez-faire economic language, although there seems no doubt that such idioms or laws of political economy became commonplace at all levels of society, ranging from the aristocratic drawing-room to the taproom of the trade union and rural savings club. Arguably too, even the sternest critics of the market and the cash nexus, including Ruskin and Carlyle, were not in fact opponents of free trade, although Ruskin liked to see this as a product of Renaissance Florence rather than of Smith's *Wealth of Nations*, while Carlyle, scornful of the Cobdenite 'calico millennium', still reckoned the survival of the aristocracy as conditional upon the repeal of the Corn Laws.[40] Arguably therefore, in the longer term, the League had succeeded in displacing the language of old moral economy, and in fulfilling Cobden's goal of diffusing the language of Adam Smith; in the short term, it continued to meet strenuous opposition from both Chartists and Tory Protectionists, but it also stood ready to benefit from the failure of both. Its campaigns had however evoked a sense of a citizenry actively involved in influencing national debate, a form of 'discursive democracy', which markedly contrasted with J. S. Mill's desire to shield policy-making from public intrusion.[41] In this way it also offered a new core component of a language of popular liberalism which would succeed the constitutional language of Whiggery.[42]

The popularisation of free trade

The success of the League in upholding the cause of the People's Bread might have proved transitory had the language of protectionist political economy proved more resilient, or had Chartist hostility to the League as a 'mill-owners' ramp' been more successful. Yet by 1850, with the League disbanded, and with the failure of Chartism, the surviving Chartist platform had largely abandoned its hostility to free trade, while seeking to promote reforms which would ensure the working classes benefited from it.[43] Over the same period, the deliquescence of protectionism proved swift and virtually complete, despite evidence of a considerable backlash against free trade in the later 1840s and early 1850s as the more optimistic predictions of dogmatic free traders proved unfounded.[44] But Protectionist attempts to utilise the language of empire, nation and defence proved unable to hold back the abolition of imperial preference and the repeal of the Navigation Acts.[45] At elite levels, the political implausibility of a return to agrarian protection after 1846 ensured that many leading Protectionists cast a veil of silence over their previous beliefs, such that those who remained attached to the cause were rapidly identified as a quixotic minority, upholding a 'lost cause'.

Arguably the last chance for a revival of protectionism was presented by the negotiation of the 'free trade' commercial treaty with France in 1860, which met some protectionist resistance on the grounds of its benefiting France far more than England, and of sacrificing 'the honour and interests of England merely for the beneficial results to a particular class'.[46] Yet no coherent opposition was offered, with the critics of the Treaty forced to defend not protection but a model of reciprocity which in the 1820s had been the bellwether of Huskissonite free trade.[47]

The parliamentary ascendancy of liberal political economy after 1846 was widely complemented by its growing rootedness at popular levels, as has been extensively shown. Hence, while into the 1830s attempts had been made to uphold traditional 'moral' norms in certain industries – above all, handloom weaving – by the 1860s, as Biagini has shown, trade unions had fully adopted the language of political economy as well as the growing practice of collective wage bargaining.[48] Wages were now sanctioned by the 'wage fund', not by customary norms, although arguably the growing practice of the 'breadwinner' wage successfully re-imported notions of family and the household in place of the atomised adult workers.[49] Free trade through the cheap loaf became the guarantee of family welfare. In the classroom, too, the 'truths' of political economy held sway, reinforced not simply by the diffusion of economic lessons but by popular historical narratives such as Martineau's *History of England*.[50] Whole genres of edifying popular literature reiterated the central ideas of political economy, especially attempts to construct new fields of knowledge such as 'social economy'.[51] While such literature did not necessarily exceed other genres in popularity, it became a staple of the new free libraries from the 1850s, as well as those of mechanics institutes and reading rooms. Nor was the fiction of the period without a strong sense of the challenge of commerce to existing norms in politics and society.[52] It is also well established that political economy became a staple of the university extension movement as well as of many lectures and classes in working men's clubs in the 1870s and 1880s.[53] Arguably the whole gamut of working-class self-help institutions, including friendly societies, savings clubs, working-men's clubs, co-operative societies and the habit of life insurance shared an approach to economic life which emphasised individual calculation within the framework of the market and the common body of practical economic knowledge.[54] Following in the tradition of Marcet and Martineau, new literary ventures such as the *English Woman's Journal* embraced a liberal model of political economy as a guide to women as consumers and philanthropists.[55] Finally, there seems little doubt that the language of the League provided the dominant idioms of the cheap press after 1855, with regular reports of politicians celebrating free trade as this 'great and glorious policy'.[56] Hence there was near editorial unanimity in 1860 that both ribbon weavers and paper manufacturers exemplified groups who upheld the principle of free trade but regarded themselves as deserving exemption from its application: typically the *Daily News* concluded that 'The interests of the consumers are to be first consulted, and those interests demand the abolition of protective duties wherever they exist.'[57] Cobden himself by 1864 could speak convincingly of the common principles which bound together 'this free trade nation'.[58]

Against this background, it proved relatively easy to articulate popular defences of free trade against subsequent challenges.[59] The most important of these was the fair trade movement between 1879 and 1892, an attempt to mobilise 'English' notions of fair play against 'foreign' competition, as well as to appeal to imperial sentiment (kith and kin), and to shape a 'national' rather than 'cosmopolitan' political economy.[60] This movement acquired some discursive momentum in challenging the hegemony of 'free trade', appealing mostly to those who felt themselves to be its losers. Yet at the level of popular political argument, the proponents of free trade were able to marshal a defence which drew on a range of ideas first articulated in the 1840s, although the religious dimension had greatly subsided in favour of linking free trade with popular affluence; with justice and welfare for the working man, with freedom of the body politic from the pressure of vested interest groups and with a Cobdenite vision of interdependence between nations.[61] Such arguments had become deeply ingrained among the urban working-class, now the bulk of the borough electorate, with the Second Reform Act giving the vote to the mass of urban consumers. This new army of citizen-consumers would become the ultimate guarantors against a return to protection in Victorian and Edwardian Britain.[62] To ensure this outcome, Cobden's heirs – now suitably organised in the Cobden Club – turned their energies to a huge propaganda effort to defeat the 'Fair Trade' assault on working class voters in the election of 1880, typically aiming, as the League had done, to 'inform' the mass electorate by swamping it with printed propaganda. This exercise in popular political argument however proved a mere rehearsal for the election of 1885, when it was feared the Third Reform Act might unleash a torrent of protectionism among the newly enfranchised agricultural labourers. But such fears were short-lived, for 'Hodge' was found to be a loyal recruit to free trade, encouraged both by fear of a return to the 'bad old days' and by the strong effort to disseminate the arguments for free trade in the countryside, not least its link with land reform. As a result, fair trade was largely a spent force by 1885, but appeals to the citizen-consumer were also brought to bear in subsidiary campaigns such as that waged by free traders successfully against attempts to restrict the imports of cheap sugar.

Here the simplicity of free trade ('free imports') was threatened by the revival of a far more complex language of bounties, restriction, subsidies and international regulation which was widely presented as alien to the case for free trade, as one identifying 'British' interests with those of the rest of the world.[63]

Nevertheless, these specific defences of free trade were part and parcel of a wider language of what have been aptly termed the 'social contract' and the 'fiscal constitution', a language which enshrined the rights of the citizen-consumer. This had two main elements: on the one hand, as McKibbin has emphasised, the state in Britain abstained from interference in essential economic relationships, so that non-interference with regard to wages (left to collective bargaining) was paralleled by not interfering in the market for goods by imposing tariffs (and working class living costs).[64] Where the state did interfere, necessarily in regard to taxation policy, as Daunton has shown, working class allegiance to the state was consolidated by a taxation policy which balanced the interests of classes, and in which the existence of income tax from the 1840s was a broad signal of equity between classes.[65] Since the 1820s fiscal policy had greatly reduced the number of dutiable articles of working class consumption, and the Huskissonite-Peelite 'liberal' approach had systematically removed privileges from particular interests to the greater benefit of consumers. This had greatly reduced the pressure of indirect taxation, a long-standing radical grievance, and ideas such as that of the 'free breakfast table' became an important successor to the idea of cheap bread in the 1840s. Overall, therefore, Gladstonian budgetary policy had consolidated the link between the consumer, free trade and the general good within popular notions of political economy, at the same time demonising tariffs as promoting the vested interests of 'producers', initially landowners but later an array of 'capitalist' tycoons and trusts.[66]

Finally this fiscal constitution was linked to the fundamental stability provided by the gold standard, removing from British workers the threat of inflation eroding wages. As a result, after the 1840s, currency did not prove a magnet for popular political argument – as Cobden warned, 'The fact is the currency question has been in the hands of very irrational and excitable parties, and sober people shun it as they would any other quackery.'[67] We know too little about working-class understandings of monetary issues, but it is clear that the Birmingham School of paper inflation, while it retained a loyal local following, did not recruit more widely.[68] Nor did the Cobbettite attack on the parasitism of the City of London spread to the industrial working class, despite the survival of a quasi-radical tradition in London ready to attack the 'Cormorant' of Threadneedle Street.[69] But, as Alborn has shown, loyalty to the gold-backed pound was deeply linked to Victorian ideas of national identity and the fiscal constitution. This was most of all firmly conveyed by the failure of the later nineteenth-century bimetallic movement to recruit popular support, despite a vigorous attempt to wrest the language of money out of the hands of the orthodox. The rhetoric of 'producers' versus 'rentiers', 'gold Bugs' versus 'silverites' proved largely unattractive to a working class – many of them now savers or 'creditors' themselves – ready to share in the conservative patriotism enshrined in the gold sovereign, newly reminted embracing Queen, empire and nation.[70]

Challenges to free trade

Nevertheless, if for the public as a whole 'free trade' remained the short-hand device linking wider understanding of the economy, state and society, that understanding was increasingly challenged by the end of the century.[71] The revived debate on poverty from the 1880s necessarily suggested that free trade had not produced prosperity for all members of society, although the 'fair trade' critics of free trade did not systematically attempt to link free trade to low living standards. Nevertheless, increasingly, a changing perception of the state as a positive contributor to the common good, for example in the works of T. H. Green, sanctioned a critique of free trade as hostile to state intervention, part and parcel of an individualistic, laissez-faire approach to the individual and the economy. It was in this context that terms such as 'Manchester School' came to acquire primarily negative connotations on the left. Likewise, perceptions of a 'Great Depression' suggested the growing failure of the economy under free trade conditions, and the need for alternative economic prescriptions to those of the 'free market'. Much of this discontent focused on new perceptions of the incidence of 'unemployment', linked in part to the trade cycle, but also to growing foreign competition affecting particular groups of workers. Although relatively new as a concept and still little used as a term in the late nineteenth century, unemployment, together with the growth of the 'sweated' trades, became one of the key concerns of the burgeoning labour movement, which also fostered a growing sense that free trade had been par excellence a 'capitalist' issue' whose continuing benefits for the working classes were no longer wholly self-evident. Thus, as Trentmann has shown, among a small group of Labour intellectuals, a new understanding of political economy was emerging which would challenge the whole trajectory of free trade, rejecting wealth in favour of welfare, providing a critique of the limitations of laissez-faire, and arguing in some cases for national rather than international solutions to the regulation of the economy.[72] At times, this extended to the view that capitalist Britain faced a future of economic decline, lower wages and failing trades, with advanced thinkers such as Snowden ready to reject the whole pattern of growth under capitalism in favour of the revival of a more balanced urban–rural economy. Even so, this new understanding left deep divisions on the British left, with the Social Democratic Federation favouring 'socialist– protectionism', while the Fabians for the most part sided with imperialism and tariffs. The Independent Labour Party retained important elements of the 'liberal' language of the critique of 'capitalist' protectionism, and continued to uphold the ethical internationalism of free trade. The latter in particular made a deep appeal to many sectors of working-class opinion, not least the co-operative movement, now reinforced by the emergence of the keenly free trade Women's Co-operative Guild. Within (and to some extent outside) this nascent socialist critique of liberal political economy lay an earlier Ruskinian/Carlylean moral analysis of the failings of the 'cash nexus', linked to the production of 'inferior goods' and the worship of 'cheapness'. This stimulated, even among free trade's long-term supporters such as Hobson, an important rethinking of earlier views of consumption, with a growing demand for 'higher' forms of consumption, transforming 'passive shoppers into active citizens' (even if such concepts remained remote from the daily lives of the bulk of the working classes).[73]

This embryonic socialist alternative to popular political economy was paralleled on the right by the emergence of historical political economy in the late nineteenth century. Its neo-mercantilist language underlay the later tariff reform challenge to free trade.[74] This primarily rejected what it saw as the abstraction of classical political economy, with its emphasis on the universal market and individual economic man, in favour of a new national and imperial framework for understanding industrialisation and welfare in Britain. In this perspective the free trade of the 1840s was considered a fundamental breach with an earlier tradition which had linked the state, economy and society in a responsible order guaranteeing economic progress and popular welfare within the nation-state. While free trade had suited Britain's mid-century industrial primacy, it now jeopardised future prosperity and power, as Britain's competitors resorted to tariffs to protect their economies. Britain, it seemed, was now ready to sacrifice 'producers' to the interests of its consumers, wedded to cheap imports, and the interests of its rentiers, seeking to export capital in vast quantities, arguably to the detriment of the domestic economy. In place of the liberal model of the small state, the historical economists favoured state intervention by tariffs to guarantee both growth and welfare. Above all, they rejected the cosmopolitanism of free trade; if Britain was to compete with the emerging imperial states of the future, she needed to return to her own imperial traditions – for the historical economists such as Cunningham and Hewins typically recalled both the Elizabethan empire and the imperial genesis of industrial prosperity in the eighteenth century. Far more effectively than the fair traders, they developed the notion of the imperial *zollverein* and, as Peter Cain has shown, there emerged a powerful new language of 'constructive imperialism'.[75] The historical economists therefore offered a new language of empire, state, production and welfare which would richly inflect the tariff reform challenge to free trade and liberal political economy.

Against this background, competing languages of political economy moved to the centre of Edwardian popular debate in the contest between free trade and tariff reform. This was a contest not only of the spoken and written word but one in which the visual languages of postcards, posters, magic lanterns and early film also played an important part.[76] In particular, the general elections of 1906 and 1910 were to generate very literally a war of words between two highly organised mass campaigns, which sought to convey two very different images of the British past, present and future. For the tariff reformers especially, it became vital that the dominant discourse of free trade should be confronted directly and totally, avoiding 'equivocation, studied ambiguity, and rhetorical evasion'.[77] Four elements were central to this attempt to de-legitimize free trade. Firstly, the case for tariff reform sought to remove the aura of quasi-religious authority attached to free trade, often presented as a secular religion which its opponents now consciously attacked as a remnant of the tribal past, a set of primitive shibboleths defending a 'fetish'; free trade was to be derided as a superstition, not a science. Secondly, having removed the aura of sanctity, free trade might be contested on its empirical foundations, hence the war of figures which redounded from meeting to meeting, blue books and commissions, tract to tract of endless 'facts and figures' without ever delivering a decisive verdict in either direction.[78] But it became a central part of the movement to claim 'scientific' validity approved by 'experts'.[79] Thirdly, the notion of 'free trade' itself was directly anatomised, with 'free' frequently identified simply with free imports, that is to say a readiness to admit 'cheap' foreign goods at the expense of the domestic producer and irrespective of 'unfair' foreign practices such as subsidies, dumping or the payment of low wages. In the vocabulary the tariff reformers inherited from the 'Fair traders', if trade was to be free it also needed to be 'fair'. This required reciprocity, bargaining and, if necessary, retaliation and tariff wars, deploying the 'big revolver'.[80] Finally, while the critique of 'unfair practices' made an appeal to the 'correct' working of economic laws of supply and demand, hitherto distorted by 'artificial' intervention, the addition of the desirability for trade to run in 'imperial channels' reflected a new understanding, inspired by the historical economists, of a state- and empire-centred approach to economic life. For in articulating the tariff reform case, the primary issue for many became 'no less than the growth and consolidation, or the decline and decay, of the British Empire'.[81] Arguably the most novel challenge of tariff reform was not its attempt to politicise employment but to politicise empire by linking tariffs with a particular vision of the contemporary vogue for 'Greater Britain', which now challenged the deeply engrained metanarrative of 'Little England'.[82] Empire, according to Chamberlain, the creator of the tariff campaign, was fundamental to the identity of the British people, to the power of the British state and to the possibility of 'the weary Titan' reversing its incipient decline.

Chamberlain's alternative political economy also attempted to reverse free trade's primacy of the consumer in favour of the producers whose goods would replace unfair 'cheap imports', reversing Britain's industrial decline and providing, in the favourite slogan of the tariff reform campaign, 'Work for All'.[83] This is turn would allow male breadwinners to regain independence, virtue and social standing. Arguably tariff reform did make some progress when it spoke the same language as the free traders, relating to living standards, employment and consumption. But to a large extent in the Edwardian period the vocabulary of 'national industry', 'self-sufficiency' and 'producers' remained on the margins of political discourse, while, as Trentmann has shown, the tariff reformers, in their attempt to create a language of the producer, failed to create an imperial language of the consumer able to compete with that of free trade.[84] Nor did they rival the language of the producer which had been central to American protectionist political economy.[85]

Imperial and producers' interests in turn helped to anchor tariff reform in its global as well as its domestic dimension. For an important part of the widely articulated 'case for tariff reform' lay in its claim to 'make the foreigner pay', the promise that increased tariffs would provide a boost to government revenue which would not only obviate the need for increased direct taxation but would moreover yield sufficient funds to pay for increased social reforms. Tariff reform typically presented free trade as a cosmopolitan creed benefiting 'foreigners' at the expense of 'Britons', exploiting a strand of economic nationalism which had been widely voiced in the 1890s – especially against cheap German goods undermining British industries[86] – but had also been widespread in the movement to restrict alien immigration, culminating in the Aliens Act of 1905. Here was a new language of exclusion of labour and foreign goods, a new language of closure in the international sphere, an economic retreat within tariff boundaries, sheltering domestic production against international competition, which reflected a much wider reaction against the economic globalisation of the early twentieth century. This led in turn to emphatically conflictual languages of political economy which sought to break sharply with the claims that free trade promoted a general community of interests among classes and peoples. As Hobson would put it in the 1930s, any sense of common civic or international society was 'perverted by a phraseology of conflict suggestive and provocative of class strife and international strife'. Hobson adhered to his Edwardian belief that 'we must displace the language which represents trade both within and in the world at large as a competitive struggle akin to the actual warfare which conflicting national interests are liable to evoke'.[87]

If the language of tariff reform linked the future welfare of Britain ineluctably to the empire in a mercantilist zero-sum game of retaliation and tariff warfare in a new era dominated by big states, that of free trade necessarily used the past and present to uphold the status quo with its traditional emphases on goodwill, peace, community and consumer welfare. Undoubtedly the strongest element in the free trade case remained the defence of the consumer against 'food taxes' and 'dear bread'. At this level, in a political culture in which popular history did much to instruct the new democracy, the re-invention of 'The Hungry Forties' proved a master-stroke of popular propaganda, warning men, women and children against the evils of a return to protection.[88] Fear of a return to the 'Hungry Forties' remained far more powerful and resonant in the popular imaginary than an appeal to the distant days of Drake, Cromwell and Chatham. Nor was the language of economic orthodoxy ignored, with the defence of free trade grounded in international trade theory, comparative advantage and the benefits of free imports spelled out for a society with which the aspirations of consumers had typically come to dominate over those of producers. Even so, those interests were far from ignored in a polity where overseas trade was vital to employment, and understandably few politicians in cotton Lancashire were yet ready to argue that jobs should migrate to the sites of raw materials, nor in mining districts that coal exports harmed the working classes.[89] But, as in the past, free trade was not wedded to laissez-faire but to increasingly interventionist policies including minimum wages, labour exchanges and nationalization, recipes for economic modernization without the potential costs of a tariff-based state. For the language of free trade still articulated notions of political justice in which tariffs were seen as promoting exploitative trusts and cartels, the products of brokerage among interest groups in tariff-dominated polities which undermined the neutrality of the hitherto 'knave-proof' state. The survival and vitality of democracy were therefore dependent upon resisting tariffs.[90]

Finally, although free trade was often linked to the need for a large navy (in part to defend trade and food supply),[91] its usage still predominantly reflected ideals of interdependence which enjoyed a renewed popularity in the newly global century. That free trade led to peace was still widely asseverated, whether among diplomats, distrustful of the 'big revolver' of tariff retaliation, or co-operative shoppers enjoying the diverse products of the world market, or idealists such as Angell purveying a futile vision in which the economic irrationality of war would become a guarantee against its outbreak.[92] As for Liberals of the Gladstonian generation, protection, as illustrated by Germany or Italy, was too easily the path to militarism. But, on the contrary, free trade Edwardian Britain saw the efflorescence of a considerable peace culture, not least in the outbreak of 'Angellism' before 1914. Thus tariff reform language linking trade with competing national interests contrasted markedly with a concurrent revitalisation of cosmopolitan language in the works of Wells, Hobson and Lowes Dickinson, with its emphasis on openness, civil society, peace, democracy and globality.[93] Winston Churchill himself now left the Unionist party over the threat tariff reform posed to international relations, while the philosopher Bertrand Russell endorsed free trade as 'the only sane internationalism left'.[94] Within the labour movement, as Trentmann has re-emphasised, ethical internationalism trumped economic arguments for tariffs.[95] Finally, however, free traders could not ignore the empire – yet for them, empire was not the limit to Britain's global role, simply one facet of a truer cosmopolitanism, which was itself linked to Kant's older global ideal of commercial exchange and perpetual peace. Paradoxically the creed of 'Little England' was in fact a cosmopolitan alternative to Greater Britain. Nor, however, was empire for free traders a means of market manipulation, material interest and political manoeuvring but was held out as a realm of sentiment, loyalty and brotherhood. The language of free trade therefore prioritised harmony, co-operation, justice, and the consumer, retaining its clothing of constitutional patriotism and its ethical as well as economic appeal. By contrast, tariff reform struggled to escape its 'squalid argument' of material prosperity, supported by images of decaying industries, competing interests, retaliation, international conflict and imperial power.[96]

For the most part, therefore, despite the alternative visions of both the tariff reformers and the Labour left, the liberal political economy of free trade remained the most politically compelling language of politics in Edwardian Britain. Hence the paradox that a language closely linked to the emerging bourgeoisie in the 1840s had by the 1900s largely become the language of the Edwardian working-class electorate. Yet this primacy was not simply residual, the lowest common denominator in the anti-tariff campaign. Rather the case for free trade had been revitalised in the late nineteenth and early twentieth centuries by the very challenges it faced, so that its language changed in the very act of communication to new audiences and in new contexts. This was not simply a negative process but built on two underlying intellectual shifts. Firstly, the economic case for free trade had if anything been strengthened by theoretical developments in economics, with the 'marginalist revolution' displacing the labour theory of value (itself the keystone of Ricardian socialism) in favour of consumer utility, a notion not only foreshadowed by Benthamites and free traders but one which the debate over the Corn Laws had already put at the forefront of political rhetoric.[97] As voiced by Marshall, Pigou, Edgworth and the early Keynes, the new economic orthodoxy vitally underpinned the Edwardian consumer-based defence of free trade, while also moving from older notions of free competition and wealth towards ideas of welfare and the community. This in turn paved the way for developments in liberal fiscal theory in which progressive taxation became the means to increased welfare. Many orthodox Liberals had endorsed the growing revolt against the 'Manchester School', and under influence of Green and Hobson now elaborated a new language of popular rights and the community. This increasingly marginalised the 'individualistic' free traders, emphasising self-help, low taxation, individual competition and personal responsibility. This minimalist old Gladstonian creed had a diminishing appeal both to the lower middle class now ready to trade-off 'personal rights' for Chamberlain's imperial splendour, and to working men and women, many of whom rallied to the revitalised popular language of free trade and consumer welfare. Here the language of free trade had moved far from the 'laws of political economy' propagated by the League, transforming itself into a language which defended consumers, jobs and justice but incorporated graduated taxation and state-provided welfare; a language of wealth and welfare which sought to avoid the perils of retaliation, war and empire.

Secondly, as in the 1840s, the language of free trade fed into wider ideologies of reform, as we have in part seen with regard to the peace movement.[98] This was most powerfully the case with regard to land reform, a complex movement but one with distinct Cobdenite hallmarks. Thus Thorold Rogers, the most Cobdenite of economists, and doyen of the adult education movement, had helped engrain the anti-aristocratic vocabulary of land reform which remained central to popular politics into the Edwardian period.[99] Thus Lloyd George readily appeared as a latter-day Anti-Corn Law Leaguer, with his land campaign of 1912 forecast as the resumption of the League campaign against 'landed monopoly'.[100] This campaign was equally fed by the strand of reformism deriving from Henry George, whose ideas had also helped move many free traders from individualism towards a more collectivist approach.[101] This radical attack on monopoly carried more purchase than any putative ILP model of autarkic land nationalization, or tariff reform schemes for labour colonies and rural regeneration. It popularised land reform, alongside free trade, as the solution to urban poverty, low wages and overcrowding.[102]

Thirdly, far more overtly than in the 1840s, free trade in the 1900s was presented in a gendered perspective, as a woman's question, central to the defence of the household budget, and the welfare of mothers and children. In a way this was already old-fashioned – as Trentmann argues other issues were now coming to the fore. Even so, in 1906 bread remained central to working-class consumption, and 'the big loaf' was as yet a far more compelling symbolic language than pure milk or the 'Buy British' and imperial consumption movements of the 1920s.[103] The Women's Free Trade Union, still too little studied, thus made a vital contribution to adding a flavour of maternalism to the defence of free trade. Typically, one of its activists, Alice Bamford Slack, defended free trade as necessary to contentment in the home, a freedom-loving empire, the interests of consumers, and the role of women as house-keepers 'upon whom...rested the burden of adjusting expenditure to income'.[104]

These vital transformations within the discourse of free trade therefore ensured its continuing primacy at the centre of Edwardian political culture, able to recreate and regenerate its language of consumerism and prosperity, freedom and welfare, domesticity and democracy, ethics and internationalism. To some extent both tariff reform and socialism offered alternative political economies posited around notions of decline and economic failure with visions which promoted the interests of producers within primarily national frameworks, although with divergent views of the goals of modernization and the managed economy. The socialist vision valorised the balanced economy, the end of capitalism and land reform; the tariff reform one empire and social reform from above, order and regulation. Neither was yet able to compete effectively in a political culture still inclined to value active citizens over state power and to look to the lessons of the recent past as the best guide to political choices for the future.

Notes

1. A. Howe, *Free Trade and Liberal England, 1846–1946* (Oxford, 1997); F. Trentmann, *Free Trade Nation* (Oxford, 2008).
2. A. Somerville, *Free Trade and the League*, 2 vols (Manchester, 1853); for Somerville's political economy and 'Saxonism', see J. Codell, 'Alexander Somerville's Rise from Serfdom: Working-Class Self-Fashioning through Journalism, Autobiography and Political Economy' in A. Krishnamurthy, ed., *The Working-Class Intellectual in Eighteenth- and Nineteenth-Century Britain* (Farnham, 2009), pp. 195–218.
3. P.J. Bowler, *Evolution: the History of an Idea*, 3rd edn (Berkeley, 2003).
4. For its survival, J. Bohstedt, *The Politics of Provisions: Food Riots, Moral Economy and Market Transition in England c. 1555–1850* (Farnham, 2010).
5. *Bristol Mercury*, 3 February 1893; *Daily News*, 24 September 1889; *Pall Mall Gazette*, 12 November 1883.
6. For the change in tone in the House of Commons by 1826, G. Philips, *Hansard's Parliamentary Debates* [hereafter H] XV 339–41, 18 April 1826; see also G.F. Langer, *The Coming of Age of Political Economy* (New York, 1987).
7. G. Stedman Jones, *Languages of Class: Studies in English Working Class History, 1832–1982* (Cambridge, 1983), ch. 3.
8. See N. W. Thompson, *The People's Science* (Cambridge, 1984), pp. 221–2; G. Claeys, *Machinery, Money, and the Millennium* (Cambridge, 1987).
9. *The Collected Works of Walter Bagehot*, ed. N. St John Stevas, 15 vols (London, 1965–86), III, p. 296; Howe, *Liberal England*, pp. 31–2; P. Pickering and A. Tyrell, *The People's Bread* (London, 2000); N. McCord, *The Anti-Corn Law League* (London, 1958).
10. See esp. C. Schonhardt-Bailey, *From the Corn Laws to Free Trade* (Cambridge, MA, 2006), pp. 75–106.
11. Martineau to R. M. Milnes, 12 June 1844 in *The Collected Letters of Harriet Martineau*, ed. D. Logan, 4 vols (London, 2007), II, p. 321.

12. *League*, 10 February 1844.
13. Ibid., 20 January 1844.
14. A. Kadish, 'Introduction', *The Corn Laws*, 6 vols (London, 1996); *The Sun* cited in M. Turner, 'The "Bonaparte of free trade" and the Anti-Corn Law League', *Historical Journal* 41 (1998), 1011.
15. A. Gambles, *Politics and Protection: Conservative Economic Discourse, 1815–1852* (Woodbridge, 1999), p. 57.
16. B. Hilton, *The Age of Atonement* (Oxford, 1989); A.M.C. Waterman, *Revolution, Economics, and Religion* (Cambridge, 1991).
17. D. Winch, *Wealth and Life: Essays on the Intellectual History of Political Economy in Britain, 1848–1914* (Cambridge, 2009), p. 14.
18. For example, see Francis Place, early Malthusian but later enthusiastic celebrant of the League.
19. Sidney Smith, 12 March 1840, Anti-Corn Law League Letters, no. 429, Manchester Central Library; on religion and the League see Rev. J.W. Massie, *Manchester Times*, 3 July 1846; the free trade leaders, especially Cobden, were often deemed 'apostles'.
20. Cobden to Henry Cole, 1 June 1839, *The Letters of Richard Cobden Vol. I, 1815–1847*, ed. A. Howe, (Oxford, 2007), p. 168.
21. E. Evans, *The Contentious Tithe* (London, 1976).
22. Cobden at Wakefield, *Bradford Observer*, 1 February 1844; *League*, 3 February 1844.
23. O.R. Ashton and P. Pickering, *Friends of the People* (London, 2002), p. 87.
24. Typically, George Thompson, *League*, 20 April 1844; S.J. Morgan, 'The Anti-Corn Law League and British Anti-Slavery in Transatlantic Perspective, 1838–1846', *Historical Journal* 52 (2009), 87–107; R. Huzzey, 'Free Trade, Free Labour, and Slave Sugar in Victorian Britain', *Historical Journal* 53 (2010), 359–79.
25. See too R. F. Spall, 'Free Trade, Foreign Relations, and the Anti-Corn Law League', *International History Review* 10 (1988), 405–32.
26. See esp. M. Ceadel, *The Origins of War Prevention* (Oxford, 1996); S. Conway, 'Bentham, the Benthamites, and the Nineteenth Century Peace Movement', *Utilitas* 2 (1990), 221–43.
27. I am grateful for this reference to Henry Miller's unpublished paper on *The Struggle*, p. 41.
28. P. Joyce, *Visions of the People* (Cambridge, 1991).
29. A. Howe, 'The "Manchester School" and the Landlords' in M. Cragoe and P. Readman, eds., *The Land Question in Britain, 1750–1950* (Basingstoke, 2010), pp. 74–91.
30. *League*, 11 November 1843, 17 February 1844. Bowring (Bolton) and J. B. Smith (Dundee) spoke of free trade as the 'Magna Charta of Labour' in their election addresses in 1841.
31. For Somerville, commercial enterprise was part of the 'Saxon inheritance', Codell, 'Somerville's Rise', p. 212.
32. *League*, 16 December 1843: 'in the League, there is a power, like that of the central fire which geologists tell us, that raises the lowest beings of creation to endow them with the capability of exhibiting all the powers of life and animation'.
33. *League*, 17 February 1844; K. Gleadle, *The Early Feminists* (London, 1995), pp. 33–5.

34. B. Polkinghorn and D. L. Thomson, *Adam Smith's Daughters* (Cheltenham, 1998); M. A. Dimand, R. Dimand and E. L. Forget, eds., *Women of Value* (Aldershot, 1995).
35. S. J. Morgan, 'Domestic Economy and Political Agitation: Women and the Anti-Corn Law League, 1839–46' in K. Gleadle and S. Richardson, eds., *The Power of the Petticoat* (Basingstoke, 2000), pp. 115–33.
36. J. Garnett, 'Political and Domestic Economy in Victorian Social Thought: Ruskin and Xenophon' in S. Collini, R. Whatmore and B. Young, eds., *Economy, Polity, Society: British Intellectual History, 1750–1950* (Cambridge, 2000), pp. 205–23; *League*, 23 December 1843 for repeal as a 'household question'.
37. Gambles, *Politics and Protection*.
38. Morgan, 'Domestic Economy'; idem, *A Victorian Woman's Place* (London, 2007), pp. 139–43.
39. *The Times*, 21 June 1844; for the failure of the language of free exchange in France, D. Todd, *L'Identité Économique de la France: Libre-Échange et Protectionnisme, 1814–1851* (Paris, 2008).
40. J. Ruskin, *Val D'Arno* (1873) in *The Works of John Ruskin*, ed. E. T. Cook and A. Wedderburn, 39 vols (London, 1903–9, 1912), XXIII, p. 75; Carlyle to Edward Fitzgerald, 19 January 1846 in *The Collected Letters of Thomas and Jane Welsh Carlyle*, ed C. R. Sanders et al, 39 vols (Duke, NC, 1970-), XX, p. 103.
41. For 'discursive democracy' see D. Torgerson, 'Democracy through Policy Discourse' in M. A. Hajer and H. Wagenaar, eds., *Deliberative Policy Analysis* (Cambridge, 2003), pp. 113–38, esp. 115. Mill was conspicuous by his absence from the Anti-Corn Law debate, Cobden noting he 'never seemed to take any interest in our free trade agitation', to T. B. Potter, 22 January 1864, West Sussex Record Office, Add. MS 2761, fo. B68.
42. K. Chittick, *The Language of Whiggism: Liberty and Patriotism, 1802–1830* (London, 2010).
43. E.g. O'Connor at Aylesbury cited in *The Letters of Richard Cobden Vol. II, 1848–1853*, ed. A. Howe, (Oxford, 2010), p. 188 n. 10.
44. A. Macintyre, 'Lord George Bentinck and the Protectionists: a Lost Cause?', *Transactions of the Royal Historical Society* 39 (1989), 141–65.
45. Howe, *Liberal England*, pp. 38–69; S. Palmer, *Politics, Shipping, and the Repeal of the Navigation Laws* (Manchester, 1990).
46. George Bentinck, H CLVI 2261, 5 March 1860.
47. Idem, H CLVII 278, 9 March 1860.
48. E. F. Biagini, 'British Trade Unions and Popular Political Economy, 1860–1880', *Historical Journal* 30 (1987), 811–40.
49. See J. Thompson, 'Political Economy, the Labour Movement and the Minimum Wage, 1880–1914' in E. H. H. Green and D. Tanner, eds., *The Strange Survival of Liberal England: Political leaders, Moral Values and the Reception of Economic Debate* (Cambridge, 2007), pp. 62–88.
50. e.g. B. Templar, *Reading Lessons in Social Economy (for use in schools)* (1862); J. E. T. Rogers, *Social Economy: a Series of Lessons for the Upper Classes of Primary Schools* (1871); Florence Fenwick Miller, *Readings in Social Economy* (1883); H. Martineau, cited in Howe, *Liberal England*, pp. 31, 32.
51. R. Gilmour, 'The Gradgrind School: Political Economy in the Classroom', *Victorian Studies* 11 (1967–8), 207–24.

52. A. Celikkol, *Romances of Free Trade* (New York, 2011).
53. A. Kadish and K. Tribe, *The Market for Political Economy* (London, 1993); K. Tribe, 'Political Economy and the Science of Economics' in M. Daunton, ed., *The Organization of Knowledge in Victorian Britain* (Oxford, 2002), pp. 115–37.
54. R. McKibbin, 'Why Was There No Marxism in Great Britain?', *English Historical Review* 99 (1984), 297–331; M. Daunton and F. Trentmann, eds., *Worlds of Political Economy* (Houndmills, 2004), p. 3.
55. Garnett, 'Political and Domestic Economy', p. 222.
56. Typically, Onslow, *Times*, 25 October 1861.
57. Cited in *Birmingham Daily Post*, 3 August 1860.
58. H CLXXIV 1116, 15 April 1864.
59. A. Howe, 'Free Trade and its Enemies' in M. Hewitt ed., *The Victorian World* (Abingdon, 2012), pp. 108–24.
60. B. H. Brown, *The Tariff Reform Movement in Great Britain 1881–1895* (New York, 1943); A. Howe and M. Duckenfield, eds., *Battles over Free Trade Vol. III: The Challenge of Economic Nationalism, 1879–1939* (London, 2008), pp. 1–44.
61. Howe, *Liberal England*, pp. 129–39.
62. A. Howe, 'Towards "The Hungry Forties": Free Trade in Britain, c. 1880–1906' in E. F. Biagini, ed., *Citizenship and Community: Liberals, Radicals and Collective Identities in the British Isles, 1865–1931* (Cambridge, 1996), pp. 193–218.
63. Howe, *Liberal England*, pp. 204–13; Trentmann, *Free Trade Nation*, pp. 154–61.
64. McKibbin, 'Why Was There No Marxism?'
65. M. Daunton, *Trusting Leviathan* (Cambridge, 2001).
66. Howe, *Liberal England*, pp. 238, 251; Trentmann, *Free Trade Nation*, pp. 65–6, 151–2.
67. To Michel Chevalier, 7 November 1858, *The Letters of Richard Cobden Vol. III, 1854–1859*, eds. A. Howe and S. J. Morgan (Oxford, 2012), p. 405.
68. S.G. Checkland, 'The Birmingham Economists', *Economic History Review* 1 (1948), 1–19.
69. For example, the anti-free trader, J. Roberts, *The Cormorant of Threadneedle Street* (London, 1875).
70. T. Alborn, 'Money's Worth: Morality, Class, Politics' in Hewitt, *Victorian World*, pp. 209–24; M. Daunton, 'Britain and Globalisation since 1850. I. Creating a Global Order, 1850–1914', *Transactions of the Royal Historical Society* 16 (2006), 1–38.
71. Although excluded here, this challenge came far sooner within the discourse of Irish nationalism, for not only had Ireland in the 1840s developed its own critique of political economy in the protectionist works of Isaac Butt but the idea of Home Rule carried with it the desire to reshape an 'Irish' economy, within its own customs boundaries, and offer protection to its own infant industries.
72. F. Trentmann, 'Wealth versus Welfare: the British Left between Free Trade and National Political Economy before the First World War', *Historical Research* 70 (1997), 70–98.
73. Trentmann, *Free Trade Nation*, p. 78.
74. B. Semmel, *Imperialism and Social Reform* (London, 1960); G. M. Koot, *English Historical Economics, 1870–1926* (Cambridge, 1987); E. H. H. Green, *The Crisis of Conservatism* (London, 1995); Winch, *Wealth and Life*.

75. P. Cain, 'Wealth, Power and Empire' in P. K. O'Brien and A. Clesse, eds., *Two Hegemonies: Britain, 1846–1914 and the United States 1841–2001* (Aldershot, 2002), pp. 106–115; idem, 'The Economic Philosophy of Constructive Imperialism' in C. Navari, ed., *British Politics and the Spirit of the Age* (Keele, 1996); B. Porter, *The Absent-Minded Imperialists* (Oxford, 2005), pp. 231–3.

76. J. Thompson, '"Pictorial lies"? Posters and Politics in Britain, 1880–1914', *Past and Present* 197 (2007), 177–210; Trentmann, *Free Trade Nation*, pp. 92–5.

77. G.R. Searle, *A New England? Peace and War, 1886–1918* (Oxford, 2004), p. 343.

78. Howe, *Liberal England*, p. 235.

79. See esp. A. Marrison, *British Business and Protection, 1903–1932* (Oxford, 1996) on the work of the 'expert' Tariff Commission.

80. For the language of 'tariff war', see Howe and Duckenfield, *Battles over Free Trade*, pp. 77–114.

81. Tariff Reform League, *Speakers' Handbook*, 2nd edn (London, December 1904), p. 9.

82. See D. Bell, *The Idea of Greater Britain* (Princeton, 2007).

83. F. Trentmann, 'National Identity and Consumer Politics: Free Trade and Tariff Reform' in D. Winch and P. O'Brien, eds., *The Political Economy of British Historical Experience, 1688–1914* (Oxford, 2002), pp. 215–40.

84. Trentmann, *Free Trade Nation*, pp. 70–80, 229.

85. A. Howe, 'Free Trade and International Order: the Anglo-American tradition, 1846–1946' in F. Leventhal and R. Quinault, eds., *Anglo-American Attitudes* (Aldershot, 2000), p. 149.

86. See Trentmann, 'National Identity and Consumer Politics'.

87. J.M. Hobson and C. Tyler, eds., *Selected Writings of John A. Hobson, 1932–1938* (Abingdon, 2011), p. 213.

88. J. Cobden-Unwin, *The Hungry-Forties* (1904); for its genesis and impact, Howe, *Liberal England*, p. 259; Trentmann, *Free Trade Nation*, pp. 39–41.

89. cf. Snowden and others, Trentmann, 'Wealth versus Welfare', 78–82.

90. Howe, *Liberal England*, pp. 266–73; Trentmann, *Free Trade Nation*, pp. 3–5, 15.

91. M. Johnson, 'The Liberal Party and the Navy League in Britain before the Great War', *Twentieth-Century British History* 22 (2011), 137–63.

92. M. Ceadel, *Living the Great Illusion: Sir Norman Angell, 1872–1967* (Oxford, 2009).

93. *Inter alia*, J. S. Partington, *Building Cosmopolis: the Political Thought of H. G. Wells* (Aldershot, 2003).

94. M. Gilbert, *Churchill and America* (London, 2005), pp. 46–7; R. Rempel, 'Conflicts and Change in Liberal Theory and Practice, 1890–1918: the Case of Bertrand Russell' in P. J. Waller, ed., *Politics and Social Change in Modern Britain* (Brighton, 1987), pp. 117–39.

95. *Free Trade Nation*, p. 183.

96. Semmel, *Imperialism*, pp. 83–97.

97. Winch, *Wealth and Life*, pp. 271–88.

98. See also P. Laity, *The British Peace Movement, 1870–1914* (Oxford, 2001); A.J.A. Morris, *Radicalism against War, 1906–1914* (London, 1972).

99. A. J. Taylor, 'Richard Cobden, J. E. Thorold Rogers and Henry George' in Cragoe and Readman, *Land Question*, pp. 146–66; Trentmann, 'Wealth versus Welfare' notes the frequent use of Rogers by the nascent labour movement, p.75 n. 14.

100. *The Times*, 23 July 1912.
101. A. Taylor, *Lords of Misrule* (Basingstoke, 2004), pp. 45–72.
102. J. Cobden-Unwin, *The Land Hunger* (1912); more generally, I. Packer, *Lloyd George, Liberalism and the Land* (Woodbridge, 2001); P. Readman, *Land and Nation in England, 1880–1914* (Woodbridge, 2008).
103. For example, see Sylvia Farnell, wife of the rector of Exeter College, 'To British Housewives', *The Times*, 20 February 1926; Trentmann, *Free Trade Nation*, pp. 229–40.
104. *The Times*, 3 June 1908, 2 June 1905.

6
Democracy

Robert Saunders

In 1897, the publishing house Blackie and Son launched a series of volumes on 'The Victorian Era'.[1] Promising to assess 'the chief movements of our age', its inaugural volume was dedicated to 'The Rise of Democracy'.[2] The theme was well chosen. As Erskine May had written in 1877, 'no political question of the present time excites more profound interest than the progress of Democracy', or the forms it might take in decades to come.[3] Democracy was the spectre haunting Europe, a 'great and unwieldy force which is advancing upon us in so many shapes, and of which we are all asking whence it came, whither it is taking us, and what we are to do with it'.[4]

The 'rise of democracy' has long been a central narrative of Victorian scholarship, though historians have been more likely to invoke the term than to define it. This is a pity, as the word has enjoyed a strange and perhaps unique career. For most of the century it was a term of rebuke – deployed, in a positive sense, only by the most violent popular radicals. Even John Bright, the self-styled 'tribune of the people', told an audience in 1882 that 'I do not pretend myself to be a Democrat; I never accepted that title, and ... those who knew me and spoke honestly of me never applied it to me'.[5] By 1914, in contrast, democracy was the common currency of political rhetoric. The First World War was commonly narrated as a struggle for democracy, and the Conservatives built their hegemony after 1918 on the defence of democratic values.[6] In less than a century, a word that once enjoyed pariah status had established itself as a universal principle, to which all parties made obeisance.

Britain's democratic history is commonly viewed as a conversion process: a slow surrender to modernity in which Britain 'became' a democracy. Yet such a narrative overstates the transformation in ideas and misrepresents the relationship between concepts and institutions. It implies that 'democracy' was a constant, to which governments gradually adapted themselves, rather than a vessel in which different meanings could be stored. Yet 'democracy', as a word, had no stable meaning. At different times and in different hands, it could be a social class, a form of government or a condition of society. Across the Atlantic, it was a political party; and contemporaries slid uneasily between different usages. As John Morley complained in 1867,

> Old ladies, if you tell them that democracy is coming on apace, think dreamily of the guillotine and Marie Antoinette. Others suppose in a vague way that its arrival will cause Mr Gladstone [and] Mr Disraeli...to chew tobacco, and to shoot at one another across the House with revolvers.[7]

Over the nineteenth century, politicians of all parties became fluent in the language of democracy; but they were not passive worshippers at the democratic shrine. By wrapping themselves in the democratic mantle, they were claiming the right to define what democracy was and to label their opponents as its enemies. This opened new battlefields for democratic debate, from Ireland and the Empire to socialism and Home Rule.

This chapter explores the language of democracy from 1832 to 1914. It begins with the changing meaning of democracy as a word, charting the elision of social and political usages and its growing association with the franchise. It then considers the relationship between democracy and 'reform', and the attempt to find forms of representation that were 'popular' but not 'democratic'. Finally, it assesses the growing willingness of politicians from all parties to take up the language of democracy – and to bend it to their own political purposes. Words are never simply descriptive, least of all in a parliamentary system that privileges rhetorical exchange. Political rhetoric is purposeful, rather than analytical; it is a weapon against opponents and a source of authority, and it structures understandings of the world that create or shut down political space. The definition of terms is inherently a political act and always serves political ends. Democracy was not a fixed principle but a word in progress, shaped as much by the needs of party warfare as by the teachings of classical literature. In the long negotiation between democracy and party politics, it was not only Britain's parliamentary institutions that were transformed.

Defining democracy

Like so many political concepts, 'democracy' had its origins in the ancient world. That classical inheritance was a constant presence in the British imagination, though it served rather as a reference than as a model. Located in small, city states, with a radically different structure of classes, the ancient democracies could not easily be mapped onto a modern, industrial society; and, in this respect, Athens was less an object of emulation than a well of useful concepts. Nor could the institutions of France or America be transferred directly onto British society. It was axiomatic, in Victorian thought, that institutions must be adapted to geography, climate and social organisation. The prospects for democracy in Britain could not be read off, in any straightforward manner, either from classical texts or from its modern exemplars.

At its simplest, 'democracy' meant 'the rule of the *demos*': a system in which 'the democracy' held preponderant power; but whether this meant the government of the *poor* or the government of the *many* was a much debated point.[8] Lord John Russell spoke in 1852 of 'the democracy of this country – meaning by that term the people of this country'; but the term was also used in a more limited sense, to denote 'the humbler citizens of a State'.[9] The Protectionist writer, J.W. Croker, applied it specifically to the industrial classes, protesting that an 'astonished country' was ruled by a 'tyrant democracy'.[10] Writing in 1897, John Holland Rose complained of the 'slipshod' use of the term 'to denote the *wage-earning classes*'; yet his near contemporary, the socialist Brougham Villiers, used it as a synonym for 'the working-class elector'.[11] Frederic Rogers described democracy in 1878 as 'the government of the numerical majority', yet Leonard Hobhouse insisted in 1904 that it was 'the government which best expresses the community as a whole'. Majoritarianism, for Hobhouse, was simply a rough test of democracy, to be operated under definite constraints.[12]

If it was unclear who constituted the '*demos*', there was further disagreement over the nature of its 'rule'. The ancient democracies had been self-governing in the most literal sense, with citizens gathering in the marketplace for the transaction of public business. That was clearly impractical in the modern state, so radicals often eschewed the term in favour of 'republicanism'. In the 1830s, the *Poor Man's Guardian* routinely described itself as 'democratic', meaning by this that it spoke for the *demos*. Yet it disclaimed any aspirations towards 'democracy', which it took to mean 'direct legislation by the people'. As it declared in 1834, 'the government we look for in England is not a democracy, but a representative republic based on universal suffrage'.[13] Others, however, used the term in a more novel sense, to connote a state in which 'the right of voting...belongs to a majority of the nation'.[14] Democracy, on this reading, described the location of sovereignty rather than the composition of government, a distinction unfamiliar to the classical mind.

This owed much to the United States, which was slowly usurping the ancient world as the standard democratic reference. Operating on a continental scale and in a liberal political culture, the United States was more plausible as a model for Britain's own institutions; and its apparent success challenged images of democracy as poor, volatile and of short duration. At least until the 1850s, the most chauvinistic observer could not deny that America was stable, prosperous and devout; and even Russell thought it 'the only country which I would at all compare with this for the enjoyment of liberty'.[15] If the United States affirmed the viability of democracy in modern society, it also entrenched the relationship between democracy and a popular franchise. This owed much to the rise of the 'Democratic Party', more commonly known simply as 'the Democracy'. A consciously demotic movement, Jacksonian 'Democracy' bound together thousands of ordinary voters through a system of 'tickets' and 'platforms', mobilising 'the democracy' of the United States against 'plutocrats', 'usurers' and other 'aristocratic' forces. Its rise was both cause and consequence of the collapse of property qualifications, affirming the connection between democratic politics and mass voting.

Yet democracy was not simply an alien growth, acting on British politics from without. Britain itself was thought to possess a 'mixed constitution', in which monarchy, aristocracy and democracy were 'so combined and blended as to form the most perfect system of government'.[16] The 'mixed constitution' was one of the central inheritances of Hanoverian political thought, but this concealed important differences on what was meant by the idea. For William Blackstone, whose *Commentaries on the Laws of England* became a foundational political text, the House of Commons was the democratic agency, operating in creative tension with the monarch and the aristocratic chamber. The Swiss jurist Jean Louis de Lolme, by contrast, played down the role of elective institutions, identifying the 'democratical' features of the constitution as 'trial by jury' and 'liberty of the press'. These practices, he believed, made Britain 'a more democratical state than any other', despite its attenuated franchise.[17]

At the heart of the mixed constitution was the notion of balance, with each part acting as a constraint upon the others. It was this delicate equilibrium that formed the central excellence of the constitution. By moderating 'the collision of antagonist powers', it prevented civil discord; by giving to all classes a voice in the constitution, it secured a genuinely universal representation; and its system of mutual checks offered the best security for freedom.[18] This had two important consequences for democratic thought. In the first instance, it shrank the space for democracy by occupying much of the same intellectual terrain.[19] Critics of democracy were not feudal bigots, beating back against the tide of freedom and progress; they saw themselves as the guardians of popular liberty against class rule and absolutism. Secondly, it presented democratisation, not as an expansion of the liberal portions of the constitution but as a threat to the very equipoise that made freedom possible. By vesting power in a single class, democracy would be *less* representative of the varied interests that composed British society. It would offer less security for freedom and increase the danger of political conflict.

Democracy rising

The 'mixed constitution' held a central place in the Victorian imagination, but its achievement was inherently fragile. The forces operating within that constitution were fluid and intangible, so the balance between them was always precarious. In the eighteenth century, it had been monarchical power that caused most anxiety. By the mid-nineteenth century, it was the democratic tide that seemed most obviously in flood. This was not just a matter of legislation. As *Fraser's Magazine* noted in 1849:

> No political institutions ever devised by the ingenuity of man, have been so democratic in their tendency as the steam-engine with all its manifold appliances. Railroads, the penny-post, the electric telegraph, have all lent assistance to develope [*sic*] the same democratic element.[20]

Drawing on Tocqueville's *Democracy in America*, commentators emphasised the role of 'mechanical inventions' and 'the spread of popular education'.[21] Railways, libraries and the penny post could all be seen as democratic forces, because they homogenised experience and opened 'to all what was once but the privilege of the few'.[22] Sir Henry Ward, quoting Jules Michelet, thought mass production the 'most powerful agent of democracy', because it brought 'within the reach of the poor many objects of comfort, luxury, and even elegance'.[23] The growth of the press, too, was credited with an 'addition of enormous moment to the influence of the democracy on the action of the legislature'. Its operation, thought the *Quarterly Review*, had transformed the relationship between Parliament and people, and threatened 'to change every other form of government into a democracy'.[24]

In this usage, democracy was not a political aspiration but a social dynamic. *Fraser's* argued that the 'increased power of democracy' was 'little, if at all, to be attributed to the Reform-act; that was a manifestation of a power already existing and gave little, perhaps we may correctly say, no increase to it'.[25] *The Sporting Gazette* found more evidence of democracy on the race-track than in the reform under discussion in 1866. There was 'more danger of the inroad of democracy through disregard of the particular social scale of the Turf', it warned, 'than in twenty such Reform Bills'.[26]

Alongside this organic movement, however, critics identified a more deliberate assault on the constitutional balance. *The Standard*, a Tory paper, distinguished in 1841 between what it called 'a natural and a spurious democracy':

> The growth of the natural democracy in a civilised country is like all the great processes of nature, perfected slowly, and by an unseen operation, and beneficial in its completion. The spurious democracy is the work of man, and like most of the works of man, the effect of a hurried and noisy effort for a temporary, and often an useless or pernicious, purpose.[27]

This democratic insurgency was by no means restricted to legislation. It was to be found in trade union action, religious voluntarism and the tide of popular protest. Yet decisions at Westminster could accelerate or retard the democratic advance, a recognition that vested all kinds of controversies with democratic significance. When repeal of the Corn Laws was under discussion in 1845–6, both sides projected themselves as bulwarks against democracy. For Sir James Graham, repeal offered the best chance 'of surviving...this odious and endless topic of democratic agitation', by stripping radicalism of its most potent 'cry'. Croker, by contrast, expected repeal to 'encourage, increase, and render irresistible, democratic agitation', augmenting the 'democratic power' of the towns and impoverishing the aristocracy.[28]

Other issues could also be read in democratic terms. Gladstone's civil service reforms in 1854 struck critics as 'an immense stride towards Self-Government in the democratic sense' – first, in the expectation that they would admit a different class to government; and second, in the belief that they would weaken the power of the executive. Gladstone was also accused of 'democratic finance' in his 1860 budget, which, by abolishing the paper duty, facilitated the expansion of the press and provoked a collision between 'popular' interests and the House of Lords. In 1876, his campaign against 'the Bulgarian Horrors' was hailed as a 'bold appeal to democratic sentiment'. By mobilising public opinion to overrule the decisions of ministers, he had given 'the first serious impulse to democratic interference with the conduct of foreign affairs'.[29]

Yet if electoral reform was not the only arena for democratic controversy, it rapidly emerged as the most important – if only because it was here that the constitutional balance was most obviously under negotiation. Even in these debates, the franchise was not necessarily the crucial ingredient. The central issue in 1832 was the redistribution of seats, which was at least as effective a mechanism for reallocating power. The increased urban representation, warned *The Age*, would 'deprive the aristocracy of all power and influence', exerting 'a more democratic tendency...than the enactment of universal suffrage'. The metropolitan Members, in particular, would constitute 'a great accession to the democratical strength'.[30] The redistribution, critics claimed, was democratic in principle as well as in effect, for it made 'population the standard rather than education or property'. By reducing the power of ministers over the Commons, the Bill would transform the relationship between Crown and legislature, converting 'our limited Monarchy into a purely democratic Government'.[31]

Even in later reform debates, when the franchise was more obviously central, there was no necessary connection between enfranchisement and democracy. The leading reformers within Parliament – like Russell and Gladstone – were emphatically not democrats, and commonly saw reform as a preservative against democracy. Conversely, an extended franchise offered no guarantee of democratic influence. Brougham Villiers claimed that there was no 'civilised country in the world where there is less democracy than in the United States', because of the strength of plutocracy.[32] But if a popular suffrage was not a sufficient condition for democracy, it was increasingly recognised as its most plausible instrument – a change that owed much to the influence of Chartism.

Chartist democracy

The 1830s saw a wave of 'democratic' organisations, modelled either on the Democratic Party in America or on the French Jacobin clubs. The most important was the London Democratic Association (LDA), founded on the birthday of Thomas Paine in 1837. Its title was both a tribute to the Jacobin tradition and a statement of class identity, eschewing cooperation with middle-class reformers in favour of an 'organisation of the proletarian classes'. 'No man is too poor to unite with us', it boasted; 'the poorer, the more oppressed, the more welcome'. Its programme paired constitutional reform with such measures as an eight-hour day and repeal of the New Poor Law. As George Julian Harney noted, 'We are generally branded as levellers'; a charge to which he was 'proud to plead guilty'.[33]

The LDA was an important influence on Chartism, whose rhetoric was steeped in the language of democracy.[34] Though the word did not appear in either the Charter or the National Petitions, it was ubiquitous in other Chartist publications. Lecturers addressed their audiences as 'Fellow Democrats' or as 'Brother and Sister Democrats', and printed material also used these forms.[35] This was a class identity, as much as a political programme: Chartists were 'democrats' because they were 'friends of the people', not simply because they favoured the Charter. Feargus O'Connor, whose family claimed descent from the high kings of Ireland, boasted of being 'promoted from the ranks of the aristocracy to a commission in the democracy' – a claim to which he gave visual expression by adopting the fustian suit of the working man.[36]

Chartist democracy envisaged a totalising process of moral and political regeneration, part of a historical process in which all obstacles to the moral, social and political development of the people were overcome. In a democratic riposte to the Whig histories of Macaulay and Russell, the Chartist lecturer Edmund Stallwood hailed

the great and growing progress of democracy during the last twenty years; embracing the Combination Act – the struggle for Reform in Parliament – the war of the unstamped Press – the starting and establishment of the NORTHERN STAR – the improvements as regards the employment of women in mines and collieries – the establishment of the right of the people to hold public meetings.[37]

This was a vision of democracy stretching far beyond the franchise. Henry Vincent insisted that '*thought* is *Democracy*', while Harney warned the 'puny Canutes' who sought 'to arrest the progress of democracy' that 'the ocean of intellect will move on'.[38] As a Chartist poet exulted,

Vain are the efforts of the human mind

To fetter reason or to chain the wind ...
As well might kings the stars take down by force
Or stop the torrent in its rapid course
As bind the men, determined to be free,
Or check the progress of Democracy.[39]

Enfranchisement, then, was not the only component of democracy; but it was commonly identified as its principal weapon. The Reform Act had disillusioned the Chartists with virtual representation, ensuring that direct, personal enfranchisement would be central to their democratic programme. Universal male suffrage was hailed as 'the birth-right of every man under a pure democratic government', the first of 'those great principles of democracy embodied in the People's Charter'.[40] The *Chartist Circular* used the terms almost interchangeably, demanding 'Universal Suffrage, or democracy if you choose'.[41] Democracy meant 'the right of every society to choose its own governors', exerted through millions of independent suffrages.[42]

Chartist democracy bound together three distinct phenomena: an exclusive organisation of the working classes; universal male suffrage; and a common identity with 'democratic' movements abroad. The *Northern Star* reported regularly on 'The Progress of Democracy' in France, Italy and Germany. Headlines like 'The French Republic – Glorious Progress of Democracy' and 'Progress of Democracy in Prussia' linked Chartism to Continental movements 'for the establishment of a Democratic and Social Republic'.[43] In its strongest form, this placed Chartism squarely within the revolutionary tradition. The Irish nationalist John Mitchel boasted in 1848 that

> Democracy had crossed the Alps and entered Austria. Last week he was in Paris, and there was smashed the strongest dynasty in the world. (Loud applause.) He would presently come to Ireland. (Cheers.) 300,000 Englishmen, Chartists, would assemble in London next week, and then they would have London in their hands.[44]

All this had an important effect on high political understandings of democracy, which were increasingly defined by reference to the Chartist programme.[45] Chartism associated 'democracy' with a rejectionist political ideology, standing in opposition to the existing constitution. Viewed from without, its defining features appeared to be class exclusivity, revolutionary violence and a majoritarian suffrage that abdicated the task of negotiating between competing interests. Like the Chartists themselves, critics commonly viewed the movement as part of an international democratic insurgency, linking the constitutional agitation in Britain to revolutionary movements abroad.[46] Democracy was also thought to be an absolutist form of government, in the same category as absolute monarchy. As *Punch* told its readers in 1867, the 'Democrat bows down to a sovereign people as basely as the Tory did to a sovereign lord'. They were as 'alike as the North Pole and the South; and each is equally remote from the Temperate Zone'.[47]

Democracy and reform

This has implications for the reform debate, which re-emerged as a parliamentary question after 1848.[48] It is tempting to think of 'reformers' and 'democrats' as travellers on the same road; moving, at greater or lesser speed, down the path to universal suffrage. Yet this was not the intention of reformers within Parliament. Russell, who sponsored reform bills in 1852, 1854, 1860 and 1866, was a convinced anti-democrat who thought universal suffrage 'the grave of all temperate liberty, and the parent of tyranny and licence'.[49] Benjamin Disraeli, who steered the Second Reform Act onto the statute book, insisted that 'we do not live, and I trust it will never be the fate of this country to live, under a democracy'.[50] They saw their task as preserving and extending a model that was superior to democracy – a 'mixed constitution' that was both more modern and more sophisticated than its democratic rival.

A poorly conceived reform might, of course, collapse into democracy, and this was a prospect that hung over every reform debate of the period. In consequence, the allegation that a reform bill had democratic tendencies became the tactic of choice for critics of these measures. 'If you establish a democracy', warned Disraeli in 1859, 'you must in due season reap the fruits of a democracy', a hideous cocktail of plunder, confiscation and despotism.[51] During the 1866 reform debates, Robert Lowe elided the social connotations of democracy with the £7 franchise proposed by Gladstone and Russell:

> *Democracy* you may have at any time. Night and day the gate is open that leads to that *bare and level plain*, where every ant's nest is a mountain and every thistle a forest tree. But *a Government* such as England has, ... this is a thing which ... once lost, we cannot recover.[52]

Thomas Carlyle, likewise, denounced reform as 'the Niagara leap of completed democracy'; yet his definition was social rather than political.

Democracy meant 'swarmery': 'any man equal to any other; Quashee Nigger to Socrates or Shakspeare [sic]; Judas Iscariot to Jesus Christ'.[53] By eliding the proposed franchise with social revolution, such claims sought to discredit reform by association. Their usage of democracy was strategic, rather than descriptive, at a time when the American Civil War and the dictatorship of Napoleon III had left the reputation of democracy at a low ebb. To call a bill 'democratic' was to identify it as 'un-English', threatening the 'Americanisation' of British institutions. As a Liberal newspaper protested in 1865,

> The word democracy has been artfully used by the enemies of reform. They have been careful to make it represent dire political ills, so that the timid, who might be disposed to admit of the justice of giving labour a voice in the people's chamber, should be deterred by a dread of some vague disaster.[54]

Far from contesting the reputation of democracy, reformers promised to 'popularise' the constitution 'without democratising it', a goal to which every reform bill of this period aspired.[55]

The Conservative achievement in 1867 was to persuade MPs that a rating franchise presented the best bulwark against democracy. Because it linked the franchise to the payment of local taxes, rather than to any particular sum of rent, it 'contained no steps, as in a value franchise, by which we can descend insensibly to the despotism of a pure democracy'.[56] *The Standard* assured its readers that 'No suffrage confined to *bonâ fide* ratepayers will ever become ... a democracy', while *The Day* called rating 'the only *permanent* barrier we can erect against democracy'.[57] As *Blackwood's* observed, the opposition of Bright proved that the bill was 'the reverse of democratic'; 'if the measure was democratic', the radical leader 'would heartily applaud it'. The new electorate, it suggested, might even be more 'aristocratic' in its sympathies than the class enfranchised in 1832: 'A steady, well-to-do working man, if he only keep himself free from the bondage of Trades-unions, is far more likely to vote as we could wish him to do, than an arrogant, Church-hating, and *democratic* £10 Dissenter.'[58]

Becoming democrats

Hopes that 1867 would erect a bulwark against democracy led to a swift disappointment. The Reform Act admitted far more voters than anticipated and numbers continued to climb over the following decade.

Propelled by party competition and changes in the rating system, the number of votes had reached 3.6 million by 1880, up from 859,000 in 1865 and 2.3 million in 1868.[59] Parliament was soon debating household suffrage for the counties, and in 1880 a Liberal government was elected with a commitment to further reform. MPs had little doubt that this would involve another 'large accession of power to ... the democratic element', or that they would soon be 'face to face with a great democratic constituency'.[60]

The Second Reform Act would come to be seen as a watershed in Britain's democratic history.[61] Yet its impact on political rhetoric was of course more subtle. In the immediate aftermath of 1867, politicians of all parties continued to distance themselves from democracy. A Liberal MP assured his colleagues that 'So long as the majority of the House was elected by classes altogether above the working classes, there would be no fear of the democratic power becoming omnipotent.' Disraeli himself, noting the exclusion of two-thirds of adult males, added dryly that this was 'not quite the form which an overpowering democracy assumes'.[62] Strikingly, however, both took as their point of comparison, not 'democracy' as such, but 'an *overpowering* democracy' in which 'the democratic power' was 'omnipotent'. The shift in emphasis was significant. If household suffrage had not made Britain '*a* democracy', it had clearly increased the weight of '*the* democracy'. In this respect, the Reform Act had been democratic in *tendency*, for it had swollen the influence of what was still widely called 'the democratic section' of the constituency.[63] Writing in 1883, Lord Salisbury identified a revolution in the balance of power. A century ago, he observed, 'the control of the machine was largely shared by the Crown and the aristocracy. Now it is entirely in the hands of the democracy.'[64]

That perception caused some dismay. Debating the Irish Land Bill in 1870, Tories accused the government of acting 'not for the good of Ireland' but in such a way as to 'secure the democratic vote'.[65] Sir John Pakington denounced the abolition of army purchase as 'a sop to democracy', while Salisbury accused ministers of doing whatever 'would catch the democratic breeze'.[66] The most bitter attack came from the Duke of Somerset, who accused Gladstone of having 'condescended to lick the very dust off the feet of democracy'.[67] Nor was the Conservative Party immune from such allegations, especially once it embarked on a programme of social reform. George Goschen lamented that the 'Conservative working man has been proved to exist ... but he coerces Conservative Members in a democratic direction. The whole attitude of the Conservative Party has been entirely changed ... by the Act of 1867.'[68]

Yet the assumption that 'the democracy' was now preponderant naturally encouraged a more respectful treatment of that cohort. First into the field were the members for great towns, who proudly announced themselves as representatives of the 'urban democracy'.[69] Radicals looked forward to a democratic millennium in which both Whig and Tory would be swept aside, clearing the way for new land taxes, a progressive income tax, disestablishment of the Church of England and abolition of the House of Lords.[70] Home Rulers appealed openly 'to the newly-enfranchised Democracy', convinced that 'the democratic constituencies of the country will not allow [ministers] to govern an enfranchised nation by force'.[71]

To their surprise, they found themselves contesting that terrain with a new generation of Tory populists. In 1874 the Conservative Party won its first parliamentary majority in 33 years, and 'the democracy' returned Unionist majorities at both the elections following Liberal Home Rule bills. There was, it appeared, a 'Tory democracy' in the constituencies, 'a democracy which has embraced the principles of the Tory party'.[72] Denoting a cohort, rather than a programme, the term was to become chiefly associated with Lord Randolph Churchill, though the first politician to apply it to a national election appears to have been A.B. Forwood. Contesting the Liverpool by-election in 1882, Forwood described himself as a 'Democratic Tory', meaning by this 'that I rely upon the people and I believe in their Conservative instincts'.[73] Churchill himself used the phrase sparingly, and his tendency to slither between 'it' and 'they' was expressive of his own uncertainty as to precisely what he meant by the idea. The term was to prove most serviceable in the power struggle within the Conservative Party itself. Drawing on a long-standing distinction in military parlance between the 'aristocracy' of the officer class and the 'democracy' of the ranks, Churchill projected himself as the champion of the party membership, pitting the 'democracy' of the National Union of Conservative Associations against an 'aristocratic' Central Committee.[74]

After the Unionist landslide in 1886, Conservatives became increasingly confident in their appeals to 'the democracy'. Debating Irish coercion in 1887, Colonel Bridgeman boasted that 'the Ministerial Members may claim to represent the Democracy of England with quite as much justice as the Opposition'; while Arthur Balfour insisted that 'the democracy of this country are as firmly determined as Her Majesty's Government to see that ... law and justice shall prevail'.[75] Paying a remarkable tribute to 'that democracy which we all serve, and whose interests are first with all of us', Balfour proclaimed himself 'a better democrat' than any radical.[76]

Tariff reformers, too, claimed that 'a democracy invariably gravitated towards Protection'.[77] Baffled Liberals concluded that the voters had in some way been deceived, and drew strained distinctions between 'what you call a Tory democracy, which you have for the time being managed to manufacture for your own particular Party purposes', and 'the genuine democracy, the people themselves'.[78] Conservatives retorted 'that the democracy are far too intelligent to be led aside by such statements'.[79] By the 1890s, the most striking feature of democratic commentary was its gushing tone. Hailing the jubilee in 1897, the Liberal Unionist Alfred Lyttelton celebrated a monarch whose 'reign had seen the establishment of the power of democracy'.[80] William Harcourt congratulated Victoria for approving 'measure after measure of democratic reform', while Salisbury applauded a reign in which the 'impulse of democracy...has made itself felt fully'.[81] When the Duke of Northumberland expressed revulsion for democracy in 1911, he was treated with derision: 'noble Lords smile', he noted; 'others raise their eyebrows. I quite expected that. It is a very unpopular sentiment in these days'.[82]

This is not to say that fears of democracy had evaporated. Within Parliament, men like Charles Newdegate and Charles Warton continued to castigate 'the tyranny of democracy', with its insistence on 'counting noses, irrespective of position, wealth, or intelligence'.[83] Learned journals and publications lamented 'the new tyranny of democratic despotism', and insisted that 'Democracy, founded on a basis of false and self-contradictory theory, can never in practice prove a satisfactory system of government'.[84] Privately, even Harcourt thought the Third Reform Act 'a frightfully democratic measure which I confess appals me'.[85] However, elected politicians, whose fortunes now lay in the hands of 'the democracy', proved wary of public criticism. Attacks on 'the democracy' were less common in the third reform debates than in 1867, and there was less attempt to bundle together the pathologies associated with a mass franchise under a common 'democratic' label.

On the contrary, those who feared the consequences of reform increasingly appealed to democracy as their principle. Even Newdegate, warning against rule by 'ignorance' and 'popular impulse', invoked 'the democracy of reason' in support of a limited, educated constituency.[86] Enthusiasts for proportional representation, anxious to safeguard the representation of all classes and interests, insisted that the '*true* principle of democracy is the government of the people by the whole people equally represented, not the government of the people by a majority of the people exclusively represented'. Joseph Cowen assured MPs that 'In the vocabulary of *genuine* democracy, the people means not a majority, but the entire body of the citizens. It means not merely the landless, but the landed – not only the leisured, but the labouring classes'.[87] This was part of a wider attempt to strip 'democracy' of its class connotations. Commending the Local Government Bill in 1888, Walter Long insisted that 'No one class was favoured more than another' by its provisions. 'It was a democratic Bill'.[88]

By such means, it was possible to reconcile democracy with principles that had previously been marshalled in opposition to it. If democracy meant the representation of all classes, not simply the *demos*, it could be viewed simply as a reworking of the 'mixed constitution'.[89] Democracy could also be integrated with the idea of an 'ancient constitution', for British constitutionalism had a historicist strand that made it peculiarly susceptible to narratives of change. In Macaulay's boast, the history of England was 'emphatically the history of progress', a tale of 'constant change in the institutions of a great society'.[90] For Russell, likewise, it was

> a part of the practical wisdom of our ancestors, to alter and vary the form of our institutions as they went on; to suit them to the circumstances of the time, and reform them according to the dictates of experience. They never ceased to work upon our frame of government, as a sculptor fashions the model of a favourite statue.[91]

From this perspective, the expansion of the suffrage could be viewed not as the agent of democratisation but as a wise response to it. Erskine May told his readers in 1877 that democracy was 'a principle or force, and not simply an institution'; a social dynamic with the force of a 'natural law'.[92] Salisbury, too, identified 'a process of political evolution' affecting 'the whole western-world'. It was 'as useless to repine at this process, as to repine because we are growing older'.[93] Looking back on the Reform Acts in 1912, Brougham Villiers viewed them not as 'the coming of democracy' but as 'an incident in a general movement'. Enfranchisement, he concluded, was rather a symptom of democracy than its cause, for 'the growing political consciousness of the working classes rendered it impossible permanently to exclude them'.[94]

Democratic battlegrounds

Democracy was no longer a rebel army, at war with constitutional convention. It was contested terrain, on which all parties sought to plant their standard. In consequence, what purported to be dispassionate analysis was more commonly a rhetorical land grab, mobilising the authority of democracy for political advantage. Anti-socialists, who had traditionally associated democracy with levelling tendencies, now deployed the authority of democracy against such principles. Erskine May told his readers that the 'highest ideal of a democracy' was freedom – including 'freedom of trade' and 'freedom of labour'. Lord Acton, likewise, distinguished 'the true democratic principle' from the false, in a way that emphasised the freedom of the individual from collective pressures.[95] While purporting to *describe* democracy, they were seeking instead to *define* it – in a manner that denied the term to their opponents.

As politicians competed for the support of 'the democracy', the most unlikely controversies were vested in 'democratic' language. For proponents of disestablishment, state religions were 'inconsistent with the principles of democratic Government'. For their opponents, establishment was 'the dogma of democracy', for 'as democracy extends, the work of the State expands'.[96] Legislation regulating the sale of alcohol might be 'an attempt to interfere with democratic rights' or a democratic exercise in 'government by the people'.[97] Debating the future of the Upper House, radicals insisted that a hereditary chamber was 'antagonistic to the principles of democracy'.[98] Salisbury, by contrast, used democratic theory to revive its veto power, arguing that the Commons had no right to pass contentious legislation without a popular mandate. On the principle 'that the nation is our Master' but 'the House of Commons is not', Salisbury claimed for the peers the right to resist all legislation for which there was no explicit mandate, yielding 'only when the judgement of the nation has been challenged at the polls'. His motives were overtly partisan – as he noted cheerfully, such a mandate was 'so rarely applicable as practically to place little fetter upon our independence' – but the tactic was only credible because it resonated with democratic ideas. Emboldened by success, he fabricated tests for Gladstone's Home Rule policy that were entirely of his own devising, including a requirement that all four parts of the United Kingdom vote in its favour.[99]

Democracy was also a battleground in debates about empire. Critics of empire, like the 'New Liberal' theorists L.T. Hobhouse and J.A. Hobson, drew a polarity between 'Democracy' – the 'government of the people by itself' – and 'Imperialism', or the 'government of one people by another'.[100] The two, they insisted, were ultimately incompatible, for a governing class habituated to imperial rule overseas would be impatient of democratic liberties at home.[101] Yet the assumption that democracy provided the only basis for legitimacy arguably lowered the bar for action against states that were not democratic. During the Second Boer War, Chamberlain stressed repeatedly that President Kruger's regime was 'nothing more than an oligarchy' – 'it is ridiculous to speak of it as a republic or democratic country'. The war, he insisted, was fundamentally democratic because it sought to extend the franchise to the settler population.[102] Democratic ideas could also be used to justify imperial rule where the conditions for self-government were absent. Lord Cranbrook thought it absurd to engraft 'Western institutions' onto 'Eastern civilisation', for there was 'no Democracy … no "demos"' on which such institutions could be founded.[103]

Similar debates raged around the Irish question. Hobhouse insisted that Ireland was not 'democratically governed', and warned that colonial rule in Ireland risked destroying 'the several conditions of democracy' in Britain.[104] Others doubted whether democracy was even possible in Ireland, a country which lacked 'the manly self-reliance of free citizens, and where the democratic sentiment of social equality is almost entirely wanting'.[105] Chamberlain, like Bright, invoked the United States as proof that democracies need not permit a right of secession. America, he proclaimed, offered 'the greatest Democracy the world has ever seen, and a Democracy which has known how to fight in order to maintain its union'.[106]

Democracy was also invoked in suffrage debates. Before 1918, the franchise never encompassed more than 60 per cent of adult men, and those votes were distributed unevenly between constituencies. This caused less disquiet than might have been expected, for power could be vested in 'the democracy' without each individual possessing a vote. Ramsay MacDonald thought the 'modern state' 'democratic' despite these exclusions; for if 'the masses of ordinary people are agreed on any policy, neither rich electors, privileged peers, nor reigning houses could stand in their way'.[107] George Bernard Shaw, likewise, described the franchise in 1902 as 'practically Manhood Suffrage', with politicians governing 'at the request of proletarian Democracy.'[108] This assumed, however, that 'the democracy' was essentially masculine, an assumption that was coming under increasing attack. Demanding the 'feminisation of democracy', female suffragists demanded the vote as 'a question, not of sex, but of democracy'. As a campaign leaflet noted, 'Mr Asquith advocates Government without the consent of the Governed. Is this Democracy?'[109]

Asquith himself rejected that argument, insisting that 'Democracy wages war against artificial, and not against natural, discriminations'.[110] Others argued that it was precisely *because* politics was now democratic that it was unsuited to women's gifts. Women, it was acknowledged, had made great rulers in the past, but they 'did not plunge into the turmoil of elections and mob assemblies, as any one must now who takes a prominent part in public life'.[111] One of the leading anti-suffragists,

Mrs Humphry Ward, founded her whole case on a form of democratic utilitarianism. The franchise, she argued, was an instrument of social control: a means of 'transmuting the physical force of men ... into the peaceful results of the ballot-box'. Enfranchising women would break that link, driving men back to physical force for the attainment of their wishes. That would be especially dangerous when 'the most anxious care of politicians ... is to keep democracy to the use of the vote'.[112]

Even suffragists disagreed on the nature of the franchise to be introduced; and here, too, they sought the authority of democracy. Urging a rating franchise, David Shackleton argued that 'No democrat can refuse the claim that in principle taxation and representation should go together'.[113] Winston Churchill, by contrast, called such proposals 'not merely ... undemocratic' but 'anti-democratic', conceding an 'unfair representation to property, as against persons'.[114] If the beneficiaries of such a franchise were propertied women, the proposal might even dilute, rather than enhance, the power of 'the democracy'. Self-styled 'democratic suffragists' argued instead for 'adult suffrage', enfranchising 'the democracy' of both sexes.[115]

Democracy or Parliament?

The fiercest battlefield was Parliament itself. Democratic theory could provide a new legitimacy for Britain's parliamentary institutions, but it also offered a platform from which to critique them. Britain in 1900 still had a limited franchise, exercised in constituencies of varying size. Party discipline placed formidable powers in the hands of the Cabinet, and constituents had little control over Parliament between elections. By convention, voters were held to have given their consent to a whole menu of policies whose only necessary connection was their inclusion in the same manifesto. As Lord Selborne grumbled in 1913, someone who voted Conservative in opposition to Welsh Disestablishment was taken to have given a mandate for Tariff Reform, while a Liberal free trader was held to favour Home Rule.[116]

In this respect, the relationship between 'the democracy' and its elective institutions was far from exact. As Balfour noted, representation meant vesting the governing power in another's hands, in contrast to the self-government practised by the ancient democracies. The 'effect of representative government', he argued, was

to take away from the electors the large power which they would have if they were allowed to act directly in their own affairs. The only reason why we tolerate representative government – which is a departure from true democracy – is that true democracy, when dealing with large numbers, is an unworkable machine.[117]

That tension divided opinion within, as well as between, parties. The Fabian Executive Committee concluded in 1906 that 'what Democracy really means is government by the consent of the people' – *not* performed *by* the people. Government, for the Fabians, was a specialised function to be performed by experts. 'The democracy' was entitled to select those experts and to hold them to account, but it should not usurp their functions.[118] The Social Democratic Federation (SDF), by contrast, viewed Parliament as an institution whose 'very traditions are anti-democratic', designed not to represent the popular will but to frustrate it.[119] *Justice* told its readers that 'We do not believe in the parliamentary system', and demanded a plebiscitary democracy in its place.[120] 'Hitherto', wrote Russell Smart, 'our conception of popular government has been to give as many people as possible the opportunity of electing their rulers. It is now asked, Why have rulers? The people should rule.'[121]

For all its intellectual firepower, the SDF lacked the following to pose a significant threat to elective institutions. A more serious challenge came from the Conservative Party, in the years before 1914.[122] Beginning from overtly democratic principles, the Conservatives evolved a critique of Liberal parliaments after 1906 that stripped them of legitimacy and came close to authorising civil war. This had its origin in the mandate theory, by which the Lords could reject any measure not foreshadowed in a manifesto. By 1910, this had evolved into a still larger doctrine: the right to force either a dissolution or a referendum on any issue that had not been *decisive* at the polls. As the *Edinburgh Review* noted in 1910, the Peers had 'taken their stand upon a principle of democracy a good deal more advanced' than their opponents. 'The representative principle they hold cheap. They look for their "mandate" directly to the people.'[123]

When the peers voted down the budget in 1909, a Tory paper hailed them as 'better democrats than any member of the government'. They would 'abide by the will of the people ... [in] January 1910'; but they would *not* accept 'the Radical-Socialist pretence in 1909 at interpreting the will of the people as expressed in 1906'.[124] This denial of the representative credentials of the Commons, just three years into a Parliament, became central to Conservative rhetoric. Writers mined election statistics to show that, if individual votes were counted, rather than the aggregate of constituency results, there would be no Liberal majority. In this manner, even the landslide result of 1906 could be explained away or shown to have evaporated long before the next election.[125] This had two important consequences. First, it rendered the Parliament Act of 1911, by which the House of Lords was stripped of its veto, an assault on democracy itself, which left the Commons independent of popular control. In the words of F.E. Smith, ministers had 'by a fraud persuaded democracy to sanction a...supreme abdication of power'.[126] Second, it allowed the verdict of the 1910 elections to be set aside for any purposes other than the issue of 'the peers versus the people'. By attempting to legislate beyond that question, on issues such as Home Rule, the government had exceeded its democratic authority. As Bonar Law proclaimed, the Cabinet had become 'a revolutionary committee which has seized by fraud upon despotic power'. Ministers had 'lost the right to that obedience which can be claimed by a constitutional government'.[127]

This provided a democratic, and not simply an imperial, platform for opposing Home Rule. The Irish question had never been before a general election in the Edwardian period, and Conservatives were confident that there was a majority against the policy in the United Kingdom as a whole. The Parliament Act, however, made it impossible for the Lords to refer the issue to the electorate; and on that basis, it was possible to construct a democratic justification for armed resistance. In a message to the Primrose League in 1914, Gerald Arbuthnot warned that if 'the Government intend to ignore the rights of Democracy and revert to the methods of Charles I...the British nation to-day will oppose tyranny as strenuously as they have done in the past'.[128] Even Dicey, who had done more than any other theorist to assert the supremacy of Parliament, concluded that 'the spirit of democratic and constitutional government' had been 'violated'.[129]

There is no reason to doubt the sincerity of this opinion, but it also served a political purpose. The democratic argument for Home Rule – that the Irish had a right to decide upon their own government – had obvious force, and had been acknowledged by Chamberlain in 1886.[130] The brilliance of the Unionist response was its capacity to fight Home Rule on its own principles, building a democratic case against Irish self-government. In the struggle for supremacy in British politics, democracy was the elder wand, a weapon that could win all battles for its acknowledged master. All parties sought to command its power, and to wield it against their political foes.

As the Ulster Crisis reminds us, the engagement with democracy could be profoundly destabilising. Like Protestantism, to which it has often been compared, democracy invoked an absolute authority that was apparently accessible to all; and it allowed for no authoritative exponent by whom its meanings could be determined. The result was a proliferation of democratic 'sects', each identifying itself with the one true Church. Democracy generated texts, laws and readings of history, but its authority lay ultimately in the concept of democracy itself, an abstract principle with no fixed definition. Democracy was in the eye of the beholder. It required interpretation, and could serve many masters.

As democracy became the common possession of British politics, it was tempting to deny the word itself any significance. As a newspaper noted wryly in 1852, 'Tory democracy is certainly not the democracy of the mere Whig; that, again, differs very materially from the democracy of the Radical. It is the same word, no more: the same c[h]ameleon coloured with other lines.'[131] Yet the language of democracy was not infinitely malleable. As an instrument of political warfare, democratic rhetoric was only useful if it seemed plausible to some larger audience. That meant, first, that appeals to democracy could not over-strain the credulity of their hearers; and second, that those who claimed the authority of democracy could not act in ways that were obviously at odds with their pretensions. As Quentin Skinner has argued, such appeals require even the most cynical agents 'to limit and direct their behaviour', in order 'to render their actions *compatible* with the claim that they were motivated by some accepted principle'.[132] Competing on the battlefield of democracy meant surrendering, or at least diluting, some of the fastnesses on which Conservatism, in particular, had built its strength. The hereditary principle, the rights of property and the political authority of the Church were now instrumental, justifiable only by reference to the authority of democracy.

Britain did not 'become' a democracy, in the conventional sense of that expression. There was no moment of conversion, a point at which Britain passed from one governing system to another; nor can Britain be said to have adopted a set of normative 'democratic' values. What happened over the nineteenth century was more complex: a prolonged negotiation between the language of democracy and the established principles of British politics. That exchange was shaped as much by strategic pressures as by the teachings of classical literature, and neither the constitutional idiom nor democracy itself was unaffected by the encounter. From the Chartists, embracing democracy both as a class identity and as an alternative to the pretensions of the British constitution; through the anti-reformers of the 1850s, who used democracy as a smear with which to discredit electoral reform; to the conservative theorists who made democracy a weapon against socialism, the language of democracy was always charged with political purpose. The meaning of democracy was constantly in flux – shaping and reshaped by the needs of political warfare.

Notes

1. I am grateful to Malcolm Chase, Joanna Innes, Jonathan Parry and the editors for their helpful comments.
2. J. Holland Rose, *The Rise of Democracy* (London, 1897), p. v.
3. T. Erskine May, *Democracy in Europe: A History*, 2 vols (London, 1877), I, p. v.
4. *Edinburgh Review* 147 (1878), p. 301.
5. *The Times*, 4 January 1882.
6. R. Quinault, *British Prime Ministers and Democracy: From Disraeli to Blair* (London, 2011), pp. 85, 143; P. Williamson, *Stanley Baldwin* (Cambridge, 1999), pp. 203–42.
7. *Fortnightly Review* 7 (1867), p. 493.
8. G.C. Lewis, *Remarks on the Use and Abuse of Some Political Terms* (London, 1832), pp. 84–5.
9. *The Times*, 27 September 1852; May, *Democracy in Europe*, I, p. vii.
10. *Quarterly Review* 83 (1848), p. 269.
11. Rose, *Rise of Democracy*, p. 5; Brougham Villiers [F.J. Shaw], *Modern Democracy: A Study in Tendencies* (London, 1912), p. 172 and *passim*.
12. *Edinburgh Review* 147 (1878), p. 302; L.T. Hobhouse, *Democracy and Reaction* (London, 1904), p. 106.
13. *The Poor Man's Guardian*, 7 June 1834.
14. Lewis, *Remarks*, pp. 85–6.
15. *Hansard's Parliamentary Debates* [hereafter H] LXIII 74–5, 3 May 1842.
16. Lord Lyndhurst, H VIII 287, 7 October 1831.
17. D. Lieberman, 'The Mixed Constitution and the Common Law', in M. Goldie and R. Wokler, eds., *The Cambridge History of Eighteenth-Century Political Thought* (Cambridge, 2006), pp. 318, 340.
18. Sir Robert Peel, H LVIII 805, 27 May 1841.
19. For the analogous function of 'Republicanism' in France, see P. Rosanvallon, 'The History of the Word "Democracy" in France', *Journal of Democracy*, 6 (1995), 140–54.
20. *Fraser's Magazine* 39 (1849), p. 235.
21. *Nineteenth Century* 14 (1883), pp. 910–12.
22. J.A. Langford, *English Democracy: Its History and Principles* (London, 1853), pp. 67, 81.
23. H LXXXVI 1013, 22 May 1846.
24. *Quarterly Review* 85 (1849), p. 308.
25. *Fraser's Magazine* 39 (1849), p. 235.
26. *Sporting Gazette Limited*, 9 June 1866.
27. *The Standard*, 4 March 1841.
28. L.J. Jennings, ed., *The Croker Papers: The Correspondence and Diaries of the Late Right Honourable John Wilson Croker*, 3 vols (London, 1885), III, p. 64. Finch, H LXXXV 91, 26 March 1846.

29. *Nineteenth Century* 14 (1883), p. 908.
30. *The Age*, 27 March 1831; 10 June 1832.
31. *Morning Post*, 18 April 1831.
32. Villiers, *Modern Democracy*, p. 262.
33. J. Bennett, 'The London Democratic Association 1837–41: A Study in London Radicalism' in J. Epstein and D. Thompson, eds., *The Chartist Experience: Studies in Working-Class Radicalism and Culture, 1830–60* (London, 1982), pp. 80–3, 87, 112.
34. A search of the *Northern Star* in the Nineteenth Century British Library Newspapers database generates 5,568 hits for Chartism, 3,999 for Democracy, and 6,627 for 'democratic' or 'democrat'; all are dwarfed, of course, by 15,154 hits for 'Chartist'. The numbers are potentially misleading: the database archives multiple copies and some refer specifically to America. But they convey the habituation of democratic terms.
35. For usages by O'Connor and Harney, see *Northern Star*, 4 December 1841; 2 April 1842.
36. M. Chase, *Chartism: A New History* (Manchester, 2007), pp. 183–4.
37. *Northern Star*, 25 December 1847.
38. Chase, *Chartism*, p. 171; *Northern Star*, 2 July 1842.
39. *Northern Star*, 25 September 1847.
40. *Northern Star*, 14 August 1841; 28 May 1842.
41. *Chartist Circular*, 19 October 1839.
42. *Chartist Circular*, 4 September 1841.
43. *Northern Star*, 18 March 1848; 23 September 1848.
44. Quoted by George Grey, H XCVIII 26, 7 April 1848.
45. Russell, H XLIX 245, 12 July 1839; Peel, LXIII 81, 3 May 1842.
46. Disraeli, H C 1307, 9 August 1848.
47. *Punch*, 13 July 1867.
48. See R. Saunders, *Democracy and the Vote in British Politics, 1848–1867: The Making of the Second Reform Act* (Farnham, 2011).
49. J. Russell, *An Essay on the History of the English Government and Constitution*, 2nd edn (London, 1823), p. 352. The phrase reappears verbatim in the 1865 edition.
50. H CLXXXVI 7, 18 March 1867.
51. H CLIII 1245, 31 March 1859.
52. R. Lowe, *Speeches and Letters on Reform with a Preface* (London, 1867), p. 212. My emphases.
53. *Macmillan's Magazine* 16 (1867), p. 321.
54. *Lloyd's Weekly Newspaper*, 9 July 1865.
55. *Edinburgh Review* 106 (1857), p. 278.
56. Edward Cox, *Representative Reform. Proposal for a Constitutional Reform Bill* (London, 1866), pp. 5–6.
57. *The Standard*, 13 March 1866; *The Day*, 22 March 1867.
58. *Blackwood's* 101 (1867), pp. 762, 777.
59. C. Rallings and M. Thrasher, *British Electoral Facts, 1832–2006* (Aldershot, 2007), pp. 9–12.
60. Charles Russell, H CCXCIII 1265, 7 November 1884; Lord Rosebery, H CCXCIX 269, 10 July 1885.

61. Fawcett, H CCV 1798, 27 April 1871; Mure, CCXXIII 1344, 20 April 1875; Goschen, CCLXXXV 420, 3 March 1884; Kimberley, CCXC 110, 7 July 1884; *Nineteenth Century*, 14 (1883), p. 907; Rose, *Rise of Democracy*, p. 180.
62. Illingworth, H CCV 1799, 27 April 1871; Disraeli, CCVIII 197, 24 July 1871.
63. Joseph Cowen, H CCXLIII 1530, 20 February 1879; Sir Henry James, H CCLXXXVI 1910, 7 April 1884.
64. *Quarterly Review* 156 (1883), p. 567.
65. H CCII 52, 14 June 1870.
66. Pakington, H CCIV 1878, 13 March 1871; Salisbury, CCVII 1858, 17 July 1871.
67. H CCXVIII 42, 19 March 1874.
68. H CCLXXXV 419, 3 March 1884; see also CCXXXVIII 234, 22 February 1878.
69. For example, George Dixon (Birmingham) and Henry Fawcett (Brighton): H CCII, 790, 23 June 1870; CCV 1798, 27 April 1871.
70. *Fortnightly Review* 33 (1883), pp. 369–81.
71. John Redmond, H CCCV 974, 13 May 1886; Sir Lyon Playfair, H CCCV 1380, 18 May 1886. See also E. Biagini, *British Democracy and Irish Nationalism, 1876–1906* (Cambridge, 2007).
72. Randolph Churchill at Manchester, *Times* 7 November 1885.
73. *Liverpool Mercury*, 5 December 1882; 6 December 1882.
74. See R. Quinault, 'Lord Randolph Churchill and Tory Democracy, 1880–1885', *Historical Journal*, 22 (1979), 141–65. For military usage, see, for example, H CCXLVII 588, 24 June 1879.
75. Balfour, H CCCX 1699, 16 February 1887; Bridgeman, CCCXII 1842, 29 March 1887.
76. H XXVII 267, 17 July 1894; CCCXXXVI 483, 17 May 1889.
77. H CCCXXII 209, 10 February 1888.
78. Randal Cremer, H CCCXLIV 1862, 3 June 1890.
79. Colomb, H CCCXXXVII 1186, 1 July 1889.
80. H XLV 46, 19 January 1897.
81. Salisbury, H L 418, 21 June 1897; Harcourt, 444, 21 June 1897.
82. H VIII 467, 16 May 1911.
83. H CCLXXIII 1563, 12 August 1882; CCXCV, 3, 4 March 1885.
84. *Edinburgh Review* 216 (1912), p. 254; W. McKechnie, *The New Democracy and the Constitution* (London, 1912), p. 167.
85. A.B. Cooke and J. Vincent, *The Governing Passion: Cabinet Government and Party Politics in Britain, 1885–86* (Brighton, 1974), p. 3.
86. H CCVII 1228, 1236–7, 6 July 1871. See Anon, *The Democracy of Reason; or, the Organization of the Press* (Southampton, 1869).
87. Blennerhassett, H CCXXXVIII 990, 8 March 1878; Cowen, CCLXXIV 1218, 10 November 1882. My emphasis.
88. H CCCXXIV 1279, 13 April 1888.
89. See, for example, May, *Democracy in Europe*, I, p. liii.
90. *The Works of Lord Macaulay*, ed. Lady Trevelyan, 8 vols (London, 1873), VI, p. 358.
91. Russell, *Essay on the History of the English Government*, pp. 18–19.
92. May, *Democracy in Europe*, I, p. xlvi.

93. *Quarterly Review* 156 (1883), p. 570.
94. Villiers, *Modern Democracy*, pp. 262–3.
95. May, *Democracy in Europe*, p. lxiv; *Quarterly Review* 145 (1878), p. 137.
96. Walton, H XXXI 1638–9, 21 March 1895; Hoare, LXI 624–5, 20 April 1914.
97. Taylor, H CCLXXIX 1212, Harcourt, 1224, 30 May 1883.
98. Labouchere, H CCCXLII 1528, 21 March 1890.
99. Quinault, *British Prime Ministers*, pp. 63–4, 69.
100. Hobhouse, *Democracy and Reaction*, p. 147.
101. Hobhouse, *Social Evolution and Political Theory* (1911) in J. Meadowcroft, ed., *Hobhouse: Liberalism and Other Writings* (Cambridge, 1994) p. 148. See also J.A. Hobson, *Imperialism* (London, 1902), pp. 158–9.
102. H LXXV 700, 28 July 1899; LXXVII 267, 19 October 1899; for a riposte, see LXXVII, 330–1, 19 October 1899.
103. H CCLXXVII 1777, 9 April 1883.
104. Hobhouse, *Democracy and Reaction*, p. 153.
105. *Nineteenth Century* 14 (1883), p. 912.
106. H CCCIV 1205, 9 April 1886.
107. L. Barrow and I. Bullock, *Democratic Ideas and the British Labour Movement, 1880–1914* (Cambridge, 1996), pp. 164–5.
108. G.B. Shaw, *Man and Superman: A Comedy and a Philosophy* (London, 1903), p. 203.
109. Sandra Stanley Holton, *Feminism and Democracy: Women's Suffrage and Reform Politics in Britain, 1900–1918* (Cambridge, 1986), pp. 5, 118, 123.
110. H XIX 247, 12 July 1910; see also III, 1513, 27 April 1892.
111. Hanbury, H CCLXIV 429, 7 March 1879.
112. *The Anti-Suffrage Review*, September 1913, p. 194. Ward used democracy in two distinct senses: signifying, *first*, 'the political machinery of democracy', or 'the mere process of voting'; and *second*, a cohort that must be 'kept to the use of the vote'.
113. H XIX 41, 11 July 1910.
114. H XIX 224, 12 July 1910.
115. H XIX 138, 11 July 1910.
116. Lord Selborne [William Waldegrave Palmer], *The State and the Citizen* (London, 1913), pp. 170–1.
117. H XVIII 1184, 17 November 1893.
118. Bullock and Barrow, *Democratic Ideas*, pp. 32, 164–5.
119. Hyndman, 1884, quoted in Bullock and Barrow, *Democratic Ideas*, p. 16. See M. Bevir, 'The British Social Democratic Federation, 1880–1885: From O'Brienism to Marxism', *International Review of Social History*, 37 (1992), 207–29.
120. Bullock and Barrow, *Democratic Ideas*, pp. 39, 44–5.
121. *Clarion*, 19 March 1909, quoted in Barrow and Bullock, *Democratic Ideas*, p. 204.
122. See R. Saunders, 'Tory Rebels and Tory Democrats: The Ulster Crisis, 1910–14' in R. Carr and B. Hart, eds., *The Foundations of the Modern British Conservative Party* (London, 2013).
123. *Edinburgh Review* 211 (1910), pp. 259–60.
124. *Fortnightly Review* 93 (1910), p. 236.

125. For example, Selborne, *The State and the Citizen*, p. 113; *Campaign Guide* (1909), p.

66; 'The Will of the People', Conservative Party Archive, Bodleian Library, Pamphlets, X Films 63/2, 1909/53; 'One Vote – One Value', CPA Pamphlets, X Films 63/2, 1913/26.

126. F.E. Smith, 'The Parliament Act Considered in Relation to the Rights of the People', in *Rights of Citizenship: A Survey of Safeguards for the People* (London, 1912), pp. 27, 36.

127. *The Campaign Guide: A Handbook for Unionist Speakers* (London, 1914), p. 57.

128. *The Primrose League Gazette* 55 (April 1914), p. 7.

129. A.V. Dicey, *A Fool's Paradise: Being a Constitutionalist's Criticism on the Home Rule Bill of 1912* (London, 1913), p. 123.

130. H CCCVI 698–9, 1 June 1886.

131. *Lloyd's Weekly Newspaper*, 3 October 1852.

132. Q. Skinner, *Visions of Politics II: Renaissance Virtues* (Cambridge, 2002), p. 367.

7
Women's Suffrage

Ben Griffin

One of the most profound transformations in the study of political history in the last generation has been the collapse of determinist models that posited a straightforward connection between an individual's life experiences and political attitudes. The work of Gareth Stedman Jones in particular forced historians to confront the fact that people do not interpret their experiences in a conceptual vacuum – they make sense of their lives using the linguistic resources available to them at a particular point in time. The idea that a particular set of experiences might give rise to particular forms of political consciousness – the idea that underpinned Marx's theory of history – proved spectacularly vulnerable once one considered 'the impossibility of abstracting experience from the language that structures its articulation'.[1] The results of this 'linguistic turn' on social history and labour history are well known, but it has also fundamentally reshaped the study of gender politics in a way that is no less profound for having been accomplished more quietly. Connections that once seemed obvious between women's experiences of oppression and the emergence of feminist protest no longer seem secure, because – just as working-class politics cannot be reduced to a set of material interests that exist prior to culture – women's political consciousness could only take shape within the historically specific set of linguistic resources available to them. No less than political historians, gender historians have had to engage with Stedman Jones's call 'to study the production of interest, identification, grievance and aspiration within political languages themselves'.[2]

The result has been the emergence of an altogether new history of women's political activity which has at its core the tradition of British radicalism that Stedman Jones identified as central to explaining the history of Chartism, and which others have used to trace the connections between the radical politics of the 1790s, Chartism, Gladstonian Liberalism and the early Labour Party.[3] Uncovering women's involvement in radical politics has transformed our understanding of the women's movement.[4] John Stuart Mill no longer appears as the father of the women's suffrage movement, but rather as one radical voice among many shaping Victorian 'feminism'. Jane Rendall has been particularly important in developing this line of argument, showing how suffragist rhetoric drew on traditional radical tropes, and charting the connections between suffragism and radicalism in the 1860s and 1870s.[5] Sandra Stanley Holton has pursued a similar line, demonstrating the ways in which a strand of 'radical suffragism' contributed to tensions within the suffrage movement, and eventually to the development of support for adult suffrage within the National Union of Women's Suffrage Societies.[6] Most provocatively, Laura Nym Mayhall has explained the development of militant suffragism in the Edwardian period by arguing that militancy had its origins in the transformation of radical discourse during the Boer War, as radicals confronted the question of whether people had a right to resist by force any law imposed on them without their democratic consent.[7]

The result of this work has been to reshape our understanding of the ideology and politics of the suffrage movement, and yet it remains incomplete. The intensive study of radicalism has not been matched by interest in the ways that gender politics were shaped by other political traditions, like the Whig-liberal or Conservative traditions, despite the intensive re-evaluation of these traditions by political historians. This leaves a significant gap in the literature, not least at the heart of the political problem facing the women's movement: the need to win over the men in parliament. It may be the case that many of the women involved in 'feminist' campaigns were products of the radical liberal culture described by Jane Rendall, but the law could not be changed without the assent of a male parliament dominated by very different traditions. For this reason, in what follows the focus will principally be on the views of male political elites, not because women's political views and activities were not instrumental in driving change but because, within parliament, radical demands for women's suffrage had to be mediated through liberal and conservative languages if politicians were to be persuaded to change the law, and that process is little understood.[8] Studying the ways in which women's suffrage was situated within the political languages of liberalism and conservatism allows us to establish with greater clarity the political and ideological structures that oppressed women and within which 'feminist' protest had to operate.

Reassessing suffragism and anti-suffragism

So how did elite male politicians understand the gendering of the political system? Until recently these questions have not been seen as a problem because the contours of the debate on women's suffrage seemed to have been well-established: on the one side stood 'feminists' inspired by John Stuart Mill, while on the other side stood a group of 'anti-feminists' who believed that physiological and intellectual differences between the sexes required that men and women ought to occupy 'separate spheres'.[9] This model will no longer do. Just as it is clear that 'feminism' was much more complicated than an adherence to Mill's ideas, it is clear that a belief in 'separate spheres' cannot explain the behaviour of anti-suffragist men.

This is obvious if we look at the behaviour of MPs debating women's rights in the 1870s – debates that were largely free of party political imperatives or whipping.[10] Certainly, there were always some extreme anti-suffragists who believed that women's place was in the home, and that '[t]he sympathetic element in the mental constitution of women absolutely blinded them to all logic', but many MPs displayed behaviour inconsistent with this stereotype of anti-suffragist attitudes.[11] For a start, many men behaved more flexibly than a rigid belief in 'separate spheres' would allow. Sir Charles Adderley, for example, voted against women's suffrage from 1867 to 1871, changed his mind in 1872 and voted in favour of the proposal on three occasions, before reverting to an anti-suffragist stance in 1876. Nor can a model of anti-suffragism based on 'separate spheres' account for the large numbers of men who supported women's entry into the public sphere through voting, but who opposed the extension of women's rights in the home, in the form of married women's property rights or child custody rights. Above all, the 'separate spheres' framework cannot account for the sudden collapse of anti-suffragism in the Conservative Party in the 1890s that Martin Pugh has identified. Attitudes towards women's social and sexual independence were changing in that decade, but not quickly enough to explain this sudden political shift among Conservative men.[12]

These findings indicate that debates on women's suffrage were more complicated than previously thought, and this chapter aims to recover one dimension of this complexity by suggesting that the debate was influenced by the changing ways in which the languages of liberalism and conservatism conceptualised the nature of representative government. Let us consider some of the ways in which people described the nature of political representation. In 1866 the Conservative Sir Hugh

Cairns said that the principle of the constitution was that parliament should represent classes, not individuals. Edward James, a Liberal, disagreed, arguing that 'no one who was acquainted with the progress of this constitution and country could fail to have seen that, although classes may not be regarded, interests are very much regarded'.[13] Spencer Walpole, for his part, thought that 'the principle of representation in England is representation by communities, not by classes'.[14] Edward Gibson preferred to base his arguments on 'the old and well-known principle of the Constitution – that representation and taxation should go together'.[15] The property qualification, in other words, was not an end in itself, but was understood as a means of securing the representation of particular groups: classes, communities, interests, taxpayers, ratepayers or householders, depending on one's point of view. There were then a number of different ways of describing the basis of the constitution: different languages of representation which sought to make sense of who could vote. Some of these languages were associated with particular party political positions, and the relative popularity of these competing political languages changed over time. So, for example, the language of class representation fell out of use among Liberals, but not Conservatives, after the Second Reform Act. The crucial point is that demands for women's suffrage could be accommodated within some of these languages of representation more easily than others (it proved easier to argue that women were ratepayers than that women formed a separate social class, for example), and therefore changes in the relative status of these languages affected the ability of suffragists to appeal for support. These changes in the discursive landscape go a long way towards explaining the changing patterns of support for women's suffrage within the Liberal and Conservative parties. In general, women's suffrage proved far more compatible with radical languages about household suffrage or representation needing to accompany taxation than Conservative or Whig-liberal languages of representation, but this was to change at the end of the nineteenth century, as we shall see.[16]

An awareness of this linguistic context requires a re-evaluation of the nature of Victorian suffragism and anti-suffragism. Models of anti-suffragism that assume that it was based solely on a set of ideas about the capacities and responsibilities of women have neglected the ways in which anti-suffragist ideas were conceived within the terms of existing political languages. If men thought that the purpose of the electoral system was to secure the representation of classes then, in order for them to support women's suffrage, they would have to be persuaded that women formed a distinct class. If women did not form a class, then demands for women's suffrage simply made no sense in terms of that model of the constitution. This would be a form of anti-suffragism that owed little or nothing to ideas about women's supposed physiological or intellectual weakness, or about 'separate spheres'. Therefore, in order to understand the gender politics of the nineteenth century it is necessary to consider the ways in which the articulation and reception of demands for women's suffrage were shaped by the various constitutional idioms that were available in that period.

Studying these idioms also draws attention to the forms of identity that men and women could claim to demand enfranchisement. If one function of political language was to define the boundaries of 'the political' (and this was tremendously important in constraining female public activity), another was to define the subject positions that were recognised within that discursive field. These were so numerous that no single chapter can attempt to survey them all: men, for example, articulated their political needs as soldiers, financiers, industrialists, country gentlemen, aristocrats, young men and old men, married men and single men, disabled and non-disabled men. The legitimacy of their demands was in part shaped by these identities, and various historically specific conceptions of masculinity were intrinsic to them all. In what follows we will confine our attention to some of the identities that were invoked in parliamentary debates on the Reform Acts of 1832, 1867 and 1884, in order to establish how some aspects of constitutional discourse impacted on gender politics.

From the representation of 'interests' to the representation of 'classes'

Before the Great Reform Act of 1832 the variety of franchises in the unreformed electoral system created a range of identities which people used to claim a voice in the political life of their localities: depending on the constituency, men could claim a vote as freemen, potwallopers, scot-and-lot voters (i.e. ratepayers), members of a corporation, owners of burgages or 40-shilling freeholders. It was through these identities that men made sense of their place in public life and it was through them that individual male political subjectivities were formed. To be a freeman, in particular, seems to have been an identity that men valued and the government was forced to preserve the hereditary voting rights of freemen with few limitations in the Act of 1832.[17] The fluidity of these identities created ambiguities and linguistic resources that women could exploit to participate in electoral politics, as the work of Elaine Chalus has shown. For example, women could use their status as freewomen to claim a place on the political stage, often with success. Women in the 92 freemen boroughs who were the daughters of freemen had the right to make their husbands freemen and voters, which gave these women status and, to an extent, influence over their husbands' votes. In Bristol in 1754, for instance, one candidate issued an election address directed specifically at the freewomen of the borough. Still greater influence was possessed by those women who owned burgages or freeholds in the 29 burgage boroughs or the six freeholder boroughs. In these constituencies the franchise was attached to property ownership, which meant that if women owned the relevant forms of property they technically had the right to vote. Although by custom they were prevented from exercising this right, in practice they were allowed to appoint male proxies to vote on their behalf.[18] In these cases the need to represent the interests embodied in the various franchises (especially forms of property ownership) allowed women to contest the gendered structures of electoral politics by claiming identities as burgage-owners, freewomen or property owners. These identities may not have facilitated women's suffrage, but they did allow women to justify their participation in political life. The 1832 Reform Act therefore effected a significant change in that it swept away many of the old small boroughs, created the new borough qualification of the £10 householder, stripped the daughters of freewomen of their ability to create new voters, and explicitly defined the electorate as male (although the Scottish Reform Act did not).[19] It thereby reduced the ability of women to claim those identities that had conferred a degree of political agency before 1832.

To focus on questions of individual agency, however, runs the risk of misrepresenting contemporary understandings of the electoral system. Individuals were not enfranchised in order that they could express their own personal preferences, but in order to ensure that a variety of interests were represented in parliament.[20] The various property qualifications were understood as securing the representation of different kinds of property, and so different economic interests. The 'fitness' of individual voters was a secondary consideration: it was thought desirable that the electoral system selected the fittest representatives of an interest to vote on its behalf, but 'fitness' was not in itself considered a claim to the vote, except in radical discourse. For this reason, the franchise was a less important element in the debates on the 1832 Reform Act than the redistribution of seats; the question of who could vote was less significant than the fact that 'the cotton manufacturers had their interests represented in Parliament by fifteen Members, the colonial interests by seven, and the silk trade by three'.[21] Lord John Russell's scheme of reform was designed to give 'to all the great manufacturing interests, such as the woollen and cotton, the mining districts, the coal trade, and the potteries...a due share in the representation'.[22] Both Whigs and Tories shared this basic conceptual framework, but the Whigs had a more expansive definition of interests than the Tories.[23] Peel in particular tended to base his arguments around a simple dichotomy of 'the agricultural interest' versus 'trade and manufactures', whereas Russell referred to a broader range of economic interests as well as the interests of property in general, intelligence and the broader welfare of the community.[24] The Whig ambition in 1832 was to construct an electoral system where all interests had a voice in parliament, so that none would feel alienated and aristocratic politicians could formulate policy without any interest group feeling that they had not had a fair hearing. It was not considered necessary for everyone connected with a particular interest to have a vote provided that the interest was represented, and it was not necessary for each interest to be represented in strict proportion to its numbers: as long as each interest had a voice in parliament, they would not be ignored. The resulting system was gendered in two ways: first, the idea that women had a distinctive set of interests separate from those of men was denied; second, the idea that women's votes might be necessary to secure the representation of legitimate interests was denied. This pattern of exclusion will be explored in greater detail below.

Between the First and Second Reform Acts the language of interests evolved into a language of class. The aim of the Whig reformers in the early 1830s had been to bring within the pale of the political nation those 'various important, commercial interests [which] had grown up in this country...[but which] had been hitherto entirely overlooked in the Representation'.[25] The term 'middle class' came to serve as a popular shorthand for these hitherto unrepresented interests and, although the Reform Act made very little difference to the class composition of the electorate, the dominance of narratives that retrospectively interpreted the 1832 Act as the triumph of the middle class meant those demanding further reform increasingly couched their demands in the language of class.[26] Consequently, the agitation leading up to the Second Reform Act of 1867 and the parliamentary debates in the 1860s were dominated by the idea that reform was needed to enfranchise the working classes. But this was to be an enfranchisement of the working classes as a class – as one interest group among others. Sir Hugh Cairns said that the principle of the constitution was that Parliament shall be...a representation of every class ...so that the various classes of this country may be heard, and their views expressed fairly in the House of Commons, without the possibility of any one class outnumbering and reducing to silence all the other classes in the kingdom.

The aim was to ensure that each class of the community had a political voice, not to ensure that each individual was represented, so it did not follow 'that because there is fitness there should also be the right to exercise the suffrage'.[27] There was no need to enfranchise all working-class men; they only needed to enfranchise enough to ensure that working-class interests were represented in parliament. This was not just a Conservative idea but was found throughout the Liberal Party, although it came under heavy fire from radicals like Forster and Bright.

In 1867 the exigencies of party political manoeuvring forced the Conservatives into supporting a more radical measure than they had ever intended.[28] As Disraeli negotiated his Reform Bill's passage through the Commons the language of balancing class interests was displaced by an intense debate over the 'fitness' of the voters that would be enfranchised, a debate ultimately settled by insisting on the virtues of the urban householder who paid rates and met the requirement of 12 months' residence. The seeming gender-neutrality of this standard prompted radical women's suffrage activists to urge suitably qualified women to put their names forward for the electoral register; consequently, in several towns across Britain women actually voted in the 1868 general election, before the courts ruled that traditional prohibitions continued to apply.[29] Nevertheless, despite all the talk of 'fitness' and 'household suffrage' in 1867, most MPs outside the radical tradition continued to see the enfranchisement of urban householders as a means of securing the representation of a class, not as a recognition that 'fitness' conferred the vote. Conservatives in particular continued to speak the language of class representation as late as the debates on the Third Reform Act in 1884.

Women's suffrage as class representation

But how did these languages of interest representation and class representation influence nineteenth-century gender politics? The answer comes in two parts. First, people conceived and articulated demands for women's suffrage in terms derived from these political languages. Since most MPs believed that the purpose of enfranchisement was to secure the representation of interests or classes, the case for women's suffrage had to made in these terms: in order for women to claim the vote they would have to claim that women formed either a class or a group with distinctive interests that needed representation. Second, it was the refusal to accept that women formed a distinctive interest group or class that lay at the heart of anti-suffragism in the early years of the women's suffrage movement, before these languages of representation fell out of favour.

The first point can be demonstrated easily. In her 1867 essay 'The Claim of Englishwomen to the Suffrage Constitutionally Considered', Helen Taylor claimed that if women chose 'to urge their claims simply as women...they would, on the theory of class representation, have been able to take up very strong ground'. Although as a radical she did not subscribe to the theory of class representation she thought that it would have special weight for 'those who group all women together, as actual or potential wives and mothers'.[30] This might explain why Lord Claud Hamilton said that 'of all people who would jump at the theory of classes none would be more eager than the ladies'.[31] Laura Ormiston Chant fell easily into using the language of class when she wrote about the need for women to have the vote.

> The class of human beings called men, having the making and admin-istering of laws in its own hands, has been so eager to recognise its own interests, it has sometimes entirely forgotten that another class existed with interests as pressing and vital as its own; and the class called women, not having the power to represent its interests – being in fact out of sight, has been out of mind.[32]

It was this idea that early opponents of the women's suffrage move-ment had to rebut. In 1876 John Bright told the House of Commons that 'the great mistake' of those who supported women's suffrage 'was in arguing that women were a class...They were not like the class of agricultural labourers or factory workers.'[33] The Liberal Edward Leatham agreed that 'The cardinal error' of the suffragist case 'was that women constituted a class as the agricultural labourers or working classes consti-tuted a class'.[34] James Bryce also insisted that 'The farm labourers...were undoubtedly a class...But it could not reasonably be contended that women were in that sense a class'.[35] These comments cannot be easily assimilated within the existing literature on anti-suffragism, which has assumed that men's opposition to women's suffrage was based solely on men's beliefs about women's capacities and 'separate spheres'. Any such framework is inadequate: the anti-suffragism of men like Bright, Leatham and Bryce only makes sense once we accept that their anti-suffragism was as much an outcome of their constitutional beliefs as their beliefs about the nature and responsibilities of women.

It is significant that at no time did anyone suggest that the enfranchisement of women might secure a more perfect representation of the working class or the middle class. Instead it was assumed that to render women's suffrage compatible with the theory of class representation one would have to prove that women were a separate class: their claims as members of the upper, middle or working classes were ignored. If anyone was to speak for the working classes it was working-class men, not working-class women. In this sense the most important effect of the rhetoric of separate spheres on the early women's suffrage movement may not have been a blanket prohibition of women's suffrage, but a more subtle process in which men naturally assumed that the spokespersons for a class would be male members of that class rather than women. The same issue had made it difficult to allow women to claim a political role as defenders of particular interests in the earlier part of the century.

Why did it prove so difficult for women to convince MPs that they formed a separate class with separate needs? Differences of social class and marital status were regularly cited as factors that disrupted any common identity as women. John Bright said that

> Nothing could be more monstrous and absurd than to describe women as a class. They were not like the class of agricultural labourers or factory workers. There were women in the highest ranks, others in the middle ranks, and others in the humblest ranks.[36]

Suffragists like Bright's brother, Jacob, regularly argued that women's legal disabilities made them a class, but focusing on legal disabilities tended to draw attention to the different interests of married and unmarried women under coverture.[37] Edward Bouverie complained that '[t]he greater part of the grievances sought to be remedied by his hon. friend were the grievances of married women, and it was by no means clear that the best way to remedy them was by conferring the franchise upon women who were not married.'[38] Since the early suffrage bills would not have enfranchised married women, the sponsors of the women's suffrage bills were in effect arguing in favour of some form of virtual representation, in which single women represented married women. The question then became one of who was best suited to represent married women: single women or husbands? To contemporaries the answer was obvious.

The 'advanced' academic liberals who contributed to *Essays on Reform* in late 1866 may have condemned class representation but they shared many of the premises of that theory, which explains why so many of them opposed women's suffrage – most famously Goldwin Smith and James Bryce. These advanced Liberals also saw politics as involving conflicts between opposing classes: the important distinction in the debates on the Second Reform Act was between those who believed that it was necessary to ensure that classes were represented in order to *protect* class interests, and those who thought that it was necessary to ensure that classes were represented in order to *transcend* class interests.[39] Advanced Liberals believed that parliamentary reform would allow divisive class loyalties to be superseded by an attachment to national institutions.[40] The root of this confidence was a belief that the science of political economy could demonstrate that there were no irreconcilable differences of interest between capitalists and labourers. But the case of recognising the interests of women was problematic because Liberal politics could not rest on claims about indefeasible differences like those attributed to sex by partisans on both sides of the suffrage issues: arguments invoking women's distinctive physiology, sensibilities and their potential for maternity. If these interests could not be transcended, only institutionalised, conflict was inevitable and the logic of accepting women into the political system was not social stability but a radical transformation of all social relationships.

Not everyone believed in this model of sex war. Jacob Bright argued that women were like the working class in that they laboured under a set of legal disabilities caused by their exclusion from the electorate. His argument was that enfranchisement was a necessary step towards the removal of those disabilities, which would allow sexual antagonism to be transcended. But many anti-suffragists saw this as a weak argument because once women's grievances were remedied they would be left with no distinctive interests. In this way women were seen as fundamentally unlike the working class, whose distinctive class interests were expected to remain after enfranchisement.

Victorian domestic ideology proved another barrier to those trying to argue that women formed a class with interests opposed to those of men. Nineteenth-century writings on domesticity made a particular fetish of household harmony, and commonly insisted that the best way to achieve that harmony was for women willingly to defer to their husbands in all things as a way of promoting marital unity.[41] Describing women's suffrage in terms of class representation was incompatible with that vision of domesticity, because it posited, in John Bright's words, 'an assumed constant and irreconcilable hostility between the sexes'. They were asked, he said, 'To arm the women of this country against the men of this country – to defend them against their husbands, their brothers, and their sons.' To him 'the idea had in it something strange and monstrous'.[42] Two things need noting here. The first is that most men had too much invested in the gender order to accept that women might need defending against 'their husbands, their brothers, and their sons'. The second is that this domestic ideology made it extremely difficult to conceptualise any kind of female political agency, because that would undermine the marital harmony created by female submission. This was the point that Goldwin Smith gave pride of place at the start of his pamphlet on *Female Suffrage*, writing that enfranchising married women would 'for the first time authorise a wife, and make it in certain cases her duty as a citizen, to act publicly in opposition to her husband'. 'A man and his wife taking opposite sides in politics would be brought into direct and public collision ... Would the harmony of most households bear the strain?'[43]

This position was not without its difficulties, because it required Smith to acknowledge that men and women might have divergent views that might promote arguments, whilst at the same time he had to deny that men and women ever had conflicting interests.

> The case of women is not that of an unenfranchised class, the interest of which is distinct from that of the enfranchised. The great mass of them are completely identified in interests with their husbands, while even those who are not married can hardly be said to form a class, or to have any common interest, other than mere sex, which is liable to be unfairly affected by class legislation.[44]

The awkwardness of the concession '*mere sex*' is striking. Nor could he sustain the idea that there was no class legislation that affected 'mere sex', arguing that 'with Female Suffrage there would probably be always a woman's question, of a kind appealing to sentiment, such as the question of the Contagious Diseases Act'. He even went as far as claiming that 'With Female Suffrage, the question of the CDA would probably have made a clean sweep at the last general election of all the best servants of the State.'[45] His position boiled down to a claim that issues like the Contagious Diseases Acts would be important to women, but were ultimately unimportant. These contradictions expose the limits of the assumptions on which Smith's politics were predicated. Ultimately, his type of Liberal politics rested on the assumption that the power relations found in the home and between the sexes were not 'political'. His belief that women had no need of the vote rested on the assumption of a harmony of interests between husband and wife secured by a wife's willingness to subordinate her will to that of her husband. He wrote that women 'have been free from political vices, because they have generally taken no part in politics, just as home has been an asylum from political rancour because political division has not been introduced between man and wife'.[46] This insistence on the divide between public and private provided the foundation for the claim that women had no political interests to speak of, and this in turn allows us to see the ways in which male political subjectivities were thought to be distinctive. Smith claimed that women's 'sphere will be one in which they do not directly feel the effects of good or bad government, which are felt by the man who goes forth to labour'.[47]

The divergence of interests between men and women that Smith tried to ignore became increasingly important to female activists in the final third of the century, as they came to assert precisely the kind of class identity that anti-suffragists denied them. Sandra Stanley Holton has argued that the 1870s saw 'a growing sense of solidarity' between women of the middle and working classes, and 'a developing analysis of women's wrongs in terms of all women's shared membership of a subordinated sex-class'.[48] Josephine Butler, for example, asserted that the Contagious Diseases Acts had evoked 'a deeply awakened common womanhood. Distinctions are levelled. We no more covet the name of ladies; we are all women'.[49] To some extent this rhetoric was the outcome of the difficulties that radical women had encountered when they tried to articulate their needs in terms of the traditional radical rhetoric of 'the people' versus the aristocracy.[50] Just as men would not accept that women could speak as the representatives of a class, or that women had needs separate from those of men, so many radicals were reluctant to accept that women were just as able to speak as representatives of 'the people', or that the needs of men and women within the category of 'the people' might diverge. The result was that 'in the 1880s women's rights activists made fewer appeals to "the People" as a body which might secure women's emancipation, and ... replaced "the People" as the primary subject and agent of liberation with "Womanhood"'.[51] This transition was to have important consequences for the women's suffrage movement, especially as it entered its militant phase in the early twentieth century, but this strand of thought remained just one of many found within the women's movement and it played a negligible role in the parliamentary debates on franchise reform in the nineteenth century.

Household suffrage and the rights of women

The discussion so far has concentrated on the ways in which activists found it difficult to articulate a case for women's suffrage using constitutional idioms that saw the end of political representation as the representation of groups, classes or interests rather than individuals. These various languages of representation dominated constitutional debate for the first two-thirds of the nineteenth century, but the discursive landscape began to change dramatically in the 1870s once the Liberal Party began to abandon the theory of class representation. It did so for three reasons. First, there was a pressing need to try and make sense of the changes made by the 1867 Reform Act. Secondly, the introduction of the secret ballot in 1872 seriously weakened the idea that the electoral system was based on the representation of classes or interests rather than individuals. Once voting became secret voters were no longer accountable to non-electors: voting became a private expression of individual conscience and it became implausible to suggest that voters represented anyone but themselves at the poll. The third factor was the Liberal defeat in the 1874 general election, which swiftly led them to embrace the idea of reforming the franchise in the Tory-dominated counties. The further extension of the franchise prompted an intense debate about the skills and knowledge that prospective voters were thought to need. In effect what happened was that the Liberals found ways of justifying giving the vote to uneducated, often illiterate, rural voters by praising their moral sense rather than their political knowledge. They did so by embracing the language of household suffrage. Liberals proposed to enfranchise the householder not because of what he knew, but because he had a stake in the community, paid taxes and displayed 'independence'. The vocabulary was similar to that used in 1867, but the meaning had changed fundamentally. In 1867 the goal had been to enfranchise householders as the most virtuous representatives of a class, but by 1884, after the transformations wrought by the secret ballot, they were to be enfranchised as individuals in their own right.[52] Although the Conservatives continued to use the language of class representation, by the time of the Third Reform Act the Liberals had embraced the idea of household suffrage with so much enthusiasm that Gladstone could say that 'The principle and the central idea' of his Franchise Bill was 'to give to every householder a vote'.[53]

Lydia Becker, the central figure in the women's suffrage movement, thought that this transformation in Liberal discourse offered an exciting opportunity. She noted that

[i]t is difficult to see how an earnest demand for the suffrage made on behalf of householders now excluded could be resisted by those who are asking for the extension of the principle to the counties, consistently with the arguments they will be compelled to use when they urge their own object.[54]

Nevertheless, the turn to household suffrage presented a number of challenges for the women's movement. It meant that it became more difficult to demand the vote for married women, because they were not the heads of households, and the suffrage movement suffered serious splits over this issue from the mid-1870s onwards.[55] The language of household suffrage also proved an obstacle to women's suffrage because, as Anna Clark has noted, the virtues of the householder were understood as peculiarly male virtues.[56] The householder was assumed to be a father and breadwinner who put a roof over his family's heads, so the language of household suffrage effectively rested the franchise on a particular conception of masculinity, with the result that the growing acceptance of this language did as much to obstruct women's suffrage as to facilitate its acceptance. Since the 1860s W.E. Forster, J.A. Roebuck and John Bright had always supported household suffrage on the grounds that it provided evidence of men's moral virtue, but all opposed women's suffrage. Anti-suffragists like Bright believed that women had separate duties from men, and the fact that some women were carrying out the responsibilities of male householders was not evidence that they were capable of voting responsibly, but a sign of a social problem – an inversion of the natural order. Nor would these men accept that the fulfilment of what they thought of as women's duties entitled women to the vote. Men could claim the vote by virtue of their paternity, but women could not make similar claims by virtue of their maternity: not least because recognition of such an idea would lead to married women being able to vote. The result was that it remained difficult to accommodate demands for women's suffrage within the language of household suffrage, and this made it easy for MPs to cave in under the party political imperatives that demanded that a women's suffrage amendment to the Franchise Bill should be rejected in 1884.[57]

The collapse of anti-suffragism

By 1884 suffragists had struggled to articulate their demands in the dominant languages of representation found in the House of Commons, but in the following decade the tide turned dramatically. By the early twentieth century both parties had adopted languages of representation that proved far more amenable to women's suffrage. Within a decade of the Third Reform Act the parliamentary Liberal Party had abandoned household suffrage in any meaningful sense. The Home Rule schism produced a Liberal Party dominated by its radical wing, and they decided that the only way to break the Conservatives' new electoral dominance in the boroughs was to alter the franchise once more. Almost as soon as the 1886 election was over, Liberals started calling for the abolition of plural voting and a reduction of the residence period from 12 months to 3 months, which required the abolition of the rating qualification.[58] Liberals even started talking about abolishing the disqualification of paupers, which amounted to a rejection of one of the most essential attributes that had historically been required of voters: 'independence'.[59] Henceforward the Liberal position was basically manhood suffrage tempered by three months' residence. In effect the idea of 'fitness' as a requirement for the franchise had been jettisoned in the process of formulating a viable policy and the Liberal Party had, for the first time, embraced a genuinely democratic doctrine. It therefore became incongruous to start discriminating against women on the grounds of fitness. One sign of this was the abandonment of long-standing claims that women and the poor should be denied the vote because they did not possess sufficient knowledge of politics to vote responsibly. As Sir Wilfrid Lawson said, 'The way to teach people politics was to let them take part in politics, else it was to act on the principle of the old lady who would not allow her son to go into the water until he had learned to swim.'[60] The idea that the responsibility of being given the vote would in itself prompt voters to acquire knowledge of political matters had been the preserve of a radical minority before 1885, but by the time of the Edwardian debates on women's suffrage it had become a commonplace in the Liberal ranks.[61] In this way support for women's suffrage became increasingly compatible with the tenets of mainstream parliamentary liberalism.

The Conservatives faced a different set of challenges after the Third Reform Act. They had to find a way of explaining their unexpected success with a mass electorate; they had to find a rhetoric which would allow them to oppose Liberal plans to abolish plural voting, reduce the residence qualification, and abolish the rating qualification; and they had to find a rhetoric that would allow them to oppose Liberal policies, without appearing as a reactionary party of privilege. Their solution to these problems was to develop the argument that the basis of the electoral system was not the representation of individuals, interests or classes but local communities. The idea that 'Our representative system is founded upon what is known as the local principle', and not 'mere personal representation', was repeated constantly from the Conservative benches from the 1890s.[62] This was not the old idea of representing groups rather than individuals: the secret ballot had got rid of that. Instead, they argued that effective representation of a community was only possible if everyone with an interest in that community could vote. That meant that plural voting was legitimate, because people with interests in more than one constituency should be able to vote in those communities. As Charles Whitmore MP explained in 1891: 'in the theory of our Constitution, it is the locality which is represented in Parliament'. This meant that if a man 'who in one locality employs labour, pays rates, discharges local duties' was deprived of his vote 'simply because in another locality he is entitled to a vote, the interests of the first locality would cease to be accurately reflected, and an injustice would be done to the man'.[63] This allowed Conservatives to defend the interests of property without adopting the rhetoric of class conflict: the rhetoric was in fact marvellously inclusive. Property ownership, rather than any other consideration of 'fitness', became the primary qualification in this rhetoric.

This new language of community appealed to the Conservatives not least because it synthesised elements of other languages of representation. In the first place it incorporated the defence of the residence and rating qualifications against Liberal plans to attack them. If the aim was to secure the representation of localities then it stood to reason that precautions 'ought to be taken to see that voters have a substantial interest in the locality', and the question for MPs was therefore 'whether 12 months' residence is too large, or whether three months is enough to give that stability'.[64] The payment of local taxes was another way of demonstrating that a voter had a genuine interest in a locality, and this allowed Conservatives to defend plural voting by appealing to the old radical doctrine that taxation and representation should go together. Above all, this language allowed Conservatives a way of justifying a franchise that secured the representation of property, at a time when the party was repositioning itself as the party for all owners of property, and not merely aristocratic landlords.[65] In this way, the development of a political language based on the representation of communities combined in a single package support for the representation of property and the maintenance of the rating and residence qualifications with opposition to the abolition of plural voting. This was a powerful rhetorical weapon.

The development of this new language had important consequences for the women's suffrage movement because it proved extremely easy to assimilate demands for women's suffrage within this language, and remarkably difficult to use this language to oppose women's suffrage. The language of community representation did not require women to be considered a separate class with separate interests, nor was it based on gendered conceptions of virtue like the language of household suffrage; it did not require any test of intellectual capacity; and it was compatible with the exclusion of married women from the franchise but it did not require it. It based its assessment of voters purely on the ownership of property. Property had always featured as an interest in need of represen-tation, but in the past it had been difficult to use this to claim votes for women due to legal restrictions on married women's property rights and a pervasive belief that female property ownership did not confer indi-vidual autonomy (because control of a woman's property rested with the male head of household).[66] After the Married Women's Property Act of 1882 these attitudes began to change, and it became a common argu-ment that propertied women ought to have the vote.

From the 1890s onwards Conservative suffragists were swimming with the tide in their party when they based their arguments on claims that women ought to have the vote because they owned property and had an interest in their local communities. Conservative anti-suffragists, on the other hand, now struggled to explain why women should not have the vote, given the party's new constitutional doctrine, in a way that they had not before. This makes the Edwardian suffrage debates qualitatively different from what had gone before. In the Edwardian period it became common to find Conservative anti-suffragists faced with the accusation that their beliefs were incompatible with their party's constitutional doctrine. This was new. In 1897 Charles Radcliffe Cooke accepted that representation was based on communities, and that property gave an interest in a community, but he went on to argue that property was merely a proxy for work, and it was work on which the franchise ulti-mately rested, allowing him to reintroduce arguments about separate spheres. But this led him perilously close to maintaining the theory of community representation by removing its essential principle, and this was obvious to suffragists like Alfred Mond, who mocked anti-suffragist Conservatives for abandoning their principles.

I remember in the Debates [sic] on the Plural Voting Bill we were continually told the old system of representation was based on prop-erty...If hon. Gentlemen on the other side of the House wish to retain that, it is curious they should deny it as soon as women are introduced. As soon as women are introduced the hon. and learned Member says it is an absurd doctrine which never existed.[67]

The difficulty of combining anti-suffragism with the Conservative Party's dominant constitutional rhetoric surely contributed to the collapse of Conservative anti-suffragism in the 1890s noted by Martin Pugh: 91 per cent of the Conservatives who had voted on women's suffrage in 1867 had voted against it, but by 1897 the figure had fallen to just under 43 per cent. From 1892 onwards, with a few exceptions, the majority of Conservative MPs taking part in divisions regularly sided with the suffragists. Nor does it seem likely that this was an artificial result created by low turnouts; the suffragists retained their lead even when the majority of MPs attended, as happened in 1897.[68] From this point onwards the major obstacles to women's suffrage would not be the lack of a majority in the House of Commons: the major obstacles were a hostile Prime Minister, constitutional battles between the Liberal government and the House of Lords, the hung parliament produced by the general elections of 1910 and the developing crisis in Ireland.

In conclusion, this chapter has argued that the political and intellectual history of women's suffrage was fundamentally shaped by the changing conceptual vocabularies that people used to make sense of Britain's unwritten constitution. Women claimed political influence not only as individuals, but as freewomen, burgage-owners, ratepayers, householders, property owners and as representatives of classes and communities. The ways in which the women's movement manipulated radical idioms is well known, but to understand the ways in which Whig, Liberal and Conservative MPs reacted to demands for women's suffrage we need to grasp how the languages of class representation, interest representation and community representation structured the articulation and reception of suffragist and anti-suffragist demands. Since women's suffrage could be accommodated within some of these languages more successfully than others, changes in the relative popularity of these languages affected the ability of suffragists to make a case that contemporaries would have regarded as persuasive. This framework helps to explain both the steady growth of suffragism within the parliamentary Liberal Party, and the sudden collapse of anti-suffragism in the Conservative Party.

Between 1867 and 1885 it had been possible to object to women's suffrage because it seemed genuinely incompatible with the dominant interpretations of the nature of the political system, but by the turn of the century the constitutional doctrines of both major political parties seemed to demand the enfranchisement of at least some women. The result was an ideological polarisation in the Edwardian period. The extreme anti-suffragists, who had always believed that physiological and intellectual differences presented an insuperable obstacle to female enfranchisement, carried on as before, but a belief in sexual difference was now the *only* legitimate source of anti-suffragism. The constitutional arguments that had underpinned opposition to women's suffrage in the 1870s had lost their power, so arguments about 'separate spheres' and pseudo-scientific ideas about sexual difference assumed a much greater importance to Edwardian anti-suffragism than they had previously possessed. The anti-suffragists were exposed as anti-democrats in an age when both parties, for different reasons and with varying levels of enthusiasm, had embraced essentially democratic constitutional doctrines that would have horrified the parliaments that passed the First and Second Reform Acts. As the Edwardian age dawned, the challenge facing defenders of the status quo was to render a patriarchal state compatible with democratic rhetoric. In the long run they were successful in finding new ways to sustain familiar inequalities, but in this task the political languages of the nineteenth century were no longer of any use: the age of Victoria was at an end.

Notes

1. Gareth Stedman Jones, *Languages of Class: Studies in English Working Class History, 1832–1982* (Cambridge, 1983), p. 20.
2. Ibid, p. 22.
3. Eugenio Biagini and Alastair Reid, eds., *Currents of Radicalism: Popular Radicalism, Organised Labour and Party Politics in Britain, 1850–1914* (Cambridge, 1991).
4. Anna Clark, *The Struggle for the Breeches: Gender and the Making of the British Working Class* (Berkeley, 1995); Helen Rogers, *Women and the People. Authority, Authorship and the Radical Tradition in Nineteenth-Century England* (Aldershot, 2000); Kathryn Gleadle, 'British Women and Radical Politics in the Late Nonconformist Enlightenment, c. 1780–1830' in Amanda Vickery, ed., *Women, Privilege and Power: British Politics, 1750 to the Present* (Stanford, 2001), pp. 123–51.
5. Jane Rendall, 'Citizenship, Culture and Civilisation: the Languages of British Suffragists, 1866–1874' in Caroline Daley and Melanie Nolan, eds., *Suffrage and Beyond: International Feminist Perspectives* (New York, 1994), pp. 127–50; 'The Citizenship of Women and the Reform Act of 1867' in Catherine Hall, Keith McClelland and Jane Rendall, eds., *Defining the Victorian Nation* (Cambridge, 2000), pp. 119–178; 'John Stuart Mill, Liberal Politics, and the

Movements for Women's Suffrage, 1865–1873' in Vickery, *Women, Privilege and Power*, pp. 168–200.

6. Sandra Stanley Holton, *Suffrage Days: Stories from the Women's Suffrage Movement* (London, 1996); idem., *Feminism and Democracy: Women's Suffrage and Reform Politics in Britain, 1900–1918* (Cambridge, 1986).

7. Laura Nym Mayhall, *The Militant Suffrage Movement: Citizenship and Resistance in Britain, 1860–1930* (Oxford, 2003), pp. 32–6.

8. On women's agency in lobbying parliament see Ben Griffin, *The Politics of Gender in Victorian Britain: Masculinity, Political Culture and the Struggle for Women's Rights* (Cambridge, 2012), pp. 6–7.

9. Brian Harrison, *Separate Spheres: the Opposition to Women's Suffrage in Britain* (London, 1978); Martin Pugh, *The March of the Women: a Revisionist Analysis of the Campaign for Women's Suffrage, 1866–1914* (Oxford, 2000); Julia Bush, *Women Against the Vote: Female Anti-Suffragism in Britain* (Oxford, 2007).

10. For a more detailed exposition see Griffin, *Politics of Gender*, pp. 14–33.

11. Sir Henry James, *The Times*, 4 May 1871.

12. Pugh, *March of the Women*, p. 115.

13. *The Times*, 27 April 1866; *Daily News*; *Morning Post*; *Standard*. In what follows, where the sources report the same substantive point, but differ as to the precise form of words used, the first citation gives the source of the wording, and subsequent citations refer to corroborating text. Where the date of the newspapers is the same, that date is given in the first reference only.

14. *The Times*, 24 April 1866.

15. *The Times*, 29 February 1884; *Morning Post*; *Standard*.

16. See especially Rendall, 'Citizenship, Culture and Civilisation'. For a more detailed account see Griffin, *Politics of Gender*, chs. 7–11.

17. Philip Salmon, 'The English Reform Legislation, 1831–1832' in D. R. Fisher, ed., *The House of Commons, 1820–1832* (Cambridge, 2009), I, pp. 378–9.

18. Elaine Chalus, *Elite Women in English Political Life, c. 1754–1790* (Oxford, 2005), p. 41; Elaine Chalus, '"That Epidemical Madness": Women and Electoral Politics in the Late Eighteenth Century', in Hannah Barker and Elaine Chalus, eds., *Gender in Eighteenth-Century England: Roles, Representations and Responsibilities* (London, 1997), pp. 151–78; idem., 'Women, Electoral Privilege and Practice in the Eighteenth Century', in Kathryn Gleadle and Sarah Richardson, eds., *Women in British Politics* (Basingstoke, 2000), pp. 19–38.

19. Kathryn Gleadle, *Borderline Citizens: Women, Gender, and Political Culture in Britain, 1815–1867* (Oxford, 2009), p. 159.

20. Miles Taylor, 'Interests, Parties and the State: the Urban Electorate in England, c. 1820–72' in Jon Lawrence and Miles Taylor, eds., *Party, State and Society: Electoral Behaviour in Britain since 1820* (Aldershot, 1997), pp. 64–6.

21. Littleton, *Hansard's Parliamentary Debates* [hereafter H] V 768, 4 August 1831.

22. H IV 338, 24 June 1831.

23. Jonathan Parry, *The Rise and Fall of Liberal Government in Britain* (New Haven, 1993), p. 78.

24. Peel, H V 667–74, 3 August 1831; Russell, IV 338, 24 June 1831; V 773, 4 August 1831.

25. Brougham, H IV 870, 6 July 1831.

26. Stedman Jones, *Languages of Class*, pp. 104–5; Dror Wahrman, *Imagining the Middle Class: the Political Representation of Class in Britain, c. 1780–1840* (Cambridge, 1995), ch. 10. On the social composition of the electorate see Frank O'Gorman, *Voters, Patrons and Parties: the Unreformed Electoral System of Hanoverian England 1734–1832* (Oxford, 1989), ch. 4.
27. *The Times*, 17 April 1866; *Daily News*; *Morning Post*; *Standard*.
28. Robert Saunders, *Democracy and the Vote in British Politics, 1848–1867* (Farnham, 2011), ch. 8.
29. Jane Rendall, 'The Citizenship of Women'.
30. Helen Taylor, *The Claim of Englishwomen to the Suffrage Constitutionally Considered* (1867), p. 8.
31. *The Times*, 5 March 1879; *Standard*.
32. Helen Blackburn, ed., *Because* (1888), p. 18.
33. *The Times*, 27 April 1876; *Daily News*; *Standard*.
34. *The Times*, 8 April 1875; *Standard*.
35. *The Times*, 13 June 1884; *Morning Post*; H III 1496, 27 April 1892.
36. *The Times*, 27 April 1876; *Standard*; *Daily News*.
37. On women's legal disabilities, see Griffin, *Politics of Gender*, pp. 9–14.
38. *The Times*, 2 May 1872; *Standard*.
39. See, for example, A.V. Dicey, 'The Balance of Classes' in A.O. Rutson, ed., *Essays on Reform* (1867), p. 81.
40. Christopher Harvie, *The Lights of Liberalism: University Liberals and the Challenge of Democracy, 1860–86* (London, 1976), pp. 142–57; Parry, *Rise and Fall*, p. 4; Jonathan Parry, *The Politics of Patriotism: English Liberalism, National Identity and Europe, 1830–1886* (Cambridge, 2006), pp. 74, 389.
41. See Griffin, *Politics of Gender*, ch. 2.
42. *The Times*, 27 April 1876; *Standard*; *Daily News*; *Morning Post*.
43. Goldwin Smith, *Female Suffrage* (1875), pp. 8, 23–4.
44. Ibid., p. 31.
45. Ibid., p. 24.
46. Ibid., p. 23.
47. Ibid., p. 24.
48. Holton, *Suffrage Days*, p. 33; cf. pp. 52–3; idem, *Feminism and Democracy*, pp. 10–12, 21, 27; Susan Kingsley Kent, *Sex and Suffrage in Britain, 1860–1914* (Princeton, 1987), p. 171 and *passim*.
49. Cited in Kent, *Sex and Suffrage*, p. 75.
50. On the populist idiom see Patrick Joyce, *Visions of the People: Industrial England and the Question of Class, 1848–1914* (Cambridge, 1991), chs. 2–3.
51. Helen Rogers, *Women and the People*, p. 285.
52. Griffin, *Politics of Gender*, chs. 8–9.
53. *The Times*, 29 February 1884; *Daily News*.
54. Helen Blackburn, *Women's Suffrage: A Record of the Women's Suffrage Movement in the British Isles* (1902), p. 123.
55. Holton, *Suffrage Days*, chs. 2–4.
56. Anna Clark, 'Gender, Class and the Nation: Franchise Reform in England, 1832–1928', in James Vernon, ed., *Re-reading the Constitution* (Cambridge, 1996), pp. 240–1. See also Eugenio Biagini, *Liberty, Retrenchment, and Reform: Popular Liberalism in the Age of Gladstone, 1860–80* (Cambridge, 1992), pp. 309–10.

57. Andrew Jones, *The Politics of Reform, 1884* (Cambridge, 1972), pp. 122–6.
58. Michael Barker, *Gladstone and Radicalism: the Reconstruction of Liberal Policy in Britain, 1885–94* (Brighton, 1975), pp. 211–17; cf. D.A. Hamer, *Liberal Politics in the Age of Gladstone and Rosebery: a Study in Leadership and Policy* (Oxford, 1972), pp. 169–72; Griffin, *Politics of Gender*, pp. 286–7.
59. Matthew McCormack, *The Independent Man: Citizenship and Gender Politics in Georgian England* (Manchester, 2005).
60. H XLV 1212, 3 February 1897.
61. Brodie, H CLXXXV 278, 28 February 1908; Bottomley, CLV 1578, 25 April 1906. Osmond Williams, *The Times*, 9 March 1907. Stanger, H II 1399, 19 March 1909; Lansbury, H XXV 767, 5 May 1911.
62. J. Lowther, *H VIII 1926, 20 February 1893. The asterisk indicates that *Hansard's* copy was approved by the individual quoted.
63. *H CCCLI 60, 3 March 1891.
64. C.T. Ritchie, *H CCCLI 127, 3 March 1891.
65. E.H.H. Green, *The Crisis of Conservatism: the Politics, Economics and Ideology of the British Conservative Party, 1880–1914* (London, 1995), pp. 79–86.
66. See Ben Griffin, 'Class, Gender and Liberalism in Parliament, 1868–1882: the Case of the Married Women's Property Acts', *Historical Journal* 46 (2003), 73–5.
67. H XIX 280, 12 July 1910.
68. Pugh, *March of the Women*, p. 115. I have recalculated Pugh's figures to exclude the Liberal Unionists from the Conservative totals.

8
Irish Nationalism

Matthew Kelly

Gareth Stedman Jones has argued that 'the growth and decline of Chartism was a function of its capacity to persuade its constituency to interpret their distress or discontent within the terms of its political language'.[1] 'A political movement', he explains, 'is not simply a manifestation of distress and pain, its existence is distinguished by a shared conviction articulating a political solution to distress and a political diagnosis of its causes.'[2] During the 1840s, he continues, Chartism lost support because government reforms undermined the movement's fundamental claim that the political system was incapable of implementing reforms that would improve the material conditions of the working class. As Chartism's established political languages ceased to describe the lived realities of its supporters, so the movement inevitably went into decline. Similar patterns can be identified in the development of Irish nationalist languages and activism in the second half of the nineteenth century. The credibility of the heightened nationalist rhetoric generated by nationalism's failures during and after 1848 was undermined by the apparent readiness of the British government, in the light of the Fenian threat of the late 1860s, to address Irish grievances. This *engageant* political environment gave credibility to Home Rule politics and its parliamentary strategy. Despite this – and notwithstanding Jon Lawrence's challenge to the traditional chronology of 'the rise of party' in Britain – Irish nationalism (and unionism) remained relatively 'outdoors' (and localist):[3] the importance of radical agrarianism enforcing the 'unwritten law' grew; Fenianism continued to attract a significant if significantly limited following; and new forms of associational culture, like the Gaelic Athletic Association (1884) and the Gaelic League (1893), generated forms of sociability that often prospected a non-constitutional politics.[4] More importantly, most constitutional nationalists, particularly the Home Rulers, expressed their commitment to parliamentary methods in strictly conditional terms. The Stedman Jones hypothesis suggests that the resilience of these oppositional political traditions were a consequence of the limited capacity of successive British governments to deliver 'justice for Ireland'. If so, expressions of nationalist conviction should not be read merely as a function of material grievance. To do so runs the danger of reproducing exactly those forms of nineteenth-century British optimism that failed to recognise the idealist and immaterial dimensions of nationalism:[5] some constitutionalist nationalists *were* ideologically committed to a form of self-government for Ireland that would leave its connection to the British Empire intact; 'advanced' nationalists, usually separatist republicans, *did* reject constitutional methods as compromising the integrity of the national demand. In practice, these distinctions were often blurred, not least because Home Rulers often sought to wean the separatists off their revolutionary ideals by presenting the constitutional agenda as Fenianism by other means. Orthodox separatists responded by insisting on fundamental ideological distinctions, arguing that the Home Rulers deliberately manipulated language in order to gain converts. To a degree this was so, though these ambiguities were also a measure of Young Ireland's success in scripting the generic language of Irish nationalism in the 1840s.[6] Under the inspired editorial direction of Charles Gavan Duffy, the uniquely successful *Nation* newspaper (established in 1842) published later anthologised contributions by Thomas Davis, James Fintan Lalor and John Mitchel, as well as much patriotic verse, often written by women.[7]

Young Ireland was more a mentality than a movement and its outlook was comprised of several key components. First, they believed that the relationship between Britain and Ireland was that of an imperial power and an imperial possession. Ireland was not a colony of England but a nation subject to a despotic form of alien government. Reforms imposed by that government, even when delivered in consultation with Irish representatives, might improve the condition of the country but could not resolve the fundamental problem of Ireland's sovereignty. Young Ireland thus opposed forms of self-government that would render Ireland a 'province' (formally subordinate to Britain), though most thought Irish nationality was compatible with O'Connell's demand for the repeal of the Act of Union. Young Ireland's cultural politics, however, engorged nationalism with a romanticism that emphasised the long continuity of Irish national life and intensified a sense of Britain's fundamental 'otherness'. Finally, Young Ireland regarded political violence – 'physical force' – as morally acceptable should circumstances appear propitious. This distinguished their thinking from O'Connellism's strict adherence to 'moral force', as deployed either through the ballot box or, most characteristically, at the 'monster meeting'. As this last contrast suggests, neither Young Ireland nor O'Connell strictly adhered to the principles of 'representative' democracy and in this they were typical Irish nationalists. O'Connell found in the assembled people an expression of Irish sovereignty and thus the democratic basis of a personal authority that far outstripped his limited influence as a Westminster MP; Young Ireland located national sovereignty in the *Nation's* citizen readers, on whose behalf they claimed to speak. Successor formations were predicated on similar ideas. Fenianism derived its authority from the 'people', which in this case was the silent masses excluded from various groups – Catholic or Protestant, upper or middle class – who were the beneficiaries of the union state; the Home Rule movement, made plausible by reforms to the Irish franchise, held the Irish people, vaguely but palpably, in reserve. By contrast, in the post-famine period O'Connell's 'not one drop of blood' principle was articulated by many within the Catholic hierarchy and their closest political allies; when taken up by Cardinal Paul Cullen it was shorn of straightforward nationalist aspirations and showed a strong preference for the 'indoors' politics of parliamentary representation rather than the 'outdoors' politics of O'Connellite acclamation.[8] Arguably, Britain's political classes feared revolutionary nationalism less than the 'direct democracy' component of Ireland's nationalisms, including its unionist forms. As Charles Maier explains, to liberal proponents of representative democracy, direct democracy 'meant the illiberal restraint of opinion, the curbing of individuality and of culture, the mobilization of mass sentiment to dominate politics and personnel' and a continual vulnerability 'to despotism, whether exercised by the mob or a tyrant'.[9] To many British observers, this might have been a definition of Parnellism.

Fenian political language dealt in separatist absolutes and this chapter offers reasons why their revolutionary speech gained political traction in the 1860s. Revolutionary politics did become less compelling after Gladstone revived the old Whig mission to deliver 'justice to Ireland' and over the following decades most Irish nationalists adapted readily to the newly receptive Westminster environment. Nonetheless, many nationalists wedded to representative politics retained core beliefs concerning the nature of British government which they frequently reiterated, handing them to the crowd for safe-keeping: most Home Rulers verbalised a politics whose mandate extended beyond the formally franchised. Moreover, and this was characteristic of Charles Stewart Parnell, the commitment to parliamentary means was often presented as conditional, constituting neither submission to Parliament nor the surrender of Irish agency to a temporarily friendly government. Eventually Gladstone, as the concluding section of the essay argues, came to recognise Irish nationalism's idealist and immaterial dimension as an enduring and legitimate political motive.

'An *Irish howl'*

England has been left in possession not only of the Soil of Ireland, with all that grows and lives thereon, to her own use, but in possession of the world's ear also. She may pour into it what tale she will; and all mankind will believe her.[10]

These famous lines open John Mitchel's *Jail Journal*. First serialised in 1854 in the *Nation* and in *Irish Citizen*, Mitchel's Irish-American newspaper, it is one of Irish nationalism's foundational texts. Mitchel began writing in 1848 during his transportation to Tasmania as a convicted treason-felon, recording the effect 1848 had on Ireland. Few would have disagreed that it saw the Repeal agitation disintegrate, the famine decimate the population and the republicans humiliated by their feeble insurrection. In sum, Irish nationalism, helped along by vigorous coercive measures, experienced organisational collapse and the ruin of its international credibility. In the decades that followed, nationalists consistently expressed their concern that they were no longer counted among the 'struggling nations' and this at a time when it was commonly believed that foreign intervention, most likely by France, was essential to the progress of those struggles. Thus, Ireland's nationalists experienced the refashioning of European politics after 1848 as a profound crisis of representation. 'Britain being in possession of the floor,' Mitchel continued, 'any hostile comment upon her way of telling our story is an unmannerly interruption; nay, is nothing short of an *Irish howl*.'[11] Fearing that England – or, more properly, Britain – acted as a barrier against the transmission of voices authentically reflective of Irish public opinion or of Irish historical experience, nationalist attempts to (re)construct a politics of the people were repeatedly articulated in terms of overcoming voicelessness. Consequently, Ireland's best friends were identified as those French Catholic radicals characterised as 'witnesses…who spoke the truth for us' and who 'reverberate the voice of our country amid the civilization of Europe'.[12] At moments of acute international crisis, such as in 1856

(Crimea), 1857 (India), 1859–60 (Italy), 1863 (Poland) and 1870 (Franco-Prussian war), nationalists showed a particular sensitivity to claims made by the London *Times* that it spoke on behalf of Irish public opinion because English and Irish interests had coalesced.[13] Thus, public meetings, spontaneous demonstrations and successive attempts to form new political organisations were represented in nationalist editorials as acts of witness, constituting attempts by nationalists to break through the barrier of English representation and to overcome the apparent indifference of the outside world. By locating their struggle in continental, transatlantic and imperial contexts, polemicists provided evidence of why oppositional nationalism was not merely a stubbornly Irish recalcitrance – a fading echo of what John Belchem calls the 'fragile opportunism' of Irish republicanism in 1848[14] – but was on the side of history. France, whether in its Napoleonic or Republican guises, was expected to catalyse the historical process that would see the empires unravel and nationality become the organising principle of a reborn Europe. As the guarantor of small nations, France was often marshalled in nationalist rhetoric as a counter-pole to the power and influence of imperial Britain.[15]

How these nationalist languages evolved becomes clearer if they are tracked against political developments after 1848. Revolutionary events in France and elsewhere raised the threshold for nationhood, reinforcing the challenge Young Ireland and its radical offshoot the Irish Confederation offered O'Connell's absolutist commitment to non-violent forms of political agitation.[16] In an exultant editorial in March 1848 (probably written by Duffy), the *Nation* expressed its confidence that for 'ages we have been known in Europe, by our constant proclamations, as the lineal and anointed champions of an old Nationality, buried under accumulated outrages'.[17] Recognising the utility of 'constant proclamations' – they *were* being heard – Duffy was also aware of the danger this posed to Irish nationalism's integrity. Addressing the Irish Confederation that same month, Duffy said 'if we are not slaves and braggarts, unworthy of liberty, Ireland will be free before the coming summer fades into winter'.[18] Marking a sudden shift away from Young Ireland's constitutional historicism, Duffy posited the limitations of political language, querying whether the expression of national feeling constituted an act of nationhood. A nation incapable of action, the new context suggested, was merely a people of boastful words rather than effective deeds, and could not be counted among the *struggling* nations.

Eighteen months later, when the humiliations of the Young Ireland rising, the transportation of rebels and his own trial for high treason before a packed jury were fresh in the memory, Duffy again pondered the national status of Ireland. Like Mitchel, he saw that the year of failed revolution, among the worst of the famine years, had 'swallowed ... the temperance reformation, the political training of the people, the labours of years, and pride of generations'.[19] If nations were developmental projects that could succeed or fail, the *Nation* recognised the destruction wrought by the famine on the capacity of the Irish people to be a national and a political people. Rebuilding was needed and it fell to the 'sound men' that read the *Nation* to develop 'an embodied public opinion empowered to think and act on the part of the people'.[20] A new political party was needed, which relied on a civic activism rather than the personality cult that had propelled the Repeal agitation.

A month later, reported by the *Nation* under the inspiring heading 'Resurgam', an 'Aggregate Meeting' of nationalists was convened. After M.R. Layne's rousing opening – repeating the refrain 'Courage, old land!' – Duffy calmly emphasised the need for unity and delineated a set of aims that combined improvement and political reform. Ireland's industrial capacity should be developed, Church temporalities should be abolished, the franchise should be extended and Irish tenant farmers should be accorded greater protections. Standard Irish radical fare, these priorities could be expected to mobilise Catholic opinion, hopefully providing a basis on which a renewed nationalist politics might emerge. Gradualism, sharply contrasting with Mitchel's Carlylean hope of a spontaneous uprising by the people, became one of the motifs of this new politics.[21] Feargus O'Connor, former radical Chartist leader but now an MP, was the meeting's special guest. His advice was telling: 'unless you are thoroughly represented in the House of Commons – you may look upon the land scheme as mere moonshine – you may look upon everything else that is proposed to you as moonshine'.[22] A challenge to O'Connellite and republican legacies, O'Connor's 'indoors' constitutionalism also questioned fundamental nationalist precepts. Suggesting that Britain's policy had been 'to excite and keep up a war between Celt and Saxon', O'Connor implied that the real issues facing Ireland were material and class-based, insinuating that the politics of nation was a form of false consciousness that divided the Irish people from the British people. From such suggestively radical but ambiguously nationalist beginnings developed the sorry history of the Irish Independent Party.[23] Tenant right was its legislative priority, but the pledge demanded of its members to remain independent of all British parties, thereby sustaining a distinct Irish political voice, was its raison d'être. Its slow decline, catalysed when John Sadleir and William Keogh accepted office in the Aberdeen coalition in 1852, generated in 1855 a famous editorial in the *Nation*. Lamenting the 'coma of Irish politics', it decried 'indifferentism' and the 'lethargy in the public mind'.[24] This was the warm-up for the main event, Duffy's address of resignation to the electors of New Ross a week later. This highly charged moment saw the founding editor of the *Nation*, one of the central figures in Young Ireland, and a driving force behind the new politics, announce he was leaving Ireland. Aged 38, he explained, his 'desire of being and doing' was 'still too strong' for him to 'subside into that desponding lethargy which has been the latter end of almost every honest public man in Ireland since the Union'.[25] Excoriating the Church hierarchy for its failure to support the Irish Independent Party according to the principles on which it was established, he said this had led to 'the fixed belief that England could now employ the powers of the Church to defeat the hopes of the people'.[26]

Sadleir and Keogh's 'betrayal' and Duffy's migration to Australia, where he enjoyed a successful political career, are emblematic of the inner failure of Irish nationalism in the immediate post-famine years. Public meetings, elections and petitions, relying much on the *Nation's* continued authority, had failed to overcome nationalism's structural weaknesses. The Church, particularly those elements alarmed by the revolutionary tendencies of nationalist rhetoric – which it associated with continental infidelity and secularism – concluded that its interests were best pursued through a constructive relationship with the government.[27] The burst of anticlericalism encouraged by Duffy's lament coincided with the hope that deteriorating Anglo-French relations might create 'Ireland's opportunity'. This generated space for a new nationalist activism driven by a generation of republicans who eschewed the representative politics of the Catholic social and clerical elite for a direct politics of 'the people'. According to the secular political language of the proto-Fenians, the Irish people were defined as those who believed that Britain had no legitimate role to play in determining Ireland's political future. For instance, the 'preamble' to O'Donovan Rossa's Skibbereen Phoenix National and Literary Society, established in 1857 and alarming enough to be suppressed in early 1859, did not suggest immediately revolutionary purposes but instead laid the emphasis on overcoming voicelessness. 'For years past, since 1848 particularly,' it opened, 'the people of Ireland have been looked upon as having silently acquiesced in their position as a conquered province, and having given up all idea of a national existence'. Though implying that the nationalist predicament could be understood by admitting what outsiders thought, the Phoenix suggested that the problem was partly one of perception rather than reality: the society aimed 'to show, as far as in us lies, the fallacy of this opinion'. To mobilise public opinion in this corner of west Cork would help make heard an Ireland that already existed, though as the modifying interpolation hinted, this was not simply a problem of perception: they needed 'to foster and rouse to action the latent spirit of nationality'.[28]

Around the same time, William Smith O'Brien, the leader of the 1848 rebellion but now thoroughly cautious in his politics, made similarly ambiguous claims. Advocating the formation of an Irish National Party, his account suggested that public opinion had an existence prior to its expression but it had become 'paralysed' because – making a barely veiled reference to Sadleir and Keogh – no political association had survived the 'seductive influences which are at the command of the British Government'.[29] Smith O'Brien admitted that an Irish party might influence policy by holding the balance of power at Westminster but this would not see the legitimacy of Ireland's demands recognised. Thus, he urged that a representative assembly be established in Dublin that could give an independent voice to Irish public opinion. In this way, Ireland's representatives, uncorrupted by Westminster's blandishments, could give authentic expression to the unified Irish voice. An exponent of similar ideas argued that an Irish legislative assembly would counteract 'the efforts made by our enemies to provincialise our country materially and in spirit'.[30] Much of this thinking was underpinned by the idea that the development of Irish national life was integral to the general improvement of life in Ireland, achieving what the Phoenix Society (and later the Fenians) described as the 'enlightenment' of the Irish people. Irish nationalism was not simply, as was once thought of Chartism, 'a passionate negation', but was an ideology of self-improvement, its aims at once instrumental and idealist.[31]

Irish nationalism's difficulty in securing international recognition could not, however, be wholly ascribed to the power of English representation. If O'Connell's continental sympathisers had been troubled by the strength of Irish Catholicism, Irish ultramontanism as manifest in its hostile responses to the Italian *Risorgimento* intensified that scepticism.[32] Catholic nationalists who recognised the contradictions in their position struggled to justify their support for the Papacy through a Faith and Fatherland rhetoric that insisted on the historicist integrity of the Papal States. They insisted that there was no fundamental incongruity between Catholicism and liberalism – indeed, the clergy 'might guard the popular cause from anarchical dangers'[33] – and that the Papal States shared with Ireland an historic right to distinct statehood. Ideological cover was provided by their consistent criticism of the despotic Austrian government, a Catholic power, in Venetia and Hungary.[34] Little, though, could undermine the belief of Europe's leading radicals that Britain's constitutional monarchy placed it in the vanguard of European liberty. It was painful to know that Mazzini thought Irish nationalism lacked a transcendental dimension and was simply a desire that the country be 'better managed', with 'all the marks of injustice and political inequality in that wide province of Great Britain' effaced.[35] Equally bruising was the rapturous reception that greeted visitor-exiles to Britain like Lojos Kossuth, Giuseppe Garibaldi and, to a lesser extent, Father Gavazzi. Each celebrated English liberty and each was prone to play the anti-clerical card.

To take Kossuth as an example: on leaving Hungary, he quoted Augustine Thierry to the effect that nationhood was natural and 'is not to be put out of her way by any devices of government or legislation'. As proof, he noted the survival, after 600 years attempted 'assimilation', of Ireland's 'peculiarities of thought and demeanour'.[36] Irish national-ists drew comfort from this orthodoxy, some regarding the apparently imminent unravelling of the European empires as the fulfilment of a divine plan. The *Nation* rarely missed an opportunity to assert the simi-larities between Ireland and Hungary,[37] presenting Kossuth as an exem-plary leader who had successfully combined 'his countrymen in peaceful leagues' that 'strove religiously to avert the horrors of war while freedom and peace were compatible; yet felt assured he was ripening them for war if war became inevitable'.[38] Such a reading vindicated Young Ireland's radicalisation in 1848, while the notion that a peaceful agitation might legitimately turn to war prefigured the distinguishing political language of Parnellism.

Kossuth's time in England left Irish nationalists bitterly disappointed. Arriving at Southampton, he expressed his 'most firm conviction that the freedom and greatness of England are in intimate connection with the destinies and liberty of Europe'.[39] England, he said, was 'the older brother to whom the Almighty has not in vain imparted the spirit to guide the tide of human destiny'.[40] He made similar claims several days later during a banquet held in his honour in the city.[41] Irish nationalists might reiterate, repeatedly and at length, the parallels between Ireland's and Hungary's histories, but Kossuth did not recognise the parallel they drew between England and Austria. Lamenting Kossuth's 'No-Popery' cry, the *Nation* insisted that the Hungarian needed to 'make reparation to Ireland' for speaking of England in terms of 'the greatness, the glory, the liberty, the magnanimity of England'.[42] Duffy, however, accepted that Ireland, once an 'angry province' whose 'dramatic agitation' had the 'world for spectators', was not on Kossuth's 'roll of nations' and was 'of no account in European politics'.[43] Some months later when speaking in the United States, Kossuth treated the Irish elements in his audience emolliently if condescendingly ('who would not sympathise with poor, unfortunate Ireland?'), but maintained that the advance of English liberty was beneficial for Ireland.[44] At least one Irish-American newspaper was unimpressed. It contrasted the 'true patriot' Thomas Meagher, who had dramatically escaped his sentence of penal servitude in Australia, with Kossuth, 'a counterfeit' on a 'money-making tour'.[45]

Kossuth's anti-Romanism was mild compared to zealously anti-Roman continental radicals like Alessandro Gavazzi. Until 1850, Gavazzi was 'emphatically a Popish preacher' but his Mazzinian allegiances placed him at odds with Pius IX and he too went into exile in England. There he converted to Protestantism and became a Barnabite monk, making a reputation by pandering to English Protestant prejudices.[46] Providing reassurance that English sectarian instincts were justifiably liberal, he maintained that Protestantism guaranteed freedom whereas Roman Catholicism was a form of slavery and Rome's 'war' against Protestantism was a 'war against civil and religious liberty'.[47] Other exiles like Louis Blanc, a veteran of 1848 known for sympathising with Ireland's nationalists, were deeply disturbed by what he observed of Catholic clerics exploiting the Irish people's 'fierce and savage love' for the Pope, which blinded them to recent improvements affected by England.[48] He regarded the Garibaldi riots in Hyde Park of 1861 as a 'disgusting spectacle' that saw an 'orderly meeting of English workmen…furiously assailed by a host of ragged Irishmen, armed with heavy bludgeons'. These 'wretched slaves of a gross fanaticism' were the victims of priests who 'inflame their passions instead of enlightening their minds'.[49]

Irish nationalists internalised much of this criticism. They worried that Irish public opinion was too weak to sustain a morally distinct position, as evident in the comparisons, often unflattering, they made between the capacity of Ireland and the other 'struggling nations' to fight their causes. For example, Polish nationalists, attempting to liberate themselves from Russian domination in the early 1860s, provided a comparison that could be both inspiring and dispiriting. Whereas Kossuth's, Mazzini's and Garibaldi's anticlericalism problematised any identification with Hungary and Italy, to identify with Poland was more straightforward. Ireland and Poland, the *Nation* claimed, were 'intensely Catholic as well as national'; both possessed an 'inextinguishable desire for Liberty!'[50] From March 1861, the newspaper's pages were saturated with news and comment on Poland, with much editorial space given over to confidently elucidating the strong parallels between these 'sister nations'. That said, a year later the *Nation* exclaimed, 'Would that we in Ireland had the same community of sentiment, the same concert of action, the same lofty resolve as our suffering brethren in Poland!'[51] Irish unity had been undermined by the machinations of the English for the '"higher" classes', seduced by the material advantages of the Union and now 'aloof...from the people', had ceased to be Irish.[52] This claim was commonly made in post-O'Connell Ireland and the Fenians in particular believed Catholic emancipation had been designed to separate the middle classes (and the priests) from 'the people' by integrating them into the system of interests that sustained the Union.[53]

The 'people', sacralised in one breath, were often found wanting in the next. British influence led the Irish to urge on 'the efforts of the [imperial] aggressor', making them a 'participator in his crimes'.[54] By raising awareness of the apparent similarities between Irish and other national experiences under 'imperial' government, including those of non-European peoples like the Indians or the Maoris, advanced nationalists fostered an international and inter-racial solidarity to combat this false consciousness.[55] At the same time, criticism of Irish public opinion was consistently tempered by the claim that no country had experienced so systematic a process of imperial denationalisation as Ireland. In the immediate context, this was thought most evident in 'the "National" education and place-hunting *systems* organized by the English', though polemicists could adeptly locate such recent developments within a continuum dating back to the twelfth century.[56] Foreign observers, because ignorant of this historical trajectory, were misled by the liberal trappings of the British state. So thorough and so demoralising had the effect been, that advanced nationalists could imagine Polish identity withstanding another century of Russian attempts to 'imperialise' them but Irish identity might not survive another century of the 'rule as now operating amongst them'.[57]

If more upbeat editorials on Irish and Polish resilience in the face of oppression drew succour from old orthodoxies, the failure of the French to fulfil their Napoleonic destiny in Poland in 1863 weakened hopes that had sustained non-Fenian advanced nationalism since 1848. Fenian revolutionaries, having equipped themselves with a newspaper, responded by complaining of a political culture that relied on flawed words rather than effective deeds. A generation after 1848, the established political class was again condemned for regarding the nation as reified through excitedly received speech rather than collective action.[58]

Particularly marked in these new separatist political languages, despite the iteration of many familiar claims, was the need for disciplined action: a Spartan ethos would restore the Irish nation's self-respect, while in time knowledge of the nation itself would be restored to the world through autonomous revolutionary action. Crucially, this alignment with international revolutionary currents was combined with a rigorous insistence on self-reliance. Notwithstanding R.V. Comerford's persuasive thesis that Fenianism originated as an opportunistic response to the Anglo-French tension in the late 1850s, the Fenians nonetheless rejected the view that a French invasion was the necessary precursor to an Irish uprising.[59] If their anticlericalism chimed with the Mazzinian views of Irish nationalism's radical critics, the Fenians nevertheless rejected a politics predicated on the notion that the Irish nation was validated by the recognition of others. According to their logic, nationalism was necessarily revolutionary for any dependency on the goodwill or the weakness of another nation, French or British, was fundamentally at odds with the principle of self-determination.

More particularly, articulators of the Fenian ideal refused to be distressed by non-recognition, finding Irish nationalism's anguished '*howl*' debasing. By rejecting a nationalist politics predicated on the possibility of reconciliation with Britain, they rejected the idea that Britain was Europe's liberal vanguard. Insisting that British liberalism was a carapace for an imperial self-interest reinforced throughout the world by force, Fenians took it for granted that British sympathy for the national claims of the Italians, the Hungarians and the Poles would not be extended to Ireland. No Fenian doubted that the charge of English hypocrisy, among the most enduring motifs in the language of Irish nationalism, could be upheld.

'Dumb Ireland will speak again'

Superficially, Fenianism failed. The most effective articulators of the Fenian ideal were imprisoned, punished and exiled in 1865 and the rising of March 1867 amounted to little. Fenianism succeeded in other ways. It bequeathed separatist nationalism a rapidly developed memory culture, central to which was the cult of the three 'Manchester Martyrs', hanged in November following the infamous van break of September 1867 during which a policeman was shot dead. Judging by the police files, the British authorities in Ireland came to treat the size of the annual November processions that occurred throughout Ireland as indicative of the strength of Fenian sentiment.[60] Also important, of course, was the widespread assumption that Fenian activity had prompted liberal reform. Gladstone's notorious public recognition of the 'intensity of Fenianism' as a significant political force expressed what many people were thinking.[61] Archbishop Croke, for instance, privately refused Cullen's demand that he condemn the Fenians outright, saying they had 'given us a tolerable land Bill and disestablished the Protestant Church'.[62]

Isaac Butt, a Tory Protestant barrister, shared Gladstone's hope that clear political boundaries could be established between Irish nationalism's 'Politics Pacific' and 'Politics Bellicose'.[63] His federal answer to the Irish question, which quickly became known as Home Rule, was not new but his timing was good.[64] To succeed, he needed to do three things. First, to coax the Fenians away from nationalisms of abstract separatist principle, second, to persuade Irish nationalists to give up their Anglophobia *and* historicist constitutionalism and, third, to convince Irish Protestants, unnerved by Gladstone's Irish legislation, that their interests would be served by a self-governing Ireland. Crucially, none of this precluded conventional expressions of nationalist sentiment or thinking. Butt claimed that 'the desire for national independence will never be plucked or torn from the heart of the Irish nation',[65] a theme he addressed at length in the extraordinary final section of his pamphlet *Irish Federalism! Its Meaning, Its Objects, and Its Hopes*.[66] Intended to 'impress upon my views and opinions a visionary character',[67] these eight pages discussed the Irish nation's ancient origins and its exceptional resilience and religious faithfulness in the face of 700 years of conquest and oppression. Federalism, Butt insisted, should appeal to those who saw the Irish question as a practical political problem and to nationalists who saw their commitments in more transcendental terms.

> The Providence that has watched over the Irish people has designed and is fitting them for some high and noble end. ... I know that we have qualities as a nation which only need self-government, with its duties and responsibilities, to bring them into great and glorious action, before which all those things that lower, and divide, and reproach us, will vanish away.[68]

Butt reiterated other traditional aspects of nationalist thinking. Believing Ireland had been misgoverned since the Act of Union, he highlighted the depth of poverty, the horrors of the famine and the level of emigration, as well as the state's frequent resort to legal persecution, its tolerance of corruption and its reliance on police despotism. Ireland's statue books, he argued, suggested 'brute force was the one expedient of Irish

Government, and the highest object of Irish Statesmanship was to crush down the spirit of the nation'.[69] Equally conventional was Butt's belief that the religious divide in Ireland was not sectarian but strictly political and stemmed from Britain having established Protestants in Ireland as 'her garrison'.[70]

Lengthy pamphlets by cautious enthusiasts like J.G. MacCarthy (a Corkman elected as a Home Ruler in 1874) and the Dublin priest Rev. Thadeus O'Malley, the self-titled 'Father of Federalism in Ireland',[71] made the case for Home Rule in terms of the twin advantages of maintaining the connection to Britain and fulfilling Lockean notions of good governance. This, MacCarthy wrote, was predicated on the 'desirableness' of finding a 'safe middle course' between 'separation' and 'over-centralisation'.[72] Answering the (phantom?) charge that Home Rule was 'communistic' or 'revolutionary', MacCarthy alluded to the recent fate of the Second Empire by explaining that it was 'beneath the shadow of great centralisation that Communism grows'.[73] O'Malley took up this theme, criticising the present system for making Irish measures of 'improvement' subject to the approval of parliamentary committees 'composed for the most part of gentlemen ignorant and heedless of the matter in hand'. This impeded 'the free action of our municipal councils and all our administrative boards'.[74] More firmly, he insisted that 'people not governed by laws of their own making are, in the strictest sense of logical terms, *slaves*'.[75] Irish disrespect for the law, so often lamented by British observers, reflected not inherent Irish characteristics but the fact that it was 'not home-made law' but 'the law of the foreigner'; this explained the widespread feeling that the law was not owed '*moral* obedience'.[76] The occasional 'unthinking recklessness' of the Irish, described by MacCarthy as 'rowdyism', was characteristic 'of slaves of whatever clime or whatever condition of slavery' and contrasted 'with the steadiness and forecast of freemen'.[77] Thus, whereas the Fenians had emphasised the moral responsibility of the individual to live according to the national ideal, early Home Rulers offered political explanations for the failings of the Irish, suggesting that new political institutions would mould the Irish people into responsible tolerant citizens. As MacCarthy explained, the Protestant minority had nothing to fear:

> It is of the very essence of civil liberty that the majority should not ride down the minority. It is the very pride of representative government that the rights of minorities are protected. It is the very glory of political philosophy to make intelligence, education, and property of more weight in social affairs than mere 'count of heads'.[78]

O'Malley expressed similar sentiments in more aggressively political terms. Taking up Fenianism's anticlerical 'priests in politics' polemics, he argued that the priests, recognising the 'sacred *duties* of patriotism', must remain outside of party politics but should strongly encourage the people to participate in the political process.[79] Strikingly, O'Malley fiercely criticised Cullen for implying that the Irish were Catholic and the Protestants 'not Irish at all' and he expressed his astonishment that 'sensible men' entertained 'the notion that the Cardinal rules Ireland'.[80] MacCarthy's pluralism was framed differently. He rejected the notion that the divisions in Ireland were racial, arguing that Celts, Normans and Saxons had become 'fused long ago'. For him, this problematised the very idea that Ireland had been conquered; instead, this historical 'intermingling' had made Ireland a distinct national community entitled to self-government but with historical and practical connections to Britain that could not be severed without doing violence to that history.[81] Federal self-government would embody these complexities and, as O'Malley argued, allow Ireland to take 'her old place in the councils of Europe', putting an end to its decline since 1800 into 'an effeminate Asiatic power'.[82] Give Ireland 'a State Legislature and a State Executive', wrote MacCarthy, and '[d]umb Ireland will then speak again'.[83]

Like much early writing on Home Rule, O'Malley's and MacCarthy's pamphlets took as their starting point the need to explain a political agenda that remained obscure to many observers. N.D. Murphy MP, in a public letter to his constituents, made the same point more directly. Surveying the range of responses to Home Rule, he correctly observed that Butt's federalist conception of Home Rule had achieved neither widespread understanding nor acceptance. John Martin, long associated with advanced nationalist causes and the first Irish MP to be elected under the Home Rule banner, was thought by Murphy to be 'basically antagonistic to the programme of the Home Government Association': Martin tended to express his Repealite nationalism in a fairly advanced register. To complicate the picture further, Murphy judged other 'Nationalists' who had adopted the Home Rule cry to be out of sympathy with the HGA *and* Martin. If, on the one hand, the *Irishman*, an advanced nationalist newspaper, argued that it would take more than 'a noisy agitation' to bring about Irish unity, on the other hand, another 'Nationalist Journal' objected to Martin's belief, often expressed by conservative advocates of Home Rule, 'that the Irish people are a monarchical race, and that they do not aspire to the full dignity of nationhood'. Accumulatively, this suggested to Murphy that the term Home Rule had 'passed out of the hands of its originators' and was generally taken to mean separation.[84]

This he could not countenance, but nor was he convinced by Repeal because he rightly thought the 1782 Parliament had been subordinate to Westminster. If Murphy believed Ireland would only be governed properly once it had an independent domestic legislature, his difficulties with the federalist idea saw him feeling his way towards the devolutionist position Gladstone adopted a decade or so later.[85]

Murphy's complaint that 'Home Rule' had quickly come to signify a generalised nationalist sentiment divorced from Butt's precise federalism can by amply justified. Sometimes this imprecision was exploited by Home Rule polemicists – O'Malley argued that *'Fenian Ireland'*, which to him meant 'the whole mass of the Irish people', wanted Home Rule[86] – other times it carried more separatist implications. Pages could be dedicated to unpicking these ambiguities, but a single illustrative example will suffice. In the preface to his *Home Rule Ballads*, John Denvir – a leading Liverpool nationalist – explained how his selection bore 'more or less on Ireland's numerous efforts to obtain Home Rule, *by whatever name the struggle*, from time to time, may have been called'.[87] Though most of the *Ballads* formed part of a long-established song tradition (Thomas Davis' 'Nationality' was second on the programme), Denvir pointedly included two new songs celebrating the involvement of Protestants in the cause ('We two shall rend her chains'). The opening song, a new ballad called 'Home Rule for Ireland' by 'Slieve Donard', associated Home Rule with Brian Boru and Hugh O'Neill, locating it within an unchanging tradition. The ballad closed:

> Our true old land ne'er faltered
>   Though chained and crushed for weary years;
> Her purpose never altered,
>   Nor yielded once to craven fears:
> And now again she's telling,
>   In tones that speak a nation's will,
> Her firm resolve—loud swelling—
> Home Rule for Ireland still![88]

Though the ballad emphasised telling and speaking – the 'nation's will' was again overcoming voicelessness – this was just this kind of baggy nationalist sentiment that irritated advanced nationalists in the 1850s and 1860s.

A more satisfactory avatar of Home Rule nationalism soon emerged in the person of Parnell. The process by which he came to the notice of the advanced nationalists, particularly in the United States, and then achieved his extraordinary ascendancy during the Land War (1879–82), has been often delineated. Of particular note, was that the leaders of Irish-American nationalism demanded that Parnell drop the federal commitment from the Home Rule agenda, though it registered little in mainstream Home Rule speech by the late 1870s anyway.[89] More generally, the contrast between his distant personality and the austerities of his speech with the verbosity and warmth of O'Connell's platform oratory has been found significant by many historians,[90] though it has not been fully recognised how the post-1848 reaction against verbosity helps account for this aspect of his appeal.[91] In any case, the reported speech – Parnell wrote little – of no other Irish politician has been subjected to such close scrutiny. Although Oliver McDonagh suggested that the peculiar power Home Rule had under Parnell's stewardship was that he never defined it – Gladstone did that in the form of primary legislation – most historical analyses have minimised the advanced nationalist component of his speech.[92]

And yet, a re-reading of Parnell's political language suggests that the constitutionalist/physical force dichotomy is not always the most helpful way of making sense of his speech. Though he did not verbalise an overt separatist politics, his speech legitimised a more radical nationalism, including at times physical force separatism. His commitment to Parliament as the site of political action was always expressed conditionally and he reserved the right to resort to the 'outdoors' as necessary. Moreover, when in September 1877 he said 'our duty is to demand', he moved parliamentary nationalism into a new key, urging that Irish MPs 'carry out a vigorous and energetic policy' at Westminster, which until then 'Irishmen had always carried out in every place except the House of Commons'.[93] Parnell's repeated insistence that Irish politicians must express the Irish people's demands directly, refusing to tailor their words to what they believed British politicians could accommodate, was portrayed as a form of self-assertion constitutive of genuine political action. Like Duffy, Smith O'Brien, the Fenians and others before him, he 'wanted the country to know its own mind', to show a 'little more disregard of what English members or English masters say', and then to act accordingly. The English government, Parnell insisted, 'must no longer trifle with the voice and wishes of Ireland'.[94] In this way, 'great good may be done', but if their demands were not met, their 'duty' – which extended to the Irish at large – was to 'show them that they must give it'. He could state the same principle more provocatively: 'No amount of eloquence could achieve what the fear of an impending insurrection – what the Clerkenwell explosion and the shot into the police van had achieved'.[95]

Such statements were less calculated gestures towards Fenian sensibilities, than acts of complicity, in which 'Clerkenwell' and the 'shot into the police van' functioned as metonyms for an Irish refusal to adhere to those British norms that sustained Irish subjecthood. Such eloquence, however, could not make good Ireland's democratic deficit, which early in the Land War Parnell linked to the system of property holding: 'You can never have civil liberty so long as strangers and Englishmen make your laws, and so long as the occupiers of the soil own not a single inch of it'.[96] Despite this, there were ways in which the Irish could express their democratic will, as Parnell explained in September 1881:

> We cannot by the law of the land declare that Irish manufactures shall be protected, but we can protect them by our unwritten law, by the public and organised opinion of the great majority of the people of this country, in accordance with whose opinions all laws governing Ireland ought to be made, and it we resolve, if we bind ourselves together into an organization to protect Irish industries, depend upon it that Irish industries will flourish and thrive in Ireland, but in no other way can you succeed.[97]

There was an important continuity here with earlier nationalist statements regarding notions of legitimate government and how public opinion was reified through unified action. And it was to the exercise of this 'unwritten law', so central to the radicalisation of the Land League, rather than to orthodox Fenianism, that Parnell referred a month later when he said that it was 'most desirable' in any movement of their kind 'that there should be a large section considerably in advance of the rest'.[98] Two days later, Parnell made the remarkable speech that led to his arrest under the provisions of the Protection of Life and Property Act. Scorning Gladstone's threat that the 'resources of civilisation were not exhausted' as being 'like a whistle of a schoolboy on his way through a churchyard at night to keep up his courage', his more substantive response synthesised much post-'48 nationalist polemic, identifying the prime minister's hypocrisy and slander as an act of misrepresentation:

> Not content with maligning you, he maligns your bishops, he maligns John Dillon. He endeavours to misrepresent the Young Ireland party of 1848. No misrepresentation is too patent, too mean, or too low for him to stoop to. And it is a good sign that this masquerading knight-errant, this pretended champion of the rights of every other nation

except those of the Irish nation, should be obliged to throw off the mask to-day, and to stand revealed as the man who by his own utterances is prepared to carry fire and sword into your homesteads unless you humbly abase yourselves before him, and before the landlords of the country.

Parnell continued, repeating the familiar claim that the government of Ireland was illegitimate because it was conducted according to the interests of a small elite.

In one last despairing wail he [Gladstone] says – 'And the Government are expected to preserve peace with no moral force behind it.' The Government has no moral force behind it in Ireland, the whole Irish people are against them. They have to depend for their support upon a self-interested and a very small minority of the people of this country, and therefore they have no moral force behind them[.]

In those 'few short words', Parnell declared to the Wexford crowd, Gladstone had admitted the 'contention' of Grattan and the volunteers of 1782, the revolutionaries of 1798, O'Connell, the Young Irelanders, 'the men of '65', and 'you in your overpowering multitudes…that England's mission in Ireland has been a failure, and that Irishmen have established their right to govern Ireland by laws made by themselves on Irish soil'.[99] Parnell's exploitation of the idea that Home Rule, despite its constitutional credentials, was continuous with previous nationalist efforts, sometimes revolutionary in nature, contrasted sharply with Butt's careful attempts to differentiate his ideas from previous nationalist thinking. As significant was the invocation of those 'overpowering multitudes'. Read in conjunction with the personal attack on Gladstone, it becomes clear that Parnell believed British government in Ireland was arbitrary and despotic and that democracy existed in Ireland only through the unified action of the people. A similar claim was evident in Parnell's response to the government's decision to move a new Coercion Bill in March 1883. He then accused Spencer – pointedly referred to as 'the noble Lord' – of behaving as though he were entitled 'to rule Ireland as if she had not a representative system and as if, in fact, she was outside the pale of the Constitution and in the position of a conquered province'.[100] The repetition of 'as if' was important: it was senior British politicians, unable to shake off an aristocratic will-to-power, rather than Irish nationalists, who stood accused of abusing a constitution that had the capacity to deliver satisfaction to Ireland.

Things changed for a brief period after Gladstone flew the Hawarden 'Kite' in December 1885. Hansard recorded lachrymose scenes of reconciliation between the prime minister and the Irish benches but as astonishment faded so the 'union of hearts' evolved a more restrained political register. In June, before an audience in Portsmouth and without evident passion, Parnell restated Isaac Butt's original definition of Home Rule, arguing that it would 'prove a more durable settlement than the restitution of the Grattan Parliament or the Repeal of the Union...Imperial unity does not require or necessitate unity of Parliaments'.[101] Two months later, in an address to a London audience, Parnell explained the shift in mood, reiterating the conditional nature of his commitment to Home Rule and historicising his earlier defiance. They could be 'more moderate' than in 1879–80 because their position was 'very much stronger'; Irish MPs and the Irish people recognised this and would 'use those weapons of legality and of moderation' that had 'so distinguished their cause up to the present' and had 'gained...the respect and sympathy of the whole civilised world'.[102] A more discordant conditional note clanged through Parnell's London speech of May 1889. Delivered in the aftermath of Parnell's appearance before the Special Commission, it was 'the only important political speech' he addressed to an Irish audience in this period:

> If our constitutional movement were to fail I would not continue twenty-four hours at Westminster. The most advanced section of the Irishmen, as well as the least advanced, have always thoroughly understood that the Parliamentary policy was to be a trial, and that we did not ourselves believe in any possibility of maintaining for all time or for any lengthened period an incorrupt and independent Irish representation at Westminster.[103]

If anomalous in the context of Parnell's 1886–90 speeches, it is hard to miss the prophetic nature of these words, for the substantive political issue underpinning the Home Rule party split of 1890–1 was 'independent opposition' at Westminster. If the speech of May 1889 is compared with one of February 1891, the paradoxical nature of the split becomes clear: continuities in argument are stronger than the breaks, but the violence of the split's political language made Parnell's commitment to constitutional methods less provisional and more fundamental:

> I took off my coat for the purpose of obtaining and consummating the future of Irish nationality.... I shall stand upon this constitutional

platform until they have torn away the last plank from under our feet. I desire to say here to-night that I believe we can win on the constitutional platform. But if we cannot win upon it, well, I shall be prepared to give way to better and stronger men, and it can never be said of us that by anything that we have done we have prevented better or abler men than ourselves from dealing with the future of our race.[104]

Parnell did indeed maintain his constitutional ethic, as analysis more sustained than this has shown,[105] but the violence of his expression was significant. Rather than the muted rhetoric of the 'union of hearts', here again were the languages of confrontation, defiance, distrust and opposition, and in being so they explicitly extended to the advanced nationalists a renewed legitimacy.[106] In early August, Parnell enlisted the revolutionaries Edward Fitzgerald and Robert Emmet as independent oppositionists;[107] later that month, standing on an amnesty platform in Dublin's Phoenix Park, he made a plea:

[O]n behalf of men who have shown by those many years of suffering how pure and how good was their love for Ireland…Had it not been for them, for the spirit which Ireland's political prisoners and Ireland's martyrs have at all times kept alive in the Irish heart, we should not to-day have an Irish nation to struggle for[.][108]

These pure-hearted men were not imprisoned Fenians or Land Leaguers but the 'dynamitards' of the early 1880s. When Isaac Butt gathered popular acclaim as a patron of the Amnesty Association in the late 1860s, he had sought the release of imprisoned Fenians on the grounds that their actions were foolish but understandable. Parnell's last speeches, here tuned to the needs of 'political prisoners' who could make no claim to represent a popular movement, went beyond a retrograde recourse to the populist certainties of his first years in politics. Nonetheless, to read the political languages of his whole career suggests it was the language of 'union of hearts' rather than the final 'appeal to the hillside men' that was the discursive aberration.

Shortly before the Fenian actions of 1867, Gladstone admitted that England's 'duty' to the Irish people had not been 'discharged', which was awkward given how they had 'gone about preaching to others that they ought to have regard to national rights, feelings, and traditions'. Around the same time, John Stuart Mill wrote that to hold Ireland by force without addressing obvious Irish grievances would place England 'in a state of open revolt against the universal conscience of Europe and Christendom'.[109] If, by admitting that the charge of British hypocrisy was plausible, this chimed with much Irish nationalist polemic, Gladstone's *The Irish Question*, published shortly after the failure of his first Home Rule Bill, was more explicitly concessional.

Insisting that the implementation of Home Rule would align the national interest with high political principle, he emphasised the 'moderate' extent of the Home Rule demand, the 'constitutional medium' through which it had been expressed, and his insistence that it would not damage 'the unity and security of the Empire'.[110] Though Gladstone conceded that the means by which the Act of Union had been passed were 'unspeakably criminal',[111] and though he admitted the integrity of the Irish people as a distinct nationality, he reserved to Britain the right to judge whether the Irish people were 'ripe' for some form of self-government. This was no more evident than in his suggestion that 'no authoritative voice from Ireland' had been heard before the 1880s.[112] If, as he maintained, the Home Rule party was the first political organ that could be judged truly representative of the Irish people as a nationality, it was equally the case that this form of representation had only become possible following the passage of reform legislation in 1884–5. By withholding the means by which Irish nationality might be judged legitimate, the British ensured that Irish nationality could not speak in a voice that Liberals were obliged to hear; what could be heard instead was the howl of Irish grievance, which British governments presumed to interpret. In a claim infused with liberal optimism that recalled early Irish arguments in favour of Home Rule, Gladstone argued that the Irish had adopted constitutional methods because the franchise had been extended. Granted responsibilities, they were behaving responsibly. 'The evil spirit of illegality and violence', he wrote, 'has thus far had no part or lot in the political action of Ireland, since, through the Franchise Act of 1885, she came into that inheritance of adequate representation, from which she had before been barred.'[113]

Gladstone's pamphlet was remarkable for its recognition of the fundamental challenge Irish nationalism posed the incorporating assumptions of the union state. He denied Ireland the right to self-determination and he did not contemplate any derogation of British sovereignty in Ireland, but he did acknowledge the truth of Irish nationalism's core complaints: Ireland had been misgoverned; Britain's support for the 'struggling nationalities' was made hypocritical by its policy in Ireland; government should manifest the national will. The Irish Question, Gladstone explained, had given 'a new place to nationality as an element in our political thought'.[114] If the union state was to be governed justly, English MPs, preponderant at Westminster, had to overcome their prejudices and learn to vote according to the particular national needs of the three smaller nations. Morality rather than weakness necessitated this, for in the age of nation a simple majoritarianism would no longer do.[115] Eleven years later, in the one of last acts of his long career, Gladstone agreed to be interviewed by R. Barry O'Brien, Parnell's biographer. In these few pages, little noticed by historians, Gladstone expressed directly what was implicit in *The Irish Question*.

I could not, of course, support Butt's movement, because it was not a national movement. I had no evidence that Ireland was behind it. Parnell's movement was very different. It came to this: we granted a fuller franchise to Ireland in 1884, and Ireland then sent eighty-five members to the Imperial Parliament. That settled the question. When the people express their determination in that decisive way, you must give them what they ask.[116]

More remarkable still was the way Gladstone adopted the language of the speech that had triggered Parnell's arrest in 1881:

The union with Ireland has no moral force. It has the force of law, no doubt, but it rests on no moral basis. That is the line that I should always take, were I an Irishman. That is the line which as an Englishman I take now.[117]

Gladstone failed to recognise how the political force of Irish Unionism, particularly in its emergent Ulster form, was also significantly re-shaped by the reforms of 1884–5. Unionism's exceptional capacity to mobilise 'outdoors' pressure would later paralyse the British government, rendering the Liberal Party's later determination to deliver Home Rule implausible. This progressively degraded the proof that representative politics could deliver 'justice for Ireland', generating in early twentieth-century Ireland new political languages and a new politics of the 'outdoors'.

Notes

1. Gareth Stedman Jones, *Languages of Class. Studies in English Working Class History 1832–1982* (Cambridge, 1983), p. 96.
2. Ibid.

3. Jon Lawrence, *Speaking for the People. Party, Language and Popular Politics in England, 1867–1914* (Cambridge, 1998); K. Theodore Hoppen, *Elections, Politics, and Society in Ireland 1832–1885* (Oxford, 1984), 341ff.

4. See Heather Laird, *Subversive Law in Ireland, 1879–1920: from 'Unwritten Law' to the Dail Courts* (Dublin, 2005); Owen McGee, *The IRB* (Dublin, 2005); M.J. Kelly, *The Fenian Ideal and Irish Nationalism, 1882–1916* (Woodbridge, 2006).

5. On how such optimism guided government reform, see Andrew Gailey, *Ireland and the Death of Kindness: the Experiences of Constructive Unionism, 1890–1905* (Cork, 1987).

6. R. F. Foster, *Words Alone. Yeats and his Inheritances* (Oxford, 2011), pp. 50–2.

7. See, for example, Thomas Davis, *Literary and Historical Essays* (Dublin, 1846); James Fintan Lalor, *Collected Writings* (Poole, 1997).

8. Matthew Kelly, 'Providence, Revolution and the Conditional Defence of the Union: Paul Cullen and the Fenians' in Dáire Keogh and Albert McDonnell, eds., *Cardinal Paul Cullen and his World* (Dublin, 2011), pp. 308–328.

9. Charles S. Maier, 'Democracy since the French Revolution' in John Dunn, ed., *Democracy. The Unfinished Journey. 508 BC to AD 1993* (Oxford, 1993), p. 128.

10. Mitchel, *Jail Journal*, p. 9.

11. Ibid.

12. *Nation*, 17 May 1862.

13. Notably, *Nation*, 3 January 1857.

14. John Belchem, 'Nationalism, Republicanism and Exile: Irish Emigrants and the Revolution of 1848', *Past and Present* 146 (1995), 113.

15. In general, see Matthew Kelly, 'Irish Nationalist Opinion and the British Empire in the 1850s and 1860s', *Past and Present* 204 (2009), 138–40 and 'Languages of Radicalism, Race, and Religion in Irish Nationalism: The French Affinity, 1848–1871', *Journal of British Studies* 49 (2010), 801–25.

16. See Foster, *Words Alone*, pp. 78–9.

17. *Nation*, 4 March 1848.

18. Ibid.

19. *Nation*, 8 September 1849.

20. Ibid.

21. T.J. Meagher, Young Irelander, transported to Australia, praised Duffy: 'The path you have pointed to is, certainly, a long and irksome one, and will painfully test the patience, the moral courage, and the endurance of the people. But, after all, it is the surest one, and the one best adapted for the progress of a nation the energies of which have been so cruelly reduced.' *Nation*, 3 August 1850.

22. *Nation*, 24 November 1849.

23. The fullest account, which questioned the traditional nationalist reading, is J.H. Whyte, *The Independent Irish Party, 1850–59* (Oxford, 1958).

24. *Nation*, 11 August 1855.

25. *Nation*, 18 August 1855; cf. R.V. Comerford, 'Churchmen, Tenants, and Independent Opposition, 1850–56' in W.E. Vaughan, ed., *A New History of Ireland. V. Ireland Under the Union, 1. 1801–70* (Oxford, 1989), pp. 410–11.

26. *Nation*, 18 August 1855.

27. Comerford, 'Churchmen', pp. 407–9.

28. *Nation*, 19 December 1857.

29. *Nation*, 3 April 1858.
30. *Nation*, 24 July 1858.
31. M. Hovell cited unfavourably by Stedman Jones, *Languages of Class*, p. 99.
32. On the Catholicity of this Irish response, see Jennifer O'Brien, 'Irish Public Opinion and the Risorgimento, 1859–1860', *Irish Historical Studies* 34 (2005), 289–305.
33. *Nation*, 29 December 1849.
34. Kelly, 'French Affinity', pp. 812–14.
35. P.A. Taylor, 'Mazzini and the Irish question' (1887), pp. 2, 4; C. Kinealy, *Repeal and Revolution: Ireland in 1848* (Manchester, 2009), p. 31.
36. *Nation*, 17 November 1849.
37. *Nation*, 10 November 1849, 18 August 1851.
38. *Nation*, 8 September 1849.
39. *Kossuth. His Speeches in England, with a Brief Sketch of his Life* (London, n.d.), p. 8.
40. Ibid.
41. Ibid., 21.
42. *Nation*, 1 November 1851.
43. *Nation*, 29 November 1851.
44. *Nation*, 24 April 1852.
45. *New York Herald* as cited in the *Nation*, 19 June 1852.
46. J.W. King, *Thirty-First Thousand. Alessandro Gavazzi: A Biography* (London, 1860), p. 3.
47. *Father Gavazzi's Oration* (London, 1854).
48. Louis Blanc, *Letters on England*, 2 vols (London, 1866), I, p. 308.
49. Ibid., II, pp. 159, 162.
50. *Nation*, 16 March 1861. Since Duffy's departure, the *Nation* was owned and edited by A.M. Sullivan, a Young Irelander whose Catholic-nationalist views shaped the newspaper's editorial line.
51. *Nation*, 12 April 1862.
52. Ibid.
53. Matthew Kelly, 'The *Irish People* and the Disciplining of Dissent' in Fearghal McGarry and James McConnel, eds., *The Black Hand of Irish Republicanism. Fenianism in Modern Ireland* (Dublin, 2009), pp. 44–6.
54. *Nation*, 28 November 1857, quoting the *Wexford People* on the Indian 'mutiny'.
55. See Kelly, 'Irish Nationalist Opinion', 140ff.
56. *Nation*, 25 May 1861. My emphasis.
57. Ibid.
58. Kelly, 'The *Irish People*', pp. 39–42.
59. R.V. Comerford, 'Anglo-French Tension and the Origins of Fenianism', in F.S.L. Lyons and R.A.J. Hawkins, eds., *Ireland Under the Union. Varieties of Tension* (Oxford, 1980).
60. Eoin McGee, '"God save Ireland": Manchester Martyr Demonstrations in Dublin 1867–1916', *Eire-Ireland* 36 (2001), 39–66.
61. Gladstone's parliamentary speech was much reproduced, including in R. Barry O'Brien, *The Life of Charles Stewart Parnell* (London, 1898), p. 53.
62. Oliver MacDonagh, *States of Mind. Two Centuries of Anglo-Irish Conflict, 1780–1980* (London, 1983), p. 100.

63. Chapter headings from MacDonagh's *States of Mind*; H.C.G. Matthew, *Gladstone 1809–1898* (Oxford, 1997), p. 194.
64. Isaac Butt, *Irish Federalism! Its Meaning, Its Objects, and Its Hopes*, 4th edn (Dublin, 1874), p. v.
65. Ibid., p. ix.
66. The technicalities but not the romance of Butt's scheme are outlined in John Kendle, *Ireland and the Federal Solution. The Debate over the United Kingdom Constitution, 1870–1921* (Kingston, 1989), pp. 12–14.
67. Butt, *Irish Federalism!*, p. 57.
68. Ibid., p. 62.
69. Ibid., pp. 42–3.
70. Ibid., p. 63.
71. Alfred Webb, *A Compendium of Irish Biography* (1878).
72. John George MacCarthy, *A Plea for the Home Government of Ireland* (Dublin, 1872), p. 9.
73. Ibid., pp. 13, 82.
74. Thadeus O'Malley, *Home Rule or The Basis of Federalism* (London, 1873), p. 6.
75. Ibid., pp. 11–12.
76. Ibid., p. 17.
77. Ibid., p. 11; MacCarthy, *A Plea*, p. 17.
78. MacCarthy, *A Plea*, pp. 76–7.
79. O'Malley, *Home Rule*, pp. 94–5.
80. Ibid., pp. 106, 110.
81. MacCarthy, *A Plea*, p. 62.
82. O'Malley, *Home Rule*, p. 16.
83. MacCarthy, *A Plea*, p. 45.
84. N.D. Murphy, *Home Rule. A Letter to His Constituents* (London, 1871), pp. 3–9.
85. Ibid., pp. 10–15.
86. O'Malley, *Home Rule*, p. 2
87. *Home Rule Ballads* (Liverpool, 1874), p. 1. My emphasis.
88. Ibid., p. 2.
89. On the 'New Departure', see T.W. Moody, *Davitt and Irish Revolution, 1846-82* (Oxford, 1981), 249ff.
90. See Donal McCartney's and Pauric Travers' introduction to the reprint of C.S. Parnell, *Words of the Dead Chief* (Dublin, 2009), pp. xiv–xx.
91. Butt had complained of this as early as 1836. See Foster, *Words Alone*, p. 27.
92. Paul Bew, *C.S. Parnell* (Dublin, 1980), pp. 124–32; Frank Callanan, *T.M. Healy* (Cork, 1996), pp. 257–404; Robert Kee, *The Laurel and the Ivy. The Story of Charles Stewart Parnell and Irish Nationalism* (London, 1993), p. 592; F.S.L. Lyons, *Charles Stewart Parnell* (Dublin, 1977), p. 642; Pauric Travers, 'Reading Between the Lines: The Political Speeches of Charles Stewart Parnell' in Pauric Travers and Donal McCartney, eds., *The Ivy Leaf. The Parnells Reconsidered* (Dublin, 2006), pp. 56–7.
93. Parnell, *Words*, p. 16.
94. Ibid., pp. 20–1, 34.
95. Ibid., pp. 15–17.
96. Ibid., pp. 33–4, spoken at Navan (12 October 1879).
97. Ibid., p. 63

98. Ibid., p. 64.
99. Ibid., pp. 64–7.
100. Ibid., p. 86.
101. Ibid., p. 113.
102. Ibid., p. 117.
103. Conor Cruise O'Brien, *Parnell and His Party* (Oxford, 1957), p. 234; Parnell, *Words*, p. 138.
104. Parnell, *Words*, p. 151.
105. See note 92.
106. On the organizational component of Parnell's neo-Fenianism, see Kelly, *Fenian Ideal*, ch. 2.
107. Parnell, *Words*, p. 164.
108. Ibid., pp. 167–8.
109. Cited in J. Parry, *The Politics of Patriotism: English Liberalism, National Identity and Europe, 1830–1886* (Cambridge, 2006), p. 259.
110. W.E. Gladstone, *The Irish Question* (London, 1886), pp. 5–6.
111. Ibid., p. 11.
112. Ibid., p. 13.
113. Ibid., p. 55.
114. Ibid., p. 36.
115. Ibid., p. 51.
116. O'Brien, *Life of Charles Stewart Parnell*, p. 562.
117. Ibid.

9

The Silence of Empire: Imperialism and India

Jon Wilson

When Charles, Marquess Cornwallis, died in 1806, British politicians were not certain what his life should be commemorated for. He died within months of William Pitt and Admiral Nelson, and, like them, had once been celebrated in the idiom of martial heroism, when his troops defeated Tipu Sultan at Seringapatam in 1792.[1] But in 1806, in his second term as Governor-General, dying on the way to negotiate peace with Maratha states, Cornwallis was seen more as an administrator and diplomat than a soldier. He was no longer a great military leader, nor was he a state-builder, an orator or a defender of the people.[2] He had become, to use the word with which Britons criticised the practitioners of empire a century later, a bureaucrat.

Like the practice of empire in India more generally, Cornwallis's life in India was difficult for Britons to assimilate into the dominant roles and idioms of metropolitan British political life. The language they used to talk and write about their place in the Indian subcontinent was shaped by arguments between British politicians, not by what they or their Indian interlocutors did in the subcontinent. This chapter traces those arguments, showing how domestic political traditions moulded attitudes to India, and prevented the very different logic which dominated colonial practice from erupting into metropolitan discourse. It is, though, with that practice that we should begin. Colonial governance in India had three characteristics which were radically out of kilter with the dominant idioms historians recognise in nineteenth-century British political discourse.

The practice of empire

Colonial practice was explicit about the dramatic break it constituted with the past of both British and Indian statecraft. Thomas Macaulay noted as much in his speech on the Charter Act of 1833, arguing that the anomalous character of British rule in India meant that 'we interrogate the past in vain' for guidance on how to rule.[3] Consequently, colonial practice was radically anti-historicist, as administrators relied on general principles more than historical narrative to explain what they did.

In the 1770s, British officers in India had spoken the historicist language which saturated politics in Britain, emphasising the East India Company's place in an Indian ancient constitution and the historical origins of its own rights in the British polity.[4] Yet this idiom was abandoned amidst the crises which led to Lord Cornwallis' arrival in Bengal in the mid-1780s. In contrast to the long, historical disquisitions in which British institutions in India were debated beforehand, Cornwallis' restructuring of the East India Company administration in Bengal after 1786 was justified in short statements of abstract reason.[5]

As Sebastien Meurer argues, the Governor-General drew from the rationalist approach to government pioneered by the commissioners of public accounts, appointed in 1780.[6] Both Cornwallis and the commissioners argued that public institutions needed to be infused with a spirit of 'administrative economy' that assumed individuals responded rationally to self-regarding financial motives. Such principles were supposed to guide all human action irrespective of space and time. Yet whilst the commissioners' work represented a short-lived moment in British administrative rationalism, a similar anti-historicist spirit endured in British attitudes towards governing India.

Secondly, with its emphasis on abstract principles and general rules rather than political storytelling, this nascent idiom of imperial governance emphasised the importance of measures rather than men. Colonial institutions treated individuals, British as well as Indian, as automata motivated by universal drives, or as members of massive, supposedly homogenous, cultural or racial categories. Colonial practice pushed aside the distinctions of individual character and personality that nineteenth-century British political argument relied on. The British government of India left little room for individual self-fashioning, for the cultivation of virtue as anything other than correct, disciplined conduct according to rules framed by the sovereign. As a man whose life was supposed to be circumscribed by rigid rules, the civil servant in India ended up as the antithesis of the manly, self-reliant Englishman celebrated in metropolitan political discourse.[7] From Cornwallis onwards, Britons often asserted the theory that their authority was founded on superior character. Honour, manliness, self-sacrifice, integrity and the capacity to make autonomous judgements were crucial. But the gap between this rhetoric and the reality of official life was frequently noted, as officials described themselves as cogs in a machine which corroded those virtues in practice. Instead of being a cadre of men who emulated each others' moral character and developed a common sense of 'public spirit', the Civil Service in India was 'a fortuitous congregation of mutually repellent atoms' as an 1872 guide for officials put it.[8]

These first two characteristics were symptomatic of a third aspect of British rule. British power in India was profoundly anxious about the basis of its authority. Security was the first priority: the dominant mood was mistrust about forces with the potential to undermine a weak state. The practice of empire was underpinned not by the will to power, but by a pervasive anxiety about the British capacity to know what its subjects were doing, and to protect its position in spite of this estrangement from its subjects.

It was this mood which led even the most conservative imperial officers to advocate governance through codified rules. They believed written texts would minimise the scope for the exercise of discretion by potentially corrupt Indians. As Governor of Bombay, it was Mountstuart Elphinstone who first formally proposed the codification of Hindu law into texts controlled by the colonial power to check the actions of Indian officials that he believed were corrupt. The *raiyatwar* revenue system – which the army officer and later Governor of Madras Thomas Munro created – was an attempt to annihilate the power of small local rulers, and to rely on supposedly more trustworthy sources of information about local society instead, not least the cultivators 'themselves'.[9] Both Elphinstone and Munro, as well as other officers who collaborated closely with Richard and Arthur Wellesley, such as John Malcolm, are often seen as romantic imperialists ruled by an historicist sensibility. Yet in practice, as Eric Stokes pointed out long ago, there was little to distinguish what they did from utilitarianism.[10]

With their emphasis on abstract reason and rule-bound systems and security, the languages employed by men in the practice of governance occupied a very different epistemological field from metropolitan discourse. The strange voice of colonial practice in India did occasionally speak in Britain. When it did, it was often heard to speak in a utilitarian voice. Utilitarianism was not a feature of the British discussion of India because Jeremy Bentham and James Mill 'influenced' British officers there. Instead, the connection occurred as the strange situation of colonial governance led colonial officers to draw sceptical conclusions about the possibility of government in India with anything other than an abstract view of law, and a mechanistic account of human motivation.

It was its visceral critique of vested interests and familiar political relationships which linked utilitarianism to an official class anxious about its ability to understand and govern India unless a small, rational elite made the rules. But it was its rationalism, and belief in a centralised bureaucracy with despotic power, that made the arguments of utilitarians so marginal in the metropole. Even Mill needed to place his utilitarian analysis of the British presence in India within a very different kind of narrative for it to be palatable to British reading tastes.

Far from enshrining a clear and confident 'progressive' narrative about imperial transformation, James Mill's *History of British India* was a book that attempted to resolve a crisis that he believed the British empire was facing in India. He argued that British administration in the subcontinent was bedevilled by semantic chaos and linguistic uncertainty, a condition he also believed afflicted British politics and law as well.[11] To make this argument, Mill drew from a recent genre written by British officers who emphasised the difficulty of understanding India, the chaos of law and government and the immoral character of its population. The former revenue official and later Governor-General John Shore, the district officials Henry Strachey and Alexander Fraser Tytler, and chaplain William Tennant were particularly important.[12] Mill argued that a coherent narrative was impossible until British imperialism itself was able to impose regularity on the subcontinent. In the meantime, he published a work that marked its own ambivalent relationship with the meaning-producing practices of his present day. Explaining why he had not consistently spelt Indian names Mill noted that 'It appeared to me to be not altogether useless, that, in a book intended to serve as an introduction to the knowledge of India, a specimen of this irregularity should appear.'[13]

But the *History* did tell a coherent story about something. Most of it conformed to the dominant idioms of eighteenth-century British narrative history, celebrating and condemning the manly virtues or effeminate vices of military and political heroes in India since the early seventeenth century. Here, Robert Clive was the villain, the French general Labourdonnais the hero and Cornwallis an ambivalent figure, criticised for not introducing written law, but praised as a military leader. Of the 150 references by name to Cornwallis, 110 discuss his role in the war in Mysore.[14] Here, it is clear Mill that knew his market. The *History's* account of the British in India as a story about heroic military exertion allowed his book to be read by a public that did not concur with his utilitarian critique.

Rather than utilitarianism, the twin poles of conquest and constitutionalism structured the debate in Britain on the relationship with India.

As we will see, both subtly changed through the nineteenth century. Occasionally, they were transformed through the influence of events and institutions in India. Usually, they were not. The forces which shaped their movement were more closely linked to politics in Britain than the practice of colonialism in India.

Conquest

Conquest, and the emphasis on India as a scene for British military prowess and power, were the dominant themes in a Tory language of empire which endured in Britain from the 1810s until at least turn of the twentieth century. This idiom celebrated the violent origins of British rule in India and saw Britain's presence there primarily from a geopolitical point of view. Its dominance in India allowed it to dominate the world, and so needed to be fiercely protected. As Lord Curzon later, famously, put it, 'as long as we rule India, we are the greatest Power in the world. If we lose it, we shall drop straight away to a third-rate Power'.[15] But conquest was seen as placing limits on the scope for British action in India. It was argued that Indian hierarchies needed to be carefully preserved, even when the practice of colonial rule eroded existing forms of interaction. The result was that metropolitan Tory imperialists had very little to say about the way in which India was actually ruled.

This Conservative strand of imperial thought had roots deep in the eighteenth century, in both the Tory idea that all regimes were rooted in violence and hierarchy and the notion that polities were sustained by sentiment not reason. It was a truism in eighteenth-century Britain that everyone loved a conqueror; it was also a cliché that the *reasons* for this admiration were difficult to understand rationally. David Hume argued that philosophers were 'more inclin'd to hate than admire the ambition of heroes', but noted that '[h]eroism, or military glory, is much admir'd by the generality of mankind'.[16] In his 1783 essay on *The Right of Conquest* the portrait painter Allan Ramsay argued that it was 'vain' for moralists to teach 'us that a man who invades the property of others at the head of fifty thousand men is but a Robber on a larger scale'. This was an unusual attempt to rationalise in philosophical terms the love of conquest.[17] In making the philosophical case for conquest, Ramsay articulated a long-standing high Tory argument that royal power was needed to create order, and that sovereignty always depended on conquest. By the time he was writing, the men and women of letters who articulated such as an absolutist position were few and far between, but the place of pride in conquest within Tory political rhetoric, in particular, endured throughout the nineteenth century. The circle around Richard and Arthur Wellesley in India and then London were most significant in shaping this Tory idiom. John Malcolm, Richard Wellesley's private secretary, Governor of Bombay, and a crucial ally of the Duke of Wellington in the 1830s was particularly important.[18] For the Wellesleys and Malcolm, British powers in India needed to be free from the constitutional limits of Company and Parliament in London in order to exercise martial virtue in the Indian subcontinent. In doing so, their purpose was to establish a stable form of authority able to counter both the nefarious actions of Indian rulers and revolutionary France.

Like Mill, the Wellesley circle saw India as a place riven by chaos. But whereas Mill believed that order came from law, regular administration and the creation of transparent rules, for Malcolm and his allies it came from the use and threat of violence. As Arthur Wellesley put it, in India 'the foundation and instrument of all power there is the sword'.[19] The East India Company's military strategy in India depended on the projection of Britain's martial power and prestige, not merely its commercial self-interest. Malcolm's language was infused with the sense that policy was not a matter of rational calculation but the projection of passions and manipulation of emotions – something that neither Hume nor Ramsay would have agreed with, but which Mill would have been appalled by.

Like later writers in the Tory tradition of thought that Malcolm shaped, the British government of India was viewed from the perspective of its fragile frontiers outwards. As long as peace was maintained and taxes sufficient to pay for an army were collected, what happened within those frontiers barely matter at all. Britain's empire in India was about national status not the way the lives of the population who lived there were administered. Cornwallis was praised as a man whose career was 'grounded on that proud but just sense of national honour which will not suffer itself to be approached by the breath of insult'.[20] His 'civil' administration merited no treatment at all in Malcolm's political history.

Unlike Mill's, this was a vision of empire concerned with a search for ways to 'reconcile to the rule of strangers the various communities which formed the vast population of India'.[21] Malcolm praised Clive's insistence that Indian political forms were upheld as his noble act of conquest. He believed the British ruled best where they used the sword to over-awe, then retained Indian forms of authority in place. This argument made sense in London, but was constantly undermined by the British obsession with abstraction and security in India. In *The Life of Clive* Malcolm praised the attempt of British officers to gain 'an acquaintance with the languages, habits and characters' of Indians and attacked Mill's 'laboured and metaphysical' arguments about the irrelevance of experience.[22] Yet he did not notice that British insecurities corroded the colonial regime's ability to trust Indian forms of hierarchy in areas under direct British rule. In practice, the paranoid tendency of the British to meddle in the affairs of 'native states' undermined Indian rulers' attachment to imperial power in some places, or made local sovereignty hollow.[23] While Malcolm wrote, his close friends in positions of administrative authority were busily remoulding Indian legal and political forms with a rationalist approach to law and government.

The purpose of *The Life of Clive* was to return the excitement and heroism to a narrative about the great deeds of heroic Britons which had, Malcolm thought, been traduced by cosmopolitan calumniators like Mill. (It seemed fitting that Mill's greatest hero was French.) Malcolm wanted to tell a story about the superior virtue of Britons acting overseas. His attempt to ensure the British polity was accountable to something more noble than the petty, commercial values that dominated the East India Company connected his narrative to a British high Tory political constituency which was profoundly uneasy about the pace of industrial and commercial change.

Within this Tory imperial tradition gallant imperial officers and proconsuls were a source of stability within the British polity. Seconding the Tory opposition to the 1831 Reform Bill in the House of Commons on behalf of his friend the Duke of Wellington, Malcolm argued that reform threatened to sever the connection between Westminster and empire, particularly India. In a long speech, he mentioned the link between imperial representatives and India's '80 million people' in only one, short sentence. It was not 'India' but the Britons who 'were extending the fame of their native land into the remotest quarters of the world' that needed to be represented. Reform would signal that Britain did not care for imperial patriots like him. If the 'Constitution was to be broken up, adieu to that patriotism which had carried England through so many difficulties.'[24]

In these texts and speeches, Malcolm articulated a consistent Tory language about Britain's place in India which endured until at least the early twentieth century. Within this tradition, empire in India was a field for noble British actions and an expression of the power of Britain in the world. As Lord Mayo, Disraeli's first Viceroy put it, Conservatives believed that holding India was demanded by 'our national character'.[25]

At the centre of this Conservative language was the belief that the British in India faced a choice between imposing violence themselves, or being subject to the conquering ambition of another power. On his voyage to India after being appointed Governor-General and Viceroy by Disraeli in 1876, Lord Lytton outlined energetic plans for British imperial expansion in Egypt and South Africa which appalled his Liberal friend John Morley.[26] The 'forward policy' which Lytton developed towards Afghanistan was rooted in the sense of the interconnection between violence and British prestige which motivated those musings. In the last quarter of the nineteenth century, fear of Russia was a dividing line between Liberals and Conservatives.[27] Liberals worried that Tories were stoking paranoia in order to justify costly imperial wars. Lytton's actions towards Afghanistan were based on what had become the Tory doctrine that Britain's security in India depended on its ability to impose itself by force on its frontiers. As a result, Lytton authorised the first instance of 'conquest' since the rebellion of 1857–8, and he and other Tory colleagues were bitterly critical of Gladstone's departure from Kandahar in 1881.[28]

Lord Curzon was the most self-conscious exponent of this Tory imperial sensibility, obsessed with the grandeur of imperial authority and continually concerned to memorialise those he believed had founded it. He spent a lot of time trying to erect monuments to Robert Clive. Like Malcolm, he believed the 'dazzling achievement' of a man who had 'planted the foundations of an Empire more enduring than Alexander's' had been unjustly maligned by 'the avenging page of history'. In 1907, Curzon won the argument with the new Liberal Secretary of State for India, John Morley, about whose statue should be erected outside the new Foreign and Commonwealth Office. Morley wanted a statue of Garibaldi. Curzon insisted it should be Clive. With its exploding cannons, Curzon's statue between the India Office and Treasury in Whitehall is the first representation of Clive to depict the violence he authored.[29]

Conservatives like Lytton and Curzon wanted to restore a form of hierarchy which Conservatives feared was being lost in liberal, increasingly democratic, England. At its centre was the monarch who, as Miles Taylor shows, called herself 'Empress' of India from before 1876, and insisted on exercising her prerogative powers over the Indian army. With her close friendship to Wellington and Ellenborough and her understanding of herself as a 'warrior queen', Queen Victoria's sense of herself was bound up with a Tory conception of empire in India.[30] 'Ornamentalist' imperialists from Victoria down projected 'chivalry and ceremony, monarchy and majesty' to try to create a stable, hierarchical order.[31] Pageantry was key. Disraeli had sent the romantic poet Robert, Lord Lytton, to India primarily to shape the lush celebration of Anglo-India's conservative social order which occurred with the formal declaration of Victoria as Queen-Empress, *Kaiser-e-Hind*, in 1877. The celebrations Lytton created portrayed India as a rigid hierarchy in which the 'feudatory' relationship between subjects, princes and supreme sovereign was central, and defined in terms of the number of guns fired in salute.[32] This vision had princely India at its centre, even though four-fifths of India was governed directly by British district officials rather than intermediate Indian sovereigns. But the district British bureaucracy which governed most of the subcontinent did not fit easily into Tory visions of rule.

Nonetheless hierarchies based on fine gradations of ceremonial authority were overladen with starker, more racially defined, forms of difference. For some, rule through a 'native aristocracy' was seen as more appropriate for people deemed less able to rule themselves than the British. But, as Lord Salisbury argued, 'the condition of a protected dependency is more acceptable to the half-civilized races.... It is cheaper, simple, less wounding to their self-esteem, gives them more careers as public officials, & spares them unnecessary contact with white men'.[33]

Missing from this language was the everyday task of governing people in India. As P.J. Marshall notes in a review of David Cannadine's *Ornamentalism*, this hierarchical view often ran out of kilter with the sensibility of men posted to empire who 'went along' with the practice of colonial governance with little enthusiasm for its ruling ideologies. There was an extraordinary gap between the language of metropolitan imperialism, and the practical situation, the actions and effects, of colonial administration. Nineteenth-century India saw what Marshall calls the 'great human tragedy' of mass mortality, as millions were killed by dearth and disease.[34] Indians died across North and West India as the colonial regime's rigid attitude to tax collection exacerbated increases in land revenue, and compounded peasants' exposure to markets they were ill-equipped to engage with. The result was what David Hall-Matthews describes as a 'slide into famine' in the 1870s and then again in the 1890s.[35]

A consistent conservative response might have attributed mass death to the demise of protective local hierarchies. In practice, officials stuck to rigid doctrines of laissez-faire and a famine policy which, at best, provided a sub-subsistence level of income for famine victims. The priority, as for Cornwallis, was cheap, secure government and an administration whose conduct was determined by a clear set of rules.

Lytton's two most important Tory projects, proclaiming Queen Victoria as Queen Empress and 'securing' Britain's dominance over Afghanistan occurred amidst famine throughout much of the subcontinent. It was Sir Richard Temple, the Conservative Lieutenant-Governor of Bengal from 1874 and then Governor of Bombay from 1877, who was most associated with the imperial regime's laissez-faire famine policy, arguing for very meagre levels of support. Yet famine relief in territory directly ruled by his government played an insignificant part in the story of his career that he told when he returned to Britain. He spent far longer talking about the 'native states' ('a bulwark of strength to the Empire') and the 1877 assemblage.[36] Conservative languages about empire were very difficult to reconcile with what men who were Conservatives actually did in the empire.

Constitutionalism

If prestige, pageantry and above all conquest were central to conservative ways of thinking about empire in India, the Liberal ideas about foreign policy which Jonathan Parry has recently outlined challenged the idea that empire was a field for the British to exercise martial valour and a place from which they gained geopolitical strength.[37] Within this language, Britain's moral character came not from the conduct of military heroes in glorious battle, but the participation of people within historically-rooted institutions that cultivated a common sense of national sentiment. Britain acted well overseas when it furthered autonomy and popular participation in the countries it was concerned with. In a constitutionalist idiom, virtue mattered more than honour, and virtue relied on institutions which had a degree of popular involvement. Conquest was an act that brought separate people together in an 'unnatural' union; it also bolstered the role of unaccountable aristocratic authority and the army within Britain's polity. As a result, it was a continual source of anxiety. If national self-belief was based on Britons belonging to what Parry calls an 'inclusive polity', an empire based on the rigid rules of 'barrack and bureau' was hard to countenance. Opposition to the dominance of the army and officials unaccountable to any representative body were a central part of Whig and then Liberal attitudes to empire from the 1820s to 1910s.

In many cases, the Liberal emphasis on the institutional, cultural and racial conditions of popular government in Britain allowed them to draw a far sharper distinction between Europe and Asia than Conservatives did. Religious belief was more commonly used by Liberals than Conservatives to explain British unity and Indian difference. The problem, instead, was that governing a society supposed to be so different involved tools that threatened to corrode Britain's own polity.

If Britain was an inclusive rather than hierarchical state, a popular rather than authoritarian regime, what place would India have within its polity? How could India be governed without undermining Britain's constitutional liberties? To answer these questions, Liberals had a far wider variety of arguments at their disposal than historians recently concerned with 'liberalism and empire' suggest. They tended to address it in one of three ways. First, they argued that colonial governance could be reformed so that British India could be an inclusive polity. Second, they defended despotism by arguing that it laid the foundations for some kind of future better state, but in the process accepted the Conservative claim that governing despotically need not corrode Britain's liberties. Finally, they diminished the centrality of India to stories about Britain's empire, some even arguing India was not part of the empire at all. But Britain's relationship with India was fraught. James Mill's emphasis on colonial India as a chaotic place that confounded rational thought was a staple of liberal discourse, which only began to be undermined at the turn of the century.

First, in the early nineteenth century it was briefly possible to argue that India's polity needed to enjoy the benefit of a participatory constitution and govern itself. The language here was of English liberties being spread abroad, through emigration and the creation of a free press and jury trials. Occasionally, radicals spoke about forms of popular political representation. As Andrew Sartori suggests, a form of political liberalism which imagined the joint governance of India by Britons and Indians was founded upon a brief period of Anglo-Asian commercial partnership. Between the 1820s and the commercial collapses of the late 1840s, cross-racial commercial organisations stretched from colonial port cities into both the hinterland and out into South Asia's global commercial networks.[38] In these decades, possible economic connections formed the basis for a colonial brand of inclusive liberalism which saw the cities of Bombay, Calcutta and Madras as multi-ethnic spaces of enlightened civility within a pan-continental English constitution. These 'English' towns, the East India Company's three presidencies, were the battleground in a conflict between the territorial jurisdiction of the British crown and the extra-territorial sovereignty of the Company. The focus was particularly on law. Calcutta, Madras and Bombay's English law courts were seen as possible parts of a mixed constitution whose rival elements would balance one another and ensure the liberty of the subject in British India.[39]

In the 1820s in Bombay this radical Whig vision of empire challenged John Malcolm's Tory emphasis on the authoritarian consequences of conquest. As Governor of Bombay, Malcolm argued that the Supreme Court's attempt to protect Indian litigants against both neighbouring Indian rulers and the Company would sow chaos. The court's actions threatened 'to seriously weaken by a supposed division in our internal rule, those impressions on the minds of our native subjects, the existence of which is indispensable to the peace, prosperity and permanence of the Indian empire'.[40]

Back in Britain, this inclusive vision of empire played a role in the discussion of the 1832 Reform Act. The radical Joseph Hume briefly made common cause with Malcolm in making the case for the inclusion of imperial representatives in Parliament. But whereas Malcolm had stressed the need to find a political home for returned pro-consuls through MPs being nominated by the Court of Directors, Hume suggested that representatives from India should be elected by everyone who qualified as a juror in India itself, including propertied Indians living in the presidency towns.[41] Hume's arguments were the last gasp of an eighteenth-century form of imperialism which believed that pockets of English rule overseas could easily be assimilated into England's constitution. Hume had nothing to say about how Indians living under British rule outside Bombay, Madras and Calcutta might be included within India's structures of rule. Accordingly, his vision of an English but multiethnic empire of trading posts and commercial connections was belied by the changing reality of British power. A maritime empire had become an intricate structure for projecting British authority over a population living in Indian-ruled states that lived off the land.

Malcolm's theory of empire did not offer any more detailed prescription for how to administer this empire than did Hume's. But its emphasis on the need for a unitary, undivided power in India for empire to survive began to be accepted beyond his own narrow political circles. Philosophical Whigs like Macaulay accepted the unphilosophically Tory argument that British India to be ruled by a single will. Unlike Joseph Hume, they argued that India needed to be made exempt from the principles which ruled Britain's constitution. India was different, British rule strange, and to incorporate the two an impossibility. In the debate on the renewal of the Company's Charter, Hume doubted whether any measure could be 'entirely free from anomalous provisions'; but the government should try to iron them out over time. Macaulay made the exception into the rule. Britain's empire in India was itself 'the strangest of all political anomalies', he argued. 'The Company is an anomaly', he went on, 'but it is part of a system where every thing is anomaly. It is the strangest of all Governments: but it is designed for the strangest of all Empires.'[42]

Macaulay offered a second solution to the constitutionalist conundrum of a self-consciously inclusive polity ruling a people who had no say in their own rule. As he argued, the future existence of an inclusive polity in India depended on the imposition of British laws and education now. He began at the same place as Mill, with the argument that India was a chaotic society, in need of order more than self-rule. Unlike Mill though, he defended the *theory* that only self-governing people were ruled well, but suggested that the real experience of British rule proved that in reality, Britons were capable of administering a despotism virtuously. '[W]e' he said, 'have established order where we found confusion'.[43]

Macaulay did not think conquest itself could be good, but it could be redeemed by the virtuous acts which followed. As he suggested in his review of Malcolm's *Life of Clive*, conquerors like Robert Clive were driven by avarice and a lust for power. But Clive's virtue came in his attempt to redeem the vice of conquest through a series of reforms that rooted out corruption and consolidated British rule. Conquest would be redeemed by improvement, and the eventual creation of a self-governing Indian public. For Macaulay, the purpose of British despotism in India was to undo itself.[44]

Macaulay's speeches and writings on India in the decade after the Reform Act show how critics of conquest had been drawn into systems of imperial rule that took the conquest story for granted. The despotic administrative power of British rule was a fact that, for men like Macaulay, needed to be justified in a way that did not undermine the liberal critique of violence and un-inclusive hierarchy as the foundation for a stable polity. Macaulay's move was to imagine that British authoritarianism could be an instrument to produce the ends of a liberal society in India. To make that argument, India and Britain needed to be seen as regions alien to one another separated not just in space but by time. India was placed within a past whose present would be similar to Britain's. Acting, for Macaulay, as the carrier of a superior civilization, imperial administration was an agent that would push Indian social relations forward in time.

These arguments have recently been treated by historians as the dominant justificatory rhetoric for nineteenth-century empire.[45] Yet they emerged late. As Karuna Mantena has recently suggested, liberal imperialism did not last long. The 'reforming' emphasis on British rule as a force of social change was continually trumped by concern with the security of British power. The idea of progressive time articulated by philosophical Whigs like Macaulay could be twisted to arouse in Britons fear that transformation threatened the sources of British authority. As Mantena argues, Henry Maine's historicist arguments justified a form of imperial practice intended to consolidate what was increasingly being defined as a 'traditional' society, and for whom imperial transformation would bring a cataclysmic social rupture.[46]

James Mill's emphasis on the chaos and insecurity of the empire in India was the first moment when the anxieties of colonial practice broke through into metropolitan discussion. The criticism of liberal imperialism by mid-nineteenth century scholar-administrators such as Maine, James Fitzjames Stephen and Alfred Lyall was the second. Maine and Stephen's 'Indian experience' led them to argue that all forms of government were ultimately based on the threat of force, an argument Stephen made most forcefully in his vituperative critique of John Stuart Mill, *Liberty, Equality, Fraternity*.[47] For them, the necessity of despotism in India proved that democracy could work nowhere. For this new generation of mid-nineteenth century authoritarian Whigs, *all* societies, in Europe as well as Asia, needed to be ruled by a virtuous elite whose main tool of governance was the promulgation of written codes of law. But codification was not seen as a vehicle for social transformation, as it had been for Macaulay and James Mill. Maine and Stephen saw it as a way of preserving social relations intact in their present state, protecting either Britain's modernity or India's tradition from destabilizing social change.

Far from confirming Liberal arguments about progressive social and political developments, empire in India undermined the sense many had of the need to maintain the inclusive, participatory character of Britain's polity. Imperial governance in India, involving the rational manly exertions of an educated elite for the protection and slow improvement of unenfranchised subjects, stood in contrast to what was seen as the increasingly chaotic, overly emotional politics which they detected in Britain with the rise of Gladstonian democracy.[48] As rationalists, sceptical about the theological claims of institutionalised religion and suspicious about the endurance of institutions when not legitimised by utility, these men were not sympathetic to the sentimentality of Conservatism. Yet on an increasing number of issues in India, Ireland and eventually Britain, they became intellectual allies of Tory administrators. Stephen, who stood and lost as a Liberal candidate for Parliament in 1873, was

Lord Lytton's main epistolary interlocutor in India, and the catalyst for the young George Curzon's obsession with empire. Lytton described Stephen's letters as 'chief among the greatest comforts and enjoyments' of his life in the subcontinent. Curzon's enthusiasm for Asia began, so the future Viceroy said, on hearing Stephen speak about India as a schoolboy at the Eton Literary Society.[49]

The reality of empire meant that stadial arguments about progress were never enough to justify the fact of despotism despite the language of inclusion. By the later years of the nineteenth century, Liberal writers developed a third strategy – to deny the reality of conquest, and insist on the continued separation between Britain's constitutional polity and India. For John Seeley, Gladstone's appointment as Regius Professor of History at Cambridge and author of *The Expansion of England*, this effectively meant denying that India was part of the British empire at all.

For Seeley, Britain's Anglophone 'settler' colonies were a necessary extension of British ways of life, but the connection with India was far more fragile and contingent. He suggested that when it first arrived to the subcontinent, the East India Company found an anarchic and fissiparous collection of peoples and polities with no unifying national sentiment. Britain did not consciously introduce order, but was dragged into the 'natural struggle' between Indian politics 'to put down the anarchy which is tearing it to pieces'. '[T]here must', he continued, 'be something wrong in the conception which is current that a number of soldiers went over from England to India and there by sheer superiority in valour and intelligence conquered the whole country'. Britain did not conquer India: all it had done was send collection of officers to the subcontinent who ruled what remained an Asian power.[50]

Seeley's argument was subtly constructed to protect the potentially corrosive effect that Britain's connection with India might have on his liberal sense of virtue. He was fiercely critical of the Tory idea that virtue had any relationship to military prowess. The celebration of conquest was 'monstrous'. Such ideas 'belong to [a] primitive and utterly obsolete class of notions', he argued. Within his liberal, constitutionalist language, a nation's character depended not on armed violence but on the people's inclusion in institutions that cultivated shared national sentiments. '[F]ar removed from us in all physical, intellectual and moral conditions', it would be impossible to unite Indians and Britons in a democratic community.[51] As a result, it was very difficult to imagine any kind of political relationship with India at all. But the unBritish character of British rule in India made it difficult for Seeley to offer a clear argument about what empire there was for.

Seeley echoed Macaulay's civilising rhetoric, but he did so far more faintly than Liberals of Macaulay's generation. Whereas Macaulay argued that the English language could create the cultural convergence between the two peoples, Seeley emphasised the permanent difference between the two societies. The absence of sentimental union with India and the 'unnatural' character of the link, made empire a 'miracle' which was impossible to comprehend.[52] Seeley ended up justifying British rule with a very thin version of the civilising mission. The only excuse for Britain's presence now was that to leave would be to abandon India to anarchy.

It is hard to over-emphasise the hesitant and perplexed tone that suffuses the second book of *The Expansion of England*, where Seeley focuses his discussion on India. If his great project was to put the mind back into Britain's policy towards an empire acquired in 'a fit of absent-mindedness', he himself found it difficult to offer a definite guide to what Britons should actually think when it came to India. The confused tone and reticent arguments of the last section of the book occur as he found the elitism and unreality of Macaulay's civilising mission implausible, and the militarism of the conquest story hard to stomach. But he could not find any way to explain the fact of Britain's connections to India without them.

So while metropolitan Tories could only discuss the British role in India by ignoring the reality of colonial governance, Liberals found India difficult to think about at all. The Liberal emphasis on the sentimental connections of national and religious feeling and a history of shared institutions made it seem as if Britain's connection to India was 'unnatural'. That sense was confirmed by Liberals' abhorrence of conquest.

In the last decades of the nineteenth century a group developed on the left of the Liberal Party who argued that India should be allowed to rule itself, and take its place within a loosely coordinated imperial federation of self-governing polities. Even here, few found it possible to imagine any kind of Anglo-Indian unity without a shared set of beliefs. As Gregory Claeys argues, the radical arguments for Indian self-government made by men like James Cruickshank Geddes and Henry J.S. Cotton were founded on the idea that positivism, and 'the religion of humanity', offered a shared spirit which could unite Hindus and Christians within a single global state.[53] Theosophy provided a possible connection for others, notably the first President of the Indian National Congress, Allan Octavian Hume.

John Morley, the Gladstonian who became Secretary of State for India in the 1906 cabinet, was more typical of mainstream liberalism. He believed that the differences between Britons and Indians were irrec-oncilable, at least in any meaningful timescale. In an essay written mid-way through his period in office, he repeated the cliché that 'British rulers of India are like men bound to make their watches keep time in two longitudes at once'.[54] Like Gladstone, he argued that democracy required an ethic of civic responsibility and the existence of a common 'public opinion' united by religion and also often blood. Christianity and a shared 'Anglo-Saxon' racial heritage were deemed crucial. Writing about India, he repeated a long-standing trope about the chaotic disu-nity of India's peoples. As he explained to a friend in 1907, 'I should be guilty of criminal folly if I were to feel bound to apply the catch-words of our European liberalism as principles fit for an Asian congeries like India'.[55] His sense of the impossibility of applying liberal principles to India meant he had very little to say about what the British should do there at all.

Morley was a disappointing Secretary of State to Indian liberals who imagined that his British political sensibilities would influence the colo-nial administration in the subcontinent. His sense of their particular rootedness in British history meant he did not believe India could be governed with participatory, English institutions. But neither did he justify despotism as a force of progressive transformation. Instead, the historical, context-dependent character of his liberal arguments left him with no guidance about how to act towards India at all.

Morley offered a consistent liberal critique of rule by 'barrack and bureau' in India. Like Seeley, he opposed the imperial cult of honor-ific violence and tried to curtail what he saw as the costly scandal of British India's aggressive frontier policy in the North-West.[56] Yet these concerns were focused primarily on the effect the British rule of India would have on the *British* polity. He was fiercest in his defence of British parliamentary institutions' capacity to keep a check on colonial admin-istration. Whilst Tories argued that British governors in India needed to be free to establish their own military authority, Morley believed that colonial 'bureaucracy' would only be tolerable if the bureaucrat 'feels the direct breath of that public opinion at home in which he was born and bred'.[57] Morley's few writings about India offer no celebration of Britain's purpose in India at all.

The failure of Liberals like Seeley and Morley to offer a coherent justification for Britain's empire in India shows that arguments that defended 'progressive despotism' did not survive the real situation of colonial power for long. As the late nineteenth-century gentry sent their children and capital to India in large numbers, the practice of colonial governance was sufficiently embedded in elite British lives to make any challenge to it an existential crisis. The failure of liberal imperialism corroded the commitment of some to an inclusive, constitutional polity but produced unease and silence amongst a larger number of British Liberals. The practice of colonial domination was a fact of life which had very little cogent ideological or cultural justification.

The one theme which allowed colonial governance to sustain itself without having a coherent language or intellectual life was the idea that India lacked any united feeling, had no 'public opinion', and was a disordered society in which no individual was able to do anything other than to represent their personal point of view. The sense that India was a place where 'chaos conquers all', as Mill put it, a 'jumble', as Morley suggested, made the very act of representing India, and the idea of Britons doing anything consistently to it, impossible. Even Henry Cotton, a Liberal who argued that Britain needed to 'abandon' India in the medium term, thought that immediate departure would be 'like a man who should kidnap a child and then in a fit of repentance abandon him to a tiger jungle'.[58]

Perhaps more than anything else, it was this sense of India as both disunited and ungovernable which Indian writers so fervently challenged throughout the nineteenth century. Indians debated the character and scale of India's unity. Liberals from Sayyid Ahmed Khan to Dadabhai Naoroji argued that its unity depended on a history of shared political institutions. Others saw common culture and social practices not only as the evidence of shared identity but as the basis for self-rule. In the early twentieth-century *Swaraj* (self-rule) meant many different things.[59] But the civilisational unity of India was a common reference point.

Paradoxically, it was their acceptance of the argument for India's national unity which enabled the renewal of a certain kind of liberal imperialism by British politicians on the left. The principle of 'nationality', of 'the nation as a useful intermediate stage between the family and humanity', as William Clark suggested, was a crucial liberal idea.[60] The socialist and Liberal visitors who travelled to India in the first decade of the twentieth century were enthusiastic about India's recent 'renaissance', as the Labour journalist Henry Nevinson described it. The growth of nationality was associated with the *Swadeshi* movement against the partition of Bengal, and the Indian assertion that '[i]n religion, in education, in industries and common life, we will follow our own national lines just as though no foreigners were pretending to rule us'.[61]

Nevinson, Keir Hardie, Ramsay MacDonald and other travellers who wrote in this vein argued that Indians had begun to escape the dead-hand of colonial bureaucracy and to create new social and cultural institutions to assert the unity and independence of national life. Their tone was fiercely critical of the practice of colonial rule but it still showed that there was a British role in the Indian story. MacDonald celebrated the moment when followers of the religious and social reformer Rammohan Roy decided no longer to meet in Calcutta's Unitarian Hall, but to find a place 'where we might meet and worship God in our own way'.[62] It was only when Indian artists left European-run art academies that they stopped painting 'ugly daubs' and created a genuinely national art. Nationalist organisation was an effort to enforce the difference between Britain and India. But, it was argued, the European presence had been essential this national revival. MacDonald claimed that 'the political philosophy and axioms of the West' had been grafted onto India's ancient religious and social traditions to create 'the politics of nationality, liberalism, freedom'.[63] Nevinson suggested that India's 'new birth in intellect, social life, and the affairs of state' was caused in part by 'the awakened stirring of Liberalism in England herself'. Britain, he argued, needed to 'welcome the spirit of freedom and nationality which we have done so much to create'.[64]

Here, we need to reverse the old-fashioned argument about the relationship between British liberalism and Indian nationalism. It was not that liberal institutions created the Indian nation. At most, Liberal and Labour pro-nationalists believed that British ideas had 'awakened' a possibility which already existed within India's shared history, culture and dormant 'nationality'. The point is perhaps the other way around. Written for a British audience, concerned as much for the moral condition of their countrymen as the state of India's society and polity, there was more of a sense, through this literature, about what India could do for Britain than the other way around. For Hardie, Nevinson and MacDonald, the idea of India's nationhood allowed Liberals in Britain to feel that their presence in India could be redeemed. The paradox, of course, is that the liberal-left in Britain thought empire was a worthwhile project at precisely the point when the practice of imperial governance was breaking down. While Macaulay's liberal empire existed only in the future, early socialism's benevolent imperialism belonged purely to the past.

It is a truism in the historiography of empire that, as Frederick Cooper and Ann Stoler suggested in 1997, historians should 'treat metropole and colony in a single analytic field' and to recognise that 'social transformations are a product of both global patterns and local struggles'.[65] But it should also follow that historians need to study how power and language work in different ways in different places. Put simply, imperial domination did not have the same meaning for historical actors in different parts of the world. As this chapter has argued, there was no single colonial discourse or imperial culture which stretched from Cornwall to Calcutta, and no single pattern of words and meanings which framed arguments and practice in both Britain and the subcontinent.

Empire was a material reality connected through the physical movement of people and machines; by personal and institutional networks which stretched around the globe; and by the exchange of commodities de-severed from the particular worlds in which they were produced and consumed. But unlike commodities, languages and ideologies require dense networks of personal interconnection to endure in a particular place. Paradoxically, that often means they lead far more parochial lives than the material beings they describe. Even where British languages about imperialism in India changed and moved, they moved to a rhythm different from the practice of imperial governance they purported to describe.

This chapter has argued that discussion of India in Britain during the nineteenth century was dominated by two continuous but slowly evolving political idioms. The capacity of Britons to celebrate violent moments of conquest, as long as they could be seen in terms of military virtue and honour, was far greater than most historians have recognised. In nineteenth-century Britain conquest did not need to be masked.[66] As the imperial statues which sprouted in London from the 1850s show, conquest could be and was actively celebrated. It formed the central notion in a conservative language that stressed British rule as the guarantor of India's order and hierarchy. But this language emphasised India's central geopolitical position as a territory whose frontiers needed protecting to secure Britain's global role. Obsessed by the perception of threats to this, conservative imperial discourse had very little to say about the practice of empire in the territories the British directly ruled.

This Tory rhetoric was challenged by Whig and later Liberal languages that asked how India could fit into Britain's inclusive, participatory polity. Empire in India was a cause of anxiety not because violence was bad, but because the tools of empire would corrode Britain's constitutional liberties. In a different way, this emphasis led liberal discourses on empire in India to be as narcissistic as their conservative counterparts. The concern with the effect of empire on Britain is nicely illustrated by the fact that Morley's essay on 'Democracy in India', published amidst a mass campaign against British authoritarianism in

India, was exclusively concerned with the effect of governing India on parliamentary government in the United Kingdom. Liberals' belief in the potentially transformative capacity of British power was never strongly argued or deeply held. As Macaulay's language makes clear, it was driven more by a concern to redeem the dishonourable character of imperial domination than by a technical interest in its effects. Paradoxically, the strongest defence of liberal imperialism came at the end of empire, when nationalist politics looked, to Britons on the left, as if it had the potential to redeem Britain's entanglement with the subcontinent.

Notes

1. P.J. Marshall, '"Cornwallis Triumphant": War in India and the British Public in the Late Eighteenth Century' in Lawrence Freedman et al. eds., *War, Strategy, and International Politics: Essays in Honour of Sir Michael Howard* (Oxford, 1992), pp. 57–74; Robert Travers, 'Death and the Nabob: Imperialism and Commemoration in Late Eighteenth-Century India', *Past and Present* 196 (2007), 83–124.
2. *Hansard's Parliamentary Debates* [hereafter H] VI 121–2, 3 February 1806; Anon, *The Life of the Most Noble, The Marquis Cornwallis, Great Friend of the Country* (London, 1806).
3. H XIX 516, 10 July 1833.
4. Robert Travers, *Ideology and Empire in Eighteenth-Century India: The British in Bengal 1757–93* (Cambridge, 2007), pp. 47–52 and chs 3 and 4, passim.
5. Jon E. Wilson, *The Domination of Strangers: Modern Governance in Eastern India, 1780–1835* (Basingstoke, 2008), ch. 2.
6. Sebastian Meurer, 'Administrative Oeconomy in the Making', unpublished paper; also John R. Breihan, 'William Pitt and the Commission on Fees, 1785–1801', *Historical Journal* 27 (1984), 59–81.
7. See, for example, Marquess Wellesley, Speech to Fort William College, 11 February 1805, *The College of Fort William in Bengal* (London, 1805), pp. 144–54.
8. Anon, *Remarks on the Education of Indian Civil Service* (London, 1872), p. 26. The argument of this paragraph is drawn from the PhD research of Amy Kavanagh.
9. Wilson, *Domination of Strangers*, pp. 124–7; Burton Stein, *Thomas Munro: The Origins of the Colonial State and His Vision of Empire* (Oxford, 1989).
10. Eric Stokes, *The English Utilitarians and India* (Oxford, 1959).
11. For the connection between Mill's critique of Britain and the British in India, see Javed Majeed, *Ungoverned Imaginings: James Mill's The History of British India and Orientalism* (Oxford, 1992).
12. See, for example, James Mill, *The History of British India*, 6 vols (London, 1820), I, pp. xxii, 368, 414–18.
13. Ibid., p. xxix.
14. Ibid., V, chs. 4–6.

15. Curzon to Balfour, 31 March 1901, Balfour Papers, British Library, Add. Mss. 49732.
16. David Hume, *A Treatise of Human Nature*, ed. L.A. Selby-Bigge (Oxford, 1978), pp. 601, 600.
17. Allan Ramsay, *An Essay on The Right of Conquest* (Florence, 1783), p.7.
18. Jack Harrington, *Sir John Malcolm and the Creation of British India* (New York, 2010).
19. Arthur Wellesley, 'Notes on the Administration of Marquis Wellesley' in Sidney Owen, ed., *A Selection from the Despatches, Treaties and Other Papers of the Marquess Wellesley* (Oxford, 1877), p. lxxvi.
20. John Malcolm, *The Political History of India, from 1784 to 1823*, 2 vols (London, 1826), I, p. 90.
21. John Malcolm, *The Life of Robert, Lord Clive*, 3 vols (London, 1836), II, p.339.
22. Ibid., I, p. 165.
23. For different perspectives see Nicholas Dirks, *The Hollow Crown: Ethnohistory of an Indian Kingdom* (Ann Arbor, 1993); Barbara Ramusack, *The Indian Princes and their States* (Cambridge, 2004).
24. H IV 736, 737, 5 July 1831. See Miles Taylor, 'Empire and Parliamentary Reform: the 1832 Reform Act Revisited' in Arthur Burns and Joanna Innes, eds., *Rethinking the Age of Reform: Britain, 1780–1850* (Cambridge, 2003), pp. 295–311.
25. Cited in Sarvepalli Gopal, *British Policy in India, 1858–1905* (Cambridge, 1965), p. 120.
26. See the correspondence to Morley, Lytton Papers, British Library, Mss. Eur. E218/43 & 44.
27. David Gilmour, *Curzon* (London, 1994), pp. 71–4.
28. H CCLIX 50–131, 3 March 1881.
29. See the correspondence collected at Curzon Papers, British Library, Mss. Eur. F111/448A.
30. Miles Taylor, 'Queen Victoria and India, 1837–61', *Victorian Studies* 46 (2004), 264–74; W.L. Arnstein, 'The Warrior Queen: Reflections on Victoria and her World', *Albion* 30 (1998), 1–28.
31. David Cannadine, *Ornamentalism: How the British saw their Empire* (London, 2001), p. 122.
32. Bernard Cohn, 'Representing Authority in Victorian India' in Eric Hobsbawm and Terence Ranger, eds., *The Invention of Tradition* (Cambridge, 1983), pp. 165–211.
33. Cited in Michael Bentley, *Sailsbury's World. Conservative Environments in Late Victorian Britain* (Cambridge, 2001), p. 223.
34. P.J. Marshall, 'Review of *Ornamentalism*', *Reviews in History* http://www.history.ac.uk/reviews/review/202, last accessed 2 January 2013
35. David Hall-Matthews, *Peasants, Famine and the State in Colonial Western India* (Basingstoke, 2005); Mike Davis, *Late Victorian Holocausts: El Niño Famines and the Making of the Third World* (London, 2001).
36. Richard Temple, *The Story of My Life*, 2 vols (London, 1896), II, p. 69.
37. Jonathan Parry, *The Politics of Patriotism: English Liberalism, National Identity and Europe, 1830–1886* (Cambridge, 2006).

38. Andrew Sartori, *Bengal in Global Concept History: Culturalism in the Age of Capital* (Chicago, 2008); Partha Chatterjee, *The Black Hole of Empire: History of a Global Practice of Power* (Princeton, 2012), pp. 104–33.

39. For Calcutta and Madras see Travers, *Ideology and Empire*, pp. 181–206; Mattison Mines, 'Courts of Law and Styles of Self in Eighteenth-Century Madras: from Hybrid to Colonial Self', *Modern Asian Studies* 35 (2001), 33–74; Niels Brimnes, 'Beyond Colonial Law: Indigenous Litigation and the Contestation of Property in the Mayor's Court in Late Eighteenth-Century Madras', *Modern Asian Studies* 37 (2003), 513–550. There is no equivalent research on Bombay.

40. *The Oriental Herald* 20 (1829), p. 561.

41. Miles Taylor, 'Joseph Hume and the Reformation of India, 1819–1833' in Glenn Burgess and Matthew Festenstein, eds., *English Radicalism, 1550–1850* (Cambridge, 2007), p. 301; also Jonathan Parry, *The Rise and Fall of Liberal Government in Victorian Britain* (New Haven, 1993), p. 100.

42. H XIX 499, 515, 516, 10 July 1833. I am indebted to Kieran Hazzard's PhD research for this argument.

43. Ibid., 521.

44. Thomas Macaulay, *Critical and Historical Essays*, 2 vols (London, 1907), I, pp. 479–549.

45. See Uday Mehta, *Liberalism and Empire: A Study in Nineteenth-Century British Liberal Thought* (Chicago, 1999); Jennifer Pitts, *A Turn to Empire: the Rise of Imperial Liberalism in Britain and France* (Princeton, 2005); Sanjay Seth, *Subject Lessons: The Western Education of Colonial India* (Durham, 2007).

46. Karuna Mantena, *Alibis of Empire: Henry Maine and the Ends of Liberal Imperialism* (Princeton, 2010).

47. James Fitzjames Stephen, *Liberty, Equality, Fraternity* (London, 1873).

48. Parry, *Liberal Government*, p. 271.

49. K.J.M. Smith, *James Fitzjames Stephen: Portrait of a Victorian Rationalist* (Cambridge, 1988), p. 140.

50. J. R. Seeley, *The Expansion of England* (London, 1883), pp. 211, 199.

51. Ibid., pp. 194, 167.

52. Ibid., p. 217.

53. Gregory Claeys, *Imperial Sceptics: British Critics of Empire, 1850–1920* (Cambridge, 2010), pp. 68–75.

54. *The Nineteenth Century and After* 69 (1911), p. 189.

55. Cited in Stephen E. Koss, *Morley at the India Office, 1905–1910* (New Haven, 1969), p. 137.

56. Beryl J. Williams, 'The Strategic Background to the Anglo-Russian Entente of August 1907', *Historical Journal* 9 (1966), p. 369.

57. *The Nineteenth Century and After* 69 (1911), p. 199.

58. Cited in Claeys, *Imperial Sceptics*, p. 75.

59. Sartori, *Bengal in Global Concept History*; Shruti Kapila, 'Self, Spencer and *Swaraj*: Nationalist Thought and Critiques of Liberalism, 1890–1920', *Modern Intellectual History* 4 (2007), 109–127.

60. Cited in Claeys, *Imperial Sceptics*, p. 261.

61. Henry W. Nevinson, *The New Spirit in India* (London, 1908), p. 330.

62. J. Ramsay Macdonald, *The Government of India* (London, 1917), p. 3.

63. Ibid., p. 2.

64. Nevinson, *New Spirit in India*, pp. 321, 322, 337.
65. Frederick Cooper and Ann Stoler, eds., *Tensions of Empire: Colonial Cultures in a Bourgeois World* (Berkeley, 1997), p. 4.
66. See Gauri Viswanathan, *Masks of Conquest: Literary Study and British Rule in India* (New York, 1989).

Select Bibliography

Introduction

Bevir, M., *The Logic of the History of Ideas* (Cambridge, 1999).

Biagini, E. F. and A. J. Reid, eds., *Currents of Radicalism: Popular Radicalism, Organised Labour and Party Politics in Britain, 1850–1914* (Cambridge, 1991).

Craig, D. M., '"High Politics" and the "New Political History"', *Historical Journal* 53 (2010), 453–75.

Francis, M. and J. Morrow, *A History of English Political Thought in the Nineteenth Century* (London, 1994).

Gunn, S. and J. Vernon, eds., *The Peculiarities of Liberal Modernity in Imperial Britain* (Berkeley, 2011).

Hall, C., K. McClelland and J. Rendall, *Defining the Victorian Nation: Class, Race, Gender and the Second Reform Act of 1867* (Cambridge, 2000).

Lawrence, J., *Speaking for the People: Party, Language and Popular Politics, 1867–1914* (Cambridge, 1998).

Mandler, P., ed., *Liberty and Authority in Victorian Britain* (Oxford, 2006).

Meisel, J., *Public Speech and the Culture of Public Life in the Age of Gladstone* (New York, 2001).

Pocock, J. G. A., *Political Thought and History: Essays on Theory and Method* (Cambridge, 2009).

Roberts, M., *Popular Movements in Urban England, 1832–1914* (Basingstoke, 2009).

Skinner, Q., *Visions of Politics I: Regarding Method* (Cambridge, 2002).

Stedman Jones, G., *Languages of Class: Studies in English Working Class History* (Cambridge, 1983).

Thompson, J., '"Pictorial lies"?: Posters and Politics in Britain, 1880–1914', *Past and Present* 197 (2007), 177–210.

Vernon, J., *Politics and the People: A Study in English Political Culture, c. 1815–1867* (Cambridge, 1993).

Good Government

Daunton, M. J., *Trusting Leviathan: The Politics of Taxation in Britain, 1799–1914* (Cambridge, 2001).

Harling, P., *The Waning of 'Old Corruption': The Politics of Economical Reform, 1779–1846* (Oxford, 1996).

Harris, J., 'Political Thought and the Welfare State 1870–1940: an Intellectual Framework for British Social Policy', *Past and Present* 35 (1992), 116–41.

Harris, J., *Private Lives, Public Spirit: Britain, 1870–1914* (Oxford, 1993).

Jones, H. S., *Victorian Political Thought* (Basingstoke, 2000).

Mandler, P., *Aristocratic Government in the Age of Reform: Whigs and Liberals 1830–1852* (Oxford, 1990).

Meadowcroft, J., *Conceptualizing the State: Innovation and Dispute in British Political Thought 1880–1914* (Oxford, 1995).

Parry, J., *The Rise and Fall of Liberal Government in Victorian Britain* (New Haven, 1993).

Searle, G. R., *The Quest for National Efficiency: A Study in British Politics and Political Thought* (Oxford, 1971).

Sutherland, G., *Studies in the Growth of Nineteenth Century Government* (London, 1972).

Thompson, J., 'Modern Liberty Redefined' in G. Claeys and G. Stedman Jones, eds., *The Cambridge History of Nineteenth-Century Political Thought* (Cambridge, 2011), pp. 720–47.

Thompson, J., *British Political Culture and the Idea of 'Public Opinion'* (Cambridge, 2013).

Vernon, J., ed., *Re-reading the Constitution: New Narratives in the Political History of England's Long Nineteenth Century* (Cambridge, 1996).

Statesmanship

Collini, S., *Public Moralists: Political Thought and Intellectual Life in Britain 1850–1930* (Oxford, 1991).

Craig, D., 'Advanced Conservative Liberalism: Party and Principle in Trollope's Parliamentary Novels', *Victorian Literature and Culture* 38 (2010), 355–71.

Craig, D., 'Burke and the Constitution' in D. Dwan and C. Insole, eds., *The Cambridge Companion to Edmund Burke* (Cambridge, 2012).

Grainger, J. H., *Character and Style in English Politics* (Cambridge, 1969).

Joyce, P., *Democratic Subjects: the Self and the Social in Nineteenth-Century England* (Cambridge, 1994)

McCormack, M., ed., *Public Men: Masculinity and Politics in Modern Britain* (Basingstoke, 2007).

Parry, J., *The Rise and Fall of Liberal Government in Victorian Britain* (New Haven, 1993).

Parry, J., 'Past and Future in the Later Career of Lord John Russell' in T. Blanning and D. Cannadine, eds, *History and Biography: Essays in Honour of Derek Beales* (Cambridge, 1996), pp. 142–72.

Parry, J., 'Disraeli and England', *Historical Journal* 43 (2000), 699–728.

Runciman, D., *Political Hypocrisy: the Mask of Power, from Hobbes to Orwell and Beyond* (Princeton, 2008).

Taylor, A., *Lords of Misrule: Hostility to Aristocracy in Late-Nineteenth and Early-Twentieth Century Britain* (Basingstoke, 2004).

Patriotism

Cunningham, H., 'The Language of Patriotism, 1750–1914', *History Workshop Journal* 12 (1981), 8–33.

Grainger, J. H., *Patriotisms: Britain 1900–1939* (London, 1986).

Koebner, R. and H. Schmidt, *Imperialism: the Story and Significance of a Political Word 1840–1960* (Cambridge, 1964).

Parry, J., *The Rise and Fall of Liberal Government in Victorian Britain* (New Haven, 1993).

Parry, J., *The Politics of Patriotism: English Liberalism, National Identity and Europe, 1830–1886* (Cambridge, 2006).

Parry, J., 'The Disciplining of the Religious Conscience in Nineteenth-Century British Politics', in I. Katznelson and G. Stedman Jones, eds., *Religion and the Political Imagination* (Cambridge, 2010), pp. 214–34.

Readman, P., 'The Conservative Party, Patriotism, and British Politics: the Case of the General Election of 1900', *Journal of British Studies* 40 (2001), 107–45.

Readman, P., 'The Liberal Party and Patriotism in Early Twentieth-Century Britain', *Twentieth Century British History* 12 (2001), 269–302.

Samuel, R., ed., *Patriotism: the Making and Unmaking of British National Identity*, 3 vols (London, 1989).

Searle, G. R., *Country before Party: Coalition and the Idea of 'National Government' in Modern Britain, 1885–1987* (London, 1995).

Worden, B., 'The Victorians and Oliver Cromwell', in S. Collini, R. Whatmore and B. Young, eds., *History, Religion and Culture: British Intellectual History 1750–1950* (Cambridge, 2000), pp. 112–35.

Religion

Bebbington, D., *The Nonconformist Conscience: Chapel and Politics, 1870–1914* (London, 2009).

Bentley, J., *Ritualism and Politics in Victorian Britain: The Attempt to Legislate for Belief* (Oxford, 1978).

Boyce, D. G. and A. O'Day, eds., *Gladstone and Ireland: Politics, Religion and Nationality in the Victorian Age* (Basingstoke, 2011).

Brent, R., *Liberal Anglican Politics: Whiggery, Religion, and Reform 1830–1841* (Oxford, 1987).

Brown, S. J., *Providence and Empire: Religion, Politics and Society in the United Kingdom 1815–1914* (Harlow, 2008).

Floyd, R. D., *Church, Chapel and Party: Religious Dissent and Political Modernization in Nineteenth-Century England* (Basingstoke, 2008).

Harrison, J. F. C., *The Second Coming: Popular Millenarianism 1780–1850* (London, 1979).

Hilton, B., *The Age of Atonement: the Influence of Evangelicalism on Social and Economic Thought, 1795–1865* (Oxford, 1991).

Koss, S., *Nonconformity in Modern British Politics* (London, 1975).

Machin, G. I. T., *Politics and the Churches in Great Britain, 1832–1868* (Oxford, 1977).

Machin, G. I. T., *Politics and the Churches in Great Britain, 1869–1921* (Oxford, 1987).

Parry, J., *Democracy and Religion: Gladstone and the Liberal Party, 1867–1875* (Cambridge, 1986).

Parry, J., *The Rise and Fall of Liberal Government in Victorian Britain* (New Haven, 1993).

Skinner, S. A., *Tractarians and the 'Condition of England': the Social and Political Thought of the Oxford Movement* (Oxford, 2004).

Warren, A., 'Disraeli, the Conservatives and the national church', *Parliamentary History* 19 (2000), 96–117.

Wolffe, J., *The Protestant Crusade in Great Britain, 1829–1860* (Oxford, 1991).

Popular Political Economy

Biagini, E. F., 'British Trade Unions and Popular Political Economy, 1860–1880', *Historical Journal* 30 (1987), 811–40.

Biagini, E.F., ed., *Citizenship and Community: Liberals, Radicals and Collective Identities in the British Isles, 1865–1931* (Cambridge, 1996).

Bohstedt, J., *The Politics of Provisions: Food Riots, Moral Economy and Market Transition in England c. 1555–1850* (Farnham, 2010).

Brown, B. H., *The Tariff Reform Movement in Great Britain, 18811–1895* (New York, 1941).

Gambles, A., *Politics and Protection: Conservative Economic Discourse, 1815–1852* (Woodbridge, 1999).

Howe, A., *Free Trade and Liberal England, 1846–1946* (Oxford, 1997).

Howe, A., 'Free Trade and its Enemies' in M. Hewitt, ed., *The Victorian World* (Abingdon, 2012), pp. 108–24.

Huzzey, R., 'Free Trade, Free Labour, and Slave Sugar in Victorian Britain', *Historical Journal* 53 (2010), 359–79.

Miller, H., 'Popular Petitioning and the Corn Laws, 1833–1846', *English Historical Review* 127 (2012), 882–919.

Morgan, S.J., 'Domestic Economy and Political Agitation: Women and the Anti-Corn Law League, 1839–46' in K. Gleadle and S. Richardson, eds., *The Power of the Petticoat* (Basingstoke, 2000).

Pickering, P. and A. Tyrrell, *The People's Bread: a history of the Anti-Corn Law League* (Leicester, 2000).

Schonhardt-Bailey, C., *From the Corn Laws to Free Trade* (Cambridge, MA, 2006).

Thompson, N.W., *The People's Science* (Cambridge, 1984).

Trentmann, F., *Free Trade Nation: Commerce, Consumption and Civil Society in Modern Britain* (Oxford, 2008).

Winch, D. and P. O'Brien, eds., *The Political Economy of British Historical Experience, 1688–1914* (Oxford, 2002).

Democracy

Barrow, L. and I. Bullock, *Democratic Ideas and the British Labour Movement, 1880–1914* (Cambridge, 1996).

Biagini, E. F., *Liberty, Retrenchment and Reform: Popular Liberalism in the Age of Gladstone, 1860–80* (Cambridge, 1992).

Biagini, E. F., *British Democracy and Irish Nationalism, 1876–1906* (Cambridge, 2007).

Holton, S.S., *Feminism and Democracy: Women's Suffrage and Reform Politics in Britain, 1900–1918* (Cambridge, 1986).

Innes, J. and M. Philp, eds., *Re-Imagining Democracy in the Age of Revolutions: America, France, Britain, Ireland 1750–1850* (Oxford, 2013).

Parry, J., *Democracy and Religion: Gladstone and the Liberal Party, 1867–1875* (Cambridge, 1986).

Quinault, R., 'Lord Randolph Churchill and Tory Democracy, 1880–1885', *Historical Journal*, 22 (1979), 141–65.

Quinault, R., *British Prime Ministers and Democracy: from Disraeli to Blair* (London, 2011).

Robertson, A.W., *The Language of Democracy: Political Rhetoric in the United States and Britain, 1790–1900* (Ithaca, 1995).

Roper, J., *Democracy and its Critics: Anglo-American Democratic Thought in the Nineteenth Century* (London, 1989).

Saunders, R., *Democracy and the Vote in British Politics, 1848–1867: The Making of the Second Reform Act* (Farnham, 2011).

Saunders, R., 'Tory Rebels and Tory Democracy: The Ulster Crisis, 1900–1914', in R. Carr and B. Hart, eds., *The Foundations of Modern British Conservatism* (London, 2013).

Women's Suffrage

Bush, J., *Women against the Vote: Female Anti-Suffragism in Britain* (Oxford, 2007).

Clark, A., *The Struggle for the Breeches: Gender and the Making of the British Working Class* (Berkeley, 1995).

Gleadle, K., *Borderline Citizens: Women, Gender, and Political Culture in Britain, 1815–1867* (Oxford, 2009).

Griffin, B., *The Politics of Gender in Victorian Britain: Masculinity, Political Culture and the Struggle for Women's Rights* (Cambridge, 2012).

Harrison, B., *Separate Spheres: the Opposition to Women's Suffrage in Britain* (London, 1978).

Holton, S.S., *Feminism and Democracy: Women's Suffrage and Reform Politics in Britain, 1900–1918* (Cambridge, 1986).

Kent, S. K., *Sex and Suffrage in Britain, 1860–1914* (Princeton, 1987).

Mayhall, L. N., *The Militant Suffrage Movement: Citizenship and Resistance in Britain, 1860–1930* (Oxford, 2003).

Pugh, M., *The March of the Women: a Revisionist Analysis of the Campaign for Women's Suffrage, 1866–1914* (Oxford, 2000).

Rogers, H., *Women and the People. Authority, Authorship and the Radical Tradition in Nineteenth-Century England* (Aldershot, 2000).

Vickery, A., ed., *Women, Privilege and Power: British Politics, 1750 to the Present* (Stanford, 2001).

Irish Nationalism

Belchem, J., 'Nationalism, Republicanism and Exile: Irish Emigrants and the Revolution of 1848', *Past and Present* 146 (1995), 103–35.

Bew, P., *C.S. Parnell* (Dublin, 1980).

Boyce, D. G. and A. O'Day, eds., *Defenders of the Union: A Survey of British and Irish Unionism since 1801* (London, 2001).

Callanan, F., *The Parnell Split, 1890–91* (Cork, 1992).

Dwan, D., *The Great Community: Culture and Nationalism in Ireland* (Dublin, 2008).

Hoppen, K.T., *Elections, Politics, and Society in Ireland 1832–1885* (Oxford, 1984).

Kelly, M., *The Fenian Ideal and Irish Nationalism, 1882–1916* (Woodbridge, 2006).

Kelly, M., 'Irish Nationalist Opinion and the British Empire in the 1850s and 1860s', *Past and Present* 204 (2009), 127–54.

Kelly, M., 'Languages of Radicalism, Race, and Religion in Irish Nationalism: The French Affinity, 1848–1871', *Journal of British Studies* 49 (2010), 801–25.

Kendle, J., *Ireland and the Federal Solution. The Debate over the United Kingdom Constitution, 1870–1921* (Kingston, 1989).

Kinealy, K., *Repeal and Revolution: Ireland in 1848* (Manchester, 2009).

Lyons, F. S. L., 'The Political Ideas of Parnell', *Historical Journal* 16 (1973), 749–75.

MacDonagh, O., *States of Mind. Two Centuries of Anglo-Irish Conflict, 1780–1980* (London, 1983).

McGee, E., '"God save Ireland": Manchester Martyr Demonstrations in Dublin 1867–1916', *Eire-Ireland* 36 (2001), 39–66.

Moody, T. W., *Michael Davitt and Irish Revolution* (Oxford, 1977).

O'Brien, J., 'Irish Public Opinion and the Risorgimento, 1859–1860', *Irish Historical Studies* 34 (2005), 289–305.

Townend, P. A., 'Between Two Worlds: Irish Nationalists and Imperial Crisis 1878–1880', *Past and Present* 194 (2007), 139–74.

The Silence of Empire: Imperialism and India

Cannadine, D., *Ornamentalism: How the British saw their Empire* (London, 2001).

Chatterjee, P., *The Black Hole of Empire: History of a Global Practice of Power* (Princeton, 2012).

Claeys, G., *Imperial Sceptics: British Critics of Empire, 1850–1920* (Cambridge, 2010).

Cohn, B., 'Representing Authority in Victorian India' in E. Hobsbawm and T. Ranger, eds., *The Invention of Tradition* (Cambridge, 1983), pp. 165–211.

Mehta, U.S., *Liberalism and Empire: A Study in Nineteenth-Century British Liberal Thought* (Chicago, 1999).

Pitts, J., *A Turn to Empire: the Rise of Imperial Liberalism in Britain and France* (Princeton, 2005).

Sartori, A., *Bengal in Global Concept History: Culturalism in the Age of Capital* (Chicago, 2008).

Stein, B., *Thomas Munro: The Origins of the Colonial State and His Vision of Empire* (Oxford, 1989).

Stokes, E., *The English Utilitarians and India* (Oxford, 1959).

Taylor, M., 'Joseph Hume and the Reformation of India, 1819–1833' in G. Burgess and M. Festenstein, eds., *English Radicalism, 1550–1850* (Cambridge, 2007), pp. 285–308.

Travers, R., *Ideology and Empire in Eighteenth-Century India: The British in Bengal 1757–93* (Cambridge, 2007).

Wilson, J. E., *The Domination of Strangers: Modern Governance in Eastern India, 1780–1835* (Basingstoke, 2008).

Index